CAMBRIDGE]
Books oj

Music

The systematic academic study of music gave rise to works of description, analysis and criticism, by composers and performers, philosophers and anthropologists, historians and teachers, and by a new kind of scholar - the musicologist. This series makes available a range of significant works encompassing all aspects of the developing discipline.

Memoirs of Doctor Burney

Charles Burney (1726–1814), the music historian, is best remembered for his *General History of Music* and the accounts of his musical tours in Europe. He was a friend of Samuel Johnson and David Garrick, corresponded with Diderot and Haydn and was made Fellow of the Royal Society in 1773. Although he was a music teacher by profession, it was his writings on music which brought him widespread recognition. Following publication of the *General History*, he began his memoirs but did not complete them. It is likely that he intended his daughter, the novelist Fanny Burney, to publish the memoirs after his death using his manuscript and other papers. Instead she created her own embellished version, adding stylised accounts of events emphasising the literary and social, rather than the musical aspects. Volume 1 takes us to the mid-1770s with the publication of the accounts of the two musical tours.

Cambridge University Press has long been a pioneer in the reissuing of out-of-print titles from its own backlist, producing digital reprints of books that are still sought after by scholars and students but could not be reprinted economically using traditional technology. The Cambridge Library Collection extends this activity to a wider range of books which are still of importance to researchers and professionals, either for the source material they contain, or as landmarks in the history of their academic discipline.

Drawing from the world-renowned collections in the Cambridge University Library, and guided by the advice of experts in each subject area, Cambridge University Press is using state-of-the-art scanning machines in its own Printing House to capture the content of each book selected for inclusion. The files are processed to give a consistently clear, crisp image, and the books finished to the high quality standard for which the Press is recognised around the world. The latest print-on-demand technology ensures that the books will remain available indefinitely, and that orders for single or multiple copies can quickly be supplied.

The Cambridge Library Collection will bring back to life books of enduring scholarly value (including out-of-copyright works originally issued by other publishers) across a wide range of disciplines in the humanities and social sciences and in science and technology.

Memoirs of Doctor Burney

Arranged from His Own Manuscripts, from Family Papers, and from Personal Recollections

VOLUME 1

EDITED BY FANNY BURNEY

CAMBRIDGE UNIVERSITY PRESS

Cambridge, New York, Melbourne, Madrid, Cape Town, Singapore,
São Paolo, Delhi, Dubai, Tokyo

Published in the United States of America by Cambridge University Press, New York

www.cambridge.org
Information on this title: www.cambridge.org/9781108013710

© in this compilation Cambridge University Press 2010

This edition first published 1832
This digitally printed version 2010

ISBN 978-1-108-01371-0 Paperback

This book reproduces the text of the original edition. The content and language reflect
the beliefs, practices and terminology of their time, and have not been updated.

Cambridge University Press wishes to make clear that the book, unless originally published
by Cambridge, is not being republished by, in association or collaboration with, or
with the endorsement or approval of, the original publisher or its successors in title.

MEMOIRS

OF

DOCTOR BURNEY,

ARRANGED

FROM HIS OWN MANUSCRIPTS, FROM FAMILY PAPERS, AND
FROM PERSONAL RECOLLECTIONS.

BY

HAS DAUGHTER, MADAME D'ARBLAY.

"O could my feeble powers thy virtues trace,
By filial love each fear should be suppress'd;
The blush of incapacity I'd chace,
And stand—Recorder of Thy worth!—confess'd."

Anonymous Dedication of Evelina, to Dr. Burney, in 1778.

IN THREE VOLUMES.

VOL. I.

LONDON:
EDWARD MOXON, 64, NEW BOND STREET.

1832.

PREFACE, OR APOLOGY.

THE intentions, or, rather, the directions of Dr. Burney that his Memoirs should be published; and the expectation of his family and friends that they should pass through the hands of his present Editor and Memorialist, have made the task of arranging the ensuing collations with her own personal recollections, appear to her a sacred duty from the year 1814.*

But the grief at his loss, which at first incapacitated her from such an effort, was soon afterwards followed by change of place, change of circumstances—almost of existence—with multiplied casualties that, eventually, separated her from all her

---

* The year of Dr. Burney's decease.

manuscript materials. And these she only recovered when under the pressure of a new affliction that took from her all power, or even thought, for their investigation. During many years, therefore, they have been laid aside, though never forgotten.

But if Time, as so often we lament, will not stand still upon happiness, it would be graceless not to acknowledge, with gratitude to Providence, that neither is it positively stationary upon sorrow: for though there are calamities which it cannot obliterate, and wounds which Religion alone can heal, Time yet seems endowed with a secret principle for producing a mental calm, through which life imperceptibly glides back to its customary operations; however powerless Time itself—earthly Time!—must still remain for restoring lost felicity.

Now, therefore,—most unexpectedly,—that she finds herself sufficiently recovered from successive indispositions and afflictions to attempt the acquittal of a debt which has long hung heavily upon her mind, she ventures to re-open her manuscript stores, and to resume, though in trembling, her long-forsaken pen.

That the life of so eminent a man should not pass away without some authenticated record, will be pretty generally thought; and the circumstances which render her its recorder, grow out of the very nature of things: she possesses all his papers and documents; and, from her earliest youth to his latest decline, not a human being was more confidentially entrusted than herself with the occurrences, the sentiments, and the feelings of his past and passing days.

Although, as biography, from time immemorial, has claimed the privilege of being more discursive than history, the Memorialist may seek to diversify the plain recital of facts by such occasional anecdotes as have been hoarded from childhood in her memory; still, and most scrupulously, not an opinion will be given as Dr. Burney's, either of persons or things, that was not literally his own: and fact will as essentially be the basis of every article, as if its object were still lent to earth, and now listening to this exposition of his posthumous memoirs with her own recollections.

Nevertheless, though nothing is related that does not belong to Dr. Burney and his history, the accounts are not always rigidly confined to his presence, where scenes, or traits, still strong in the remembrance of the Editor, or still before her eyes in early letters or diaries, invite to any characteristic details of celebrated personages.

Not slight, however, is the embarrassment that struggles with the pleasure of these mingled reminiscences, from their appearance of personal obtrusion: yet, when it is seen that they are never brought forward but to introduce some incident or speech, that must else remain untold of Dr. Johnson, Mr. Burke, Mrs. Delany, Mrs. Thrale, Mr. Bruce—nay, Napoleon—and some other high-standing names, of recent date to the aged, yet of still living curiosity to the youthful reader—these apparent egotisms may be something more,—perhaps—than pardoned.

Where the life has been as private as that of Dr. Burney, its history must necessarily be simple, and can have little further call upon the attention of the world, than that which may belong to a wish of tracing the progress of a nearly abandoned Child, from a small village of Shropshire, to a Man allowed throughout Europe to have risen to the head of his profession; and thence, setting his profession aside, to have been elevated to an intellectual rank in society, as a Man of Letters—

" Though not First, in the very first line"

with most of the eminent men of his day,—Dr. Johnson and Mr. Burke, soaring above any cotemporary mark, always, like Senior Wranglers, excepted.

And to this height, to which, by means and resources all his own, he arose, the Genius that impelled him to Fame, the Integrity that established his character, and the Amiability that magnetized all hearts,—in the phrase of Dr. Johnson—*to go forth to meet him*, were the only materials with which he worked his way.

INTRODUCTION.

COPIED FROM A MANUSCRIPT MEMOIR IN THE DOCTOR'S
OWN HAND-WRITING.

If the life of a humble individual, on whom neither splendid appointments, important transactions, nor atrocious crimes have called the attention of the public, can afford amusement to the friends he leaves behind, without being offered either as a model to follow, or a precipice to shun, the intention of the writer of these Memoirs will be fully accomplished. But there is no member of society who, by diligence, talents, or conduct, leaves his name and his race a little better than those from which he sprung, who is totally without some claim to attention on the means by which such advantages were achieved.

My life, though it has been frequently a tissue of toil, sickness, and sorrow, has yet been, upon the whole, so much more pleasant and prosperous than I had a title to expect, or than many others with higher claims have enjoyed, that its incidents, when related, may, perhaps, help to put mediocrity in good-humour, and to repress the pride and overrated worth and expectations of indolence.

Perhaps few have been better enabled to describe, from an actual survey, the manners and customs of the age in which he lived than myself; ascending from those of the most humble cottagers, and lowest mechanics, to the first nobility, and most elevated personages, with whom circumstances, situation, and accident, at different periods of my life, have rendered me familiar. Oppressed and laborious husbandmen; insolent and illiberal yeomanry; overgrown farmers; generous and hospitable merchants; men of business and men of pleasure; men of letters; men of science; artists; sportsmen and country 'squires; dissipated and extravagant voluptuaries; gamesters; ambassadors; statesmen; and even sovereign princes, I have had opportunities of examining in almost every point of view: all these it is my intention to display in their respective situations; and to delineate their virtues, vices, and apparent degrees of happiness and misery.

A book of this kind, though it may mortify and offend a few persons of the present age, may be read with avidity at the distance of some centuries, by antiquaries and lovers of anecdotes; though it will have lost the poignancy of personality.

My grandfather, James Macburney, who, by letters which I have seen of his writing, and circumstances concerning him which I remember to have heard from my father and mother, was a gentleman of a considerable patrimony at Great Hanwood, a village in Shropshire, had received a very good education; but, from what cause does not appear, in the latter years of his life, was appointed land steward to the Earl of Ashburnham. He had a house in Privy Garden, Whitehall. In the year 1727, he walked as esquire to one of the knights, at the coronation of King George the Second.

My father, James, born likewise at Hanwood, was well educated also, both in school learning and accomplishments. He was a day scholar at Westminster School, under the celebrated Dr. Busby, while my grandfather resided at Whitehall. I remember his telling a story of the severe chastisement he received from that terrific disciplinarian,

Dr. Busby, for playing truant after school hours, instead of returning home. My grandfather, who had frequently admonished him not to loiter in the street, lest he should make improper and mischievous acquaintance, finding no attention was paid to his injunctions, gave him a letter addressed to the Reverend Dr. Busby; which he did. not fail to deliver, with ignorant cheerfulness, on his entrance into the school. The Doctor, when he had perused it, called my father to him, and, in a very mild, and seemingly good-humoured voice, said, " Burney, can you read writing?" " Yes, Sir," answered my father, with great courage and flippancy. " Then read this letter aloud," says the Doctor; when my father, with an audible voice, began : " Sir, My son, the bearer of this letter, having long disregarded my admonitions against stopping to play with idle boys in his way home from school—" Here my father's voice faultered. " Go on," says his master; " you read very well." " I am sorry to be under the necessity of entreating you to—to—to—to cor—" Here he threw down the letter, and fell on his knees, crying out: " Indeed, Sir, I'll never do so again !—Pray forgive me !" " O, you read perfectly well," the

Doctor again tells him, " pray finish the Letter : " And making him pronounce aloud the words, " correct him ; " complied with my grandfather's request in a very liberal manner.

Whether my father was intended for any particular profession, I know not, but, during his youth, besides his school learning, he acquired several talents and accomplishments, which, in the course of his life, he was obliged professionally to turn to account. He danced remarkably well; performed well on the violin, and was a portrait painter of no mean talents.

Notwithstanding the Mac which was prefixed to my grandfather's name, and which my father retained for some time, I never could find at what period any of my ancestors lived in Scotland or in Ireland, from one of which it must have been derived. My father and grandfather were both born in Shropshire, and never even visited either of those countries.

Early in his life, my father lost the favour of his sire, by eloping from home, to marry a young actress of Goodman's-fields' theatre, by whom he had a very large family. My grandfather's affection was completely alienated by this marriage ;

joined to disapproving his son's conduct in other respects. To the usual obduracy of old age, he afterwards added a far more than similar indiscretion himself, by marrying a female domestic, to whom, and to a son, the consequence of that marriage, he bequeathed all his possessions, which were very considerable. Joseph, this son, was not more prudent than my father; for he contrived, early in life, to dissipate his patrimony; and he subsisted for many years in Norfolk, by teaching to dance. I visited him in 1756, in a tour I made to Yarmouth. He lived then at Ormsby, a beautiful village near that town, with an amiable wife, and a large family of beautiful children, in an elegant villa, with a considerable garden; and he appeared, at that time, in perfectly restored and easy circumstances.

N. B.—The fragment whence this is taken here stops.

This Introduction, which is copied literally from the hand-writing of Dr. Burney, was both begun and dropped, as appears by a marginal note, in the year

1782; but, from what cause is unknown, was neither continued, nor resumed, save by occasional memorandums, till the year 1807, when the Doctor had reached the age of eighty-one, and was under the dejecting apprehension of a paralytic seizure. From that time, nevertheless, he composed sundry manuscript volumes, of various sizes, containing the history of his life, from his cradle nearly to his grave.

Out of the minute amplitude of this vast mass of matter, it has seemed the duty of his Editor and Memorialist, to collect all that seemed to offer any interest for the general reader; but to commit nothing to the public eye that there is reason to believe the author himself would have withheld from it at an earlier period; or would have obliterated, even at a much later, had he revised his writings after the recovery of his health and spirits.

MEMOIRS

OF

DOCTOR BURNEY.

CHARLES BURNEY was born at Shrewsbury, on the twelfth of April, 1726.

He was issue of a second marriage, of a very different colour with respect to discretion, or to prejudice, from that with the account of which he has opened his own narration. The poor actress was no more; but neither her hardly judged, though enthusiastically admired profession, nor her numerous offspring, nor the alienation she had unhappily caused in the family, proved obstacles to the subsequent union of her survivor with Miss * * * who in those days, though young and pretty, was called Mrs. Ann Cooper, a Shropshire young lady, of bright parts and great personal beauty; as well as an inheritress of a fortune which, for the times, was by no means inconsiderable. The parchments of the marriage settlement upon this occasion are still remaining amongst the few family records that Dr. Burney preserved.

Whether attracted by her beauty, her sprightliness, or her portion; or by the aggregate influence of those three mighty magnetizers of the passions of man, is not known; but Wycherley, the famous poet, fine gentleman, and Wit of the reign of Charles the Second, had been so enamoured with Mrs. Ann Cooper in her earliest youth, which flourished in his latest decadency, that he sought her for his bride.

The romance, however, of his adoration, did not extend to breaking his heart; for though he expired within a few months after her rejection, it was not from wearing the willow: another fair one, yet younger, proved less cruel, and changed it to a wreath of myrtle. But the fates were adverse to his tender propensities, and he outlived his fair fortune and his nuptials only a fortnight.

A few years after this second marriage, Mr. Burney senior, finally, and with tolerable success, fixed himself to the profession of portrait-painting; and, quitting Shrewsbury, established himself in the city of Chester; where, to his reputation in the delightful arts of the pencil, he joined a far surpassing pre-eminence in those of society. His convivial spirit, his ready repartee, and his care-chasing pleasantry, made his intercourse sought by all to whom such qualifications afford pleasure : and we are yet, I believe, to learn where coin of such sterling value for exhilarating our fellow-creatures, fails of passing current.

The then Earl of Cholmondeley was particularly partial to him, and his most essential friend.

Charles, who was Mr. Burney's last-born son, had a twin sister, called Susanna, whom he early lost, but for whom he cherished a peculiar fondness that he seemed tenderly to transmit to the beloved and meritorious daughter to whom he gave her name.*

CONDOVER.

From what cause is not known, and it is difficult to conceive any that can justify such extraordinary neglect, young Charles was left in Shropshire, upon the removal of his parents to Chester; and aban-

---

* Afterwards Mrs. Phillips.

doned, not only during his infancy, but even during his boyhood, to the care of an uncultivated and utterly ignorant, but worthy and affectionate old nurse, called Dame Ball, in the rustic village of Condover, not far from Shrewsbury.

His reminiscences upon this period were amongst those the most tenaciously minute, and the most agreeable to his fancy for detail, of any part of his life; and the uncommon gaiety of his narratory powers, and the frankness with which he set forth the pecuniary embarrassments and provoking mischances, to which his thus deserted childhood was exposed, had an ingenuousness, a good-humour, and a comicality, that made the subject of Condover not more delectable to himself than entertaining to his hearer.

Nevertheless, these accounts, when committed to paper, and produced without the versatility of countenance, and the vivacious gestures that animated the colloquial disclosures, so lose their charm, as to appear vapid, languid, and tedious: and the editor only thus slightly recurs to them for the purpose of pointing out how gifted must be the man who, through disadvantages of so lowering a species, could become, in after life, not only one of the best informed, but one of the most polished, members of society.

There were few subjects of his childish remembrance with which he was himself more amused, than with the recital of the favourite couplets which the good nurse Ball most frequently sang to him at her spinning wheel; and which he especially loved to chaunt, in imitating her longdrawn face, and the dolorous tones of her drawling sadness.

> "Good bye, my dear neighbours! My heart it is sore,
> For I must go travelling all the world o'er.
> And if I should chance to come home very rich,
> My friends and relations will make of me mich;
> But if I should chance to come home very poor,
> My friends and relations will turn me out of door,
> After I have been travelling, travelling, travelling, all the world o'er."

CHESTER.

The education of the subject of these memoirs, when, at length, he was removed from this his first instructress, whom he quitted, as he always protested, with agony of grief, was begun at the Free School at Chester.

It can excite no surprise, his brilliant career

through life considered, that his juvenile studies were assiduous, ardent, and successful. He was frequently heard to declare that he had been once only chastised at school, and that not for slackness, but forwardness in scholastic lore. A favourite comrade, who shared his affections, though not his application or his genius, was hesitating through an ill-learnt lesson, and on the point of incurring punishment, when young Burney, dropping his head on his breast to muffle his voice, whispered the required answer.

"Burney prompts, Sir!" was loudly called out by a jealous, or malevolent fellow-student: and Burney paid the ignoble tax at which his incautious good nature, and superior talents, were assessed.

The resources of practical education ought, perhaps, to be judged only by the experience which puts them into play; but incongruous, at least to all thinking, though it may be incompetent, observers, must seem the discipline that appoints to the instinctive zeal of youthful friendship, the same degrading species of punishment that may be necessary for counteracting the sluggard mischiefs of indolence, or the dangerous examples of misconduct.

The prominent talents of young Burney for music fixed that tuneful art for his profession; and happily so; for while its pursuit was his business, its cultivation was his never-ceasing delight.

Yet not exclusively: far otherwise. He had a native love of literature, in all its branches, that opened his intellects to observation, while it furnished his mind with embellishments upon almost every subject; a thirst of knowledge, that rendered science, as far as he had opportunity for its investigation, an enlargement to his understanding; and an imagination that invested all the arts with a power of enchantment.

SHREWSBURY.

His earliest musical instructor was his eldest half brother, Mr. James Burney, who was then, and for more than half a century afterwards, organist of St. Margaret's, Shrewsbury; in which city the young musician elect began his professional studies.

It was, however, in age only that Mr. James Burney was his brother's senior or superior; from him, therefore, whatever could be given or received, was finished almost ere it was begun, from the quickness with which his pupil devoted himself to what he called the slavery of conquering unmeaning difficulties in the lessons of the times.

The following spirited paragraph on his juvenile progress is transcribed from his early memorandums.

" The celebrated Felton, and after him, the first Dr. Hayes, came from Oxford to Shrewsbury on a tour, while I was studying hard, without instruction or example; and they amazed and stimulated me so forcibly by their performance on the organ, as well as by their encouragement, that I thenceforward went to work with an ambition and fury that would hardly allow me to eat or sleep.

" The quantity of music which I copied at this time, of all kinds, was prodigious; and my activity and industry surprised every body; for, besides writing, teaching, tuning, and playing for my brother, at my *momens perdus*, I was educating myself in every way I was able. With copy-books, I improved my hand-writing so much, that my father did not believe I wrote my letters to him myself. I tried hard to at least keep up the little Latin I had learned; and I diligently practised both the spinet and violin; which, with reading, transcribing music for business, and poetry for pleasure; attempts at composition, and attention to my brother's affairs, filled up every minute of the longest day.

" I had, also, a great passion for angling; but whenever I could get leisure to pursue that sport, I ran no risk of losing my time, if the fish did not bite; for I had always a book in my pocket, which enabled me to wait with patience their pleasure."

Another paragraph, which is singular and amusing, is transcribed, also, from the Shrewsbury Annals :—

"CHARACTER OF LADY TANKERVILLE.*

"This lady was the daughter of Sir John Ashley, of the Abbey Foregate, Shrewsbury. She manifested a passion for music very early, in practising on the German flute, which was then little known in the country, Sir William Fowler and this lady being the only performers on that instrument that obtained, or deserved the least notice. Miss Ashley practised the harpsichord likewise, and took lessons of my brother: and she used to make little Matteis, the language master, and first violinist of the place, accompany her. She was an *espiegle*, and doted on mischief; and no sooner found that Matteis was very timid and helpless at the slightest distress or danger, than she insisted, during summer, upon taking her lessons in the middle of an old and lofty oak tree; placing there a seat and a desk, adroitly well arranged for her accommodation; while another seat and desk, upon a thick but tottering branch, was put up for poor Matteis, who was so terrified, that he could not stop a note in tune ; yet so fearful, that he could not bring himself to resist her orders.

"In 1738, she married Lord Ossulston, son of the Earl of Tankerville : and I remember leading off a choral song, or hymn, by her direction, to chaunt her out of St. Julian's Church. I was then quite a boy; and I heard no more of her till I was grown up, and settled in London."

---

* Afterwards Dame d'Atour to the celebrated sister of Frederick the Great.

CHESTER.

On quitting Shrewsbury to return to his parents at Chester, the ardour of young Burney for improvement was such as to absorb his whole being; and his fear lest a moment of daylight should be profitless, led him to bespeak a labouring boy, who rose with the sun, to awaken him regularly with its dawn. Yet, as he durst not pursue his education at the expense of the repose of his family, he hit upon the ingenious device of tying one end of a ball of pack-thread round his great toe, and then letting the ball drop, with the other end just within the boy's reach, from an aperture in the old-fashioned casement of his bed-chamber window.

This was no contrivance to dally with his diligence; he could not choose but rise.

He was yet a mere youth, when, while thus unremittingly studious, he was introduced to Dr. Arne, on the passage of that celebrated musician through the city of Chester, when returning from Ireland: and this most popular of English vocal composers since the days of Purcel, was so much pleased with the talents of this nearly self-instructed performer, as to make an offer to Mr. Burney senior, upon such conditions as are usual to such sort of patronage, to complete the musical education of this lively and aspiring young man; and to bring him forth to the world as his favourite and most promising pupil.

To this proposal Mr. Burney senior was induced to consent; and, in the year 1744, at the age of seventeen, the eager young candidate for fame rapturously set off, in company with Dr. Arne, for the metropolis.

LONDON.

Arrived in London, young Burney found himself unrestrainedly his own master, save in what regarded his articled agreement with Dr. Arne. Every part of his numerous family was left behind him, or variously dispersed, with the single exception of his elder and only own brother, Richard Burney, afterwards of Worcester, but who, at this period, was settled in the capital.

This brother was a man of true worth and vigorous understanding, enriched with a strong vein of native humour. He was an indefatigable and sapient collector of historical portraits, and passionately fond of the arts; and he was father of a race of children who severally, and with distinction, shone in them all; and who superadded to their ingenuity and their acquirements the most guileless hearts and scrupulous integrity.

DR. ARNE.

Dr. Arne, professionally, has been fully portrayed by the pupil who, nominally, was under his guidance; but who, in after times, became the historian of his tuneful art.

Eminent, however, in that art as was Dr. Arne, his eminence was to that art alone confined. Thoughtless, dissipated, and careless, he neglected, or rather scoffed at all other but musical reputation. And he was so little scrupulous in his ideas of propriety, that he took pride, rather than shame, in being publicly classed, even in the decline of life, as a man of pleasure.

Such a character was ill qualified to form or to protect the morals of a youthful pupil; and it is probable that not a notion of such a duty ever occurred to Dr. Arne; so happy was his self-complacency in the fertility of his invention and the ease of his compositions, and so dazzled by the brilliancy of his success in his powers of melody—which, in truth, for the English stage, were in sweetness and variety unrivalled—that, satisfied and flattered by the practical exertions and the popularity of his fancy, he had no ambition, or, rather, no thought concerning the theory of his art.

The depths of science, indeed, were the last that the gay master had any inclination to sound; and, in a very short time, through something that mingled jealousy with inability, the disciple was wholly left to work his own way as he could through the difficulties of his professional progress.

Had neglect, nevertheless, been the sole deficiency that young Burney had had to lament, it would effectually have been counteracted by his own industry: but all who are most wanting to others, are most rapacious of services for themselves; and the time in which the advancement of the scholar ought to have been blended with the advantage of the teacher, was almost exclusively seized upon for the imposition of laborious tasks of copying music: and thus, a drudgery fitted for those who have no talents to cultivate; or those who, in possessing them, are driven from their enjoyment by distress, filled up nearly the whole time of the student, and constituted almost wholly the directions of the tutor.

MRS. CIBBER.

Young Burney, now, was necessarily introduced to Dr. Arne's celebrated sister, the most enchanting actress of her day, Mrs. Cibber; in whose house, in Scotland-yard, he found himself in a constellation of wits, poets, actors, authors, and men of letters.

The social powers of pleasing, which to the very end of his long life endeared him to every circle in which he mixed, were now first lighted up by the sparks of convivial collision which emanate, in kindred minds, from the electricity of conversation. And though, as yet, he was but a gazer himself in the splendour of this galaxy, he had parts of such quick perception, and so laughter-loving a taste for wit and humour, that he not alone received delight from the sprightly sallies, the ludicrous representations, or the sportive mimicries that here, with all the frolic of high-wrought spirits, were bandied about from guest to guest; he contributed personally to the general enjoyment, by the gaiety of his participation; and appeared, to all but his modest self, to make an integral part of the brilliant society into which he was content, nay charmed, to seem admitted merely as an auditor.

GARRICK.

Conspicuous in this bright assemblage, Garrick, then hardly beyond the glowing dawn of his unparalleled dramatic celebrity, shone forth with a blaze of lustre that struck young Burney with enthusiastic admiration.

And nearly as prompt was the kind impression made in return, by the new young associate, on the fancy and the liking of this inimitable outward delineator of the inward human character; who, to the very close of that splendid circle which he described in the drama and in literature, retained for this early conquest a distinguishing, though not, perhaps, a wholly unremitting partiality; for where is the spoilt child, whether of the nursery or of the public, who is uniformly exempt from fickleness or caprice,—those wayward offsprings of lavish indulgence?

Not dense, however, nor frequent, were the occasional intermissions to the serenity of their intercourse; and the sunshine by which they were dispersed, beamed from an heightened esteem that, in both parties, terminated in cordial affection.

THOMSON.

With Thomson, too, whose fame, happily for posterity, hung not upon the ephemeral charm of accent, variety of attitude, or witchery of the eye, like that of even the most transcendent of the votaries of the buskins; with Thomson, too, his favoured lot led him to the happiness of early and intimate, though, unfortunately, not of long-enduring acquaintance, the destined race of Thomson, which was cut short nearly in the meridian of life, being already almost run.

It was not in the house only of Mrs. Cibber that he met this impressive and piety-inspiring painter of Nature, alike in her rural beauties and her elemental sublimities: the young musician had the advantage of setting to music a part of the mask of Alfred,* which brought him into close

---

* Upon its revival; not upon its first coming out.

contact with the author, and rivetted good will on one side by high admiration on the other.

With various persons, renowned or interesting, of the same set, who were gaily basking, at this period, in the smiles of popular sunshine, the subject of these memoirs daily mixed; but, unfortunately, not a memorandum of their intercourse has he left, beyond their names.

Mrs. Cibber herself he considered as a pattern of perfection in the tragic art, from her magnetizing powers of harrowing and winning at once every feeling of the mind, by the eloquent sensibility with which she pourtrayed, or, rather, personified, Tenderness, Grief, Horror, or Distraction.

KIT SMART.

With a different set, and at a different part of the town, young Burney formed an intimacy with Kit Smart, the poet; a man then in equal possession of those finest ingredients for the higher call of his art, fire and fancy, and, for its comic call, of sport and waggery. No indication, however, of such possession was granted to his appearance; not a grace was bestowed on his person or manners; and his physiognomy was of that round and stubbed form that seemed appertaining to a common dealer behind a common counter, rather than to a votary of the Muses. But his intellects, unhappily, were more brilliant than sound; and his poetic turn, though it never warped his sentiments or his heart, was little calculated to fortify his judgment.

DOCTOR ARMSTRONG.

And, at this same epoch, the subject of these memoirs began also an intercourse with the celebrated Dr. Armstrong, as high, then, in the theory of his art, medicine, as he was far from lucratively prosperous in its practice. He had produced upon it a didactic poem, " The Art of Preserving Health," which young Burney considered to be as nervous in diction as it was enlightening in precept. But Dr. Armstrong, though he came from a part of the island whence travellers are by no means proverbially smitten with the reproach of coming in vain; nor often stigmatized with either meriting or being addicted to failure, possessed not the personal skill usually accorded to his countrymen, of adroitness in bringing himself forward. Yet he was as gaily amiable as he was eminently learned; and though, from a keen moral sense of right, he was a satirist, he was so free from malevolence, that the smile with which he uttered a remark the most ironical, had a cast of good-humoured pleasantry that nearly turned his sarcasm into simple sport.

MISS MOLLY CARTER.

Now, also, opened to him an acquaintance with Miss Molly Carter, a lady who, ultimately, proved the oldest friend that he sustained through life; a sacred title, of which the rights, on both sides, were affectionately acknowledged. The following account of her is copied from Dr. Burney's early manuscripts.

" Miss Molly Carter, in her youth a very pretty girl, was, in the year 1745, of a large party of young ladies, consisting of five or six Miss Gores, and Miss Anderson, at William Thompson's Esq., in the neighbourhood of Elsham, near Brig. Bob Thompson, Mr. Thompson's brother, Billy Le Grand, and myself, composed the rest of the set, which was employed in nothing but singing, dancing, romping, and visiting, the whole time I was there; which time was never surpassed in hilarity at any place where I have been received in my life."

QUEEN MAB.

Neither pleasure, however, nor literary pursuits, led young Burney to neglect the cultivation of his musical talents. The mask of Alfred was by no means his sole juvenile composition: he set to music the principal airs in the English burletta called Robin Hood, which was most flatteringly received at the theatre; and he composed the whole of the music of the pantomime of Queen Mab.

He observed at this time the strictest incognito concerning all these productions, though no motive for it is found amongst his papers; nor does there remain any recollective explanation.

With regard to Queen Mab, it excited peculiar remark, from the extraordinary success of that diverting pantomime; for when the uncertainties of the representation were over, there was every stimulus to avowal that could urge a young author to come forward; not with adventurous boldness, nor yet with trembling timidity, but with the frank delight of unequivocal success.

Queen Mab had a run which, to that time, had never been equalled, save by the opening of the Beggar's Opera; and which has not since been surpassed, save by the representation of the Duenna.

Its music, pleasing and natural, was soon so popular, that it was taught to all young ladies, set to all barrel organs, and played at all familiar music parties. It aimed not at Italian refinement, nor at German science; but its sprightly melody, and utter freedom from vulgarity, made its way even with John Bull, who, while following the hairbreadth agility of Harlequin, the skittish coquetries of Columbine, and the merry dole of the disasters of the Clown and Pantaloon, found himself insensibly caught, and unconsciously beguiled into ameliorated musical taste.

In the present day, when English singers sometimes rise to the Italian opera, and when Italian singers are sometimes invited to the English, the music of Queen Mab could be received but in common with the feats of its pantomime; so rapidly has taste advanced, and so generally have foreign improvements become nearly indigenous.

To give its due to merit, and its rights to invention, we must always go back to their origin, and judge them, not by any comparison with what has followed them, but by what they met when they first started, and by what they were preceded.

Why, when success was thus ascertained, the name of the composer was concealed, leaving him thus singularly as unknown as he was popular, may the more be regretted, as his disposition, though chiefly domestic, was not of that effeminatively sensitive cast that shrinks from the world's notice with a dread of publicity. His mind, on the contrary, belonged to his sex; and was eminently formed to expand with that manly ambition, which opens the portals of hope to the attainment of independence, through intellectual honours.

The music, when printed, made its appearance in the world as the offspring of *a society of the sons of Apollo:* and Oswald, a famous bookseller, published it by that title, and knew nothing of its real parentage.*

Sundry airs, ballads, cantatas, and other light musical productions, were put forth also, as from

---

* Even to Thomson, young Burney had appeared but as a delegate from that nominal society.

that imaginary society; but all sprang from the same source, and all were equally unacknowledged.

The sole conjecture to be formed upon a self-denial, to which no virtue seems attached; and from which reason withdraws its sanction, as tending to counteract the just balance between merit and recompense, is, that possibly the articles then in force with Dr. Arne, might disfranchise young Burney from the liberty of publication in his own name.

EARL OF HOLDERNESSE.

The first musical work by the subject of these memoirs that he openly avowed, was a set of six sonatas for two violins and a bass, printed in 1747, and dedicated to the Earl of Holdernesse; to whose notice the author had been presented by some of the titled friends and protectors to whom he had become accidentally known.

The Earl not only accepted with pleasure the music and the dedication, but conceived a regard for the young composer, that soon passed from his talents to his person and character. Many notes of Lord Holdernesse still remain of kind engagements for meetings, even after his time was under the royal, though honourable restraint, of being governor of the heir apparent.* That high, and nearly exclusive occupation, lessened not the favour which his lordship had had the taste and discernment to display so early for a young man whom, afterwards, with pleasure, if not with pride, he must have seen rise to equal and general favour in the world.

At Holdernesse House,† the fine mansion of this earl, young Burney began an acquaintance, which in after years ripened into intimacy, with Mr. Mason, the poet, who was his lordship's chaplain.

FULK GREVILLE.

While connexions thus various, literary, classical, noble, and professional, incidentally occurred, combatting the deadening toil of the copyist, and keeping his mind in tune for intellectual pursuits and attainments, new scenes, most unexpectedly, opened to him the world at large, and suddenly brought him to a familiar acquaintance with high life.

Fulk Greville, a descendant of *The Friend of*

---

* His late Majesty, George the Fourth, when Prince of Wales.
† Now the mansion of the Marquis of Londonderry.

Sir Philip Sydney, and afterwards author of Characters, Maxims, and Reflections, was then generally looked up to as the finest gentleman about town. His person, tall and well-proportioned, was commanding; his face, features, and complexion, were striking for masculine beauty; and his air and carriage were noble with conscious dignity.

He was then in the towering pride of healthy manhood and athletic strength. He excelled in all the fashionable exercises, riding, fencing, hunting, shooting at a mark, dancing, tennis, &c.; and worked at every one of them with a fury for preeminence, not equalled, perhaps, in ardour for superiority in personal accomplishments, since the days of the chivalrous Lord Herbert of Cherbury.

His high birth, and higher expectation—for a coronet at that time, from some uncertain right of heritage, hung almost suspended over his head—with a splendid fortune, wholly unfettered, already in his hands, gave to him a consequence in the circles of modish dissipation that, at the clubs of St. James's-street, and on the race ground at Newmarket, nearly crowned him as chief. For though there were many competitors of more titled importance, and more powerful wealth, neither the blaze of their heraldry, nor the weight of their gold, could preponderate, in the buckish scales of the day, over the elegance of equipment, the grandeur, yet attraction of demeanour, the supercilious brow, and the resplendent smile, that marked the lofty yet graceful descendant of Sir Philip Sydney.

This gentleman one morning, while trying a new instrument at the house of Kirkman, the first harpsichord maker of the times, expressed a wish to receive musical instruction from some one who had mind and cultivation, as well as finger and ear; lamenting, with strong contempt, that, in the musical tribe, the two latter were generally dislocated from the two former; and gravely asking Kirkman whether he knew any young musician who was fit company for a gentleman.

Kirkman, with honest zeal to stand up for the credit of the art by which he prospered, and which he held to be insulted by this question, warmly answered that he knew many; but, very particularly, one member of the harmonic corps, who had as much music in his tongue as in his hands, and who was as fit company for a prince as for an orchestra.

Mr. Greville, with much surprise, made sundry

and formal inquiries into the existence, situation, and character of what he called so great a phenomenon; protesting there was nothing he so much desired as the extraordinary circumstance of finding any union of sense with sound.

The replies of the good German were so exciting, as well as satisfactory, that Mr. Greville became eager to see the youth thus extolled; but charged Mr. Kirkman not to betray a word of what had passed, that the interview might be free from restraint, and seem to be arranged merely for shewing off the several instruments that were ready for sale, to a gentleman who was disposed to purchase one of the most costly.

To this injunction Mr. Kirkman agreed, and conscientiously adhered.

A day was appointed, and the meeting took place.

Young Burney, with no other idea than that of serving Kirkman, immediately seated himself at an instrument, and played various pieces of Geminiani, Corelli, and Tartini, whose compositions were then most in fashion. But Mr. Greville, secretly suspicious of some connivance, coldly and proudly walked about the room; took snuff from a finely enamelled snuff-box, and looked at some prints, as if wholly without noticing the performance.

He had, however, too much penetration not to perceive his mistake, when he remarked the incautious carelessness with which his inattention was returned; for soon, conceiving himself to be playing to very obtuse ears, young Burney left off all attempt at soliciting their favour; and only sought his own amusement by trying favourite passages, or practising difficult ones, with a vivacity which shewed that his passion for his art rewarded him in itself for his exertions. But coming, at length, to keys of which the touch, light and springing, invited his stay, he fired away in a sonata of Scarlatti's, with an alternate excellence of execution and expression, so perfectly in accord with the fanciful flights of that wild but masterly composer, that Mr. Greville, satisfied no scheme was at work to surprise or to win him; but, on the contrary, that the energy of genius was let loose upon itself, and enjoying, without premeditation, its own lively sports and vagaries; softly drew a chair to the harpsichord, and listened, with unaffected earnestness, to every note.

Nor were his ears alone curiously awakened; his eyes were equally occupied to mark the peculiar performance of intricate difficulties; for the young musician had invented a mode of adding neatness to brilliancy, by curving the fingers, and rounding the hand, in a manner that gave them a grace upon the keys quite new at that time, and entirely of his own devising.

To be easily pleased, however, or to make acknowledgment of being pleased at all, seems derogatory to strong self-importance; Mr. Greville, therefore, merely said, "You are fond, Sir, it seems, of Italian music?"

The reply to this was striking up, with all the varying undulations of the crescendo, the diminuendo, the pealing swell, and the "dying, dying fall," belonging to the powers of the pedal, that most popular masterpiece of Handel's, the Coronation Anthem.

This quickness of comprehension, in turning from Italian to German, joined to the grandeur of the composition, and the talents of the performer, now irresistibly vanquished Mr. Greville; who, convinced of Kirkman's truth with regard to the harmonic powers of this son of Apollo, desired next to sift it with regard to the wit.

Casting off, therefore, his high reserve, with his

jealous surmises, he ceased to listen to the music, and started some theme that was meant to lead to conversation.

But as this essay, from not knowing to what the youth might be equal, consisted of such inquiries as, "Have you been in town long, Sir?" or, "Does your taste call you back to the country, Sir?" &c. &c., his young hearer, by no means preferring this inquisitorial style to the fancy of Scarlatti, or the skill and depth of Handel, slightly answered, "Yes, Sir," or "No, Sir;" and, perceiving an instrument not yet tried, darted to it precipitately, and seated himself to play a voluntary.

The charm of genuine simplicity is nowhere more powerful than with the practised and hackneyed man of the world; for it induces what, of all things, he most rarely experiences, a belief in sincerity.

Mr. Greville, therefore, though thwarted, was not displeased; for in a votary of the art he was pursuing, he saw a character full of talents, yet without guile; and conceived, from that moment, an idea that it was one he might personally attach. He remitted, therefore, to some other opportunity, a further internal investigation.

Mr. Kirkman now came forward to announce,

that in the following week he should have a new harpsichord, with double keys, and a deepened bass, ready for examination.

They then parted, without any explanation on the side of Mr. Greville; or any idea on that of the subject of these memoirs, that he and his acquirements were objects of so peculiar a speculation.

At the second interview, young Burney innocently and eagerly flew at once to the harpsichord, and tried it with various recollections from his favourite composers.

Mr. Greville listened complacently and approvingly; but, at the end of every strain, made a speech that he intended should lead to some discussion.

Young Burney, however, more alive to the graces of melody than to the subtleties of argument, gave answers that always finished with full-toned chords, which as constantly modulated into another movement; till Mr. Greville, tired and impatient, suddenly proposed changing places, and trying the instrument himself.

He could not have devised a more infallible expedient to provoke conversation; for he thrummed his own chosen bits by memory with so little skill or taste, yet with a pertinacity so wearisome, that young Burney, who could neither hearken to such playing, nor turn aside from such a player, caught with alacrity at every opening to discourse, as an acquittal from the fatigue of mock attention.

This eagerness gave a piquancy to what he said, that stole from him the diffidence that might otherwise have hung upon his inexperience; and endued him with a courage for uttering his opinions, that might else have faded away under the trammels of distant respect.

Mr. Greville, however, was really superior to the mawkish parade of unnecessary etiquette in private circles, where no dignity can be offended, and no grandeur be let down by suffering nature, wit, or accident to take their bent, and run their race, unfettered by punctilio.

Yet was he the last of men to have borne any designed infringement upon the long established claims of birth, rank, or situation; which, in fact, is rarely practised but to lead to a succession of changes, that circulate, like the names written in a round robin, to end just where they began;—

> " Such choas, where degree is suffocate,
> Follows the choaking."*

---

* Troilus and Cressida.

In the subject of these memoirs, this effervescence of freedom was clearly that of juvenile artlessness and overflowing vivacity; and Mr. Greville desired too sincerely to gather the youth's notions and fathom his understanding, for permitting himself to check such amusing spirits, by proudly wrapping himself up, as at less favourable moments he was wont to do, in his own consequence. He grew, therefore, so lively and entertaining, that young Burney became as much charmed with his company as he had been wearied by his music; and an interchange of ideas took place, as frankly rapid, equal, and undaunted, as if the descendant of *the friend of Sir Philip Sydney* had encountered a descendant of Sir Philip Sydney himself.

This meeting concluded the investigation; music, singing her gay triumph, took her stand at the helm; and a similar victory for capacity and information awaited but a few intellectual skirmishes, on poetry, politics, morals, and literature,—in the midst of which Mr. Greville, suddenly and gracefully holding out his hand, fairly acknowledged his scheme, proclaimed its success, and invited the unconscious victor to accompany him to Wilbury House.

The amazement of young Burney was boundless;

but his modesty, or rather his ignorance that not to think highly of his own abilities merited that epithet, was most agreeably surprised by so complicate a flattery to his character, his endowments, and his genius.

But his articles with Dr. Arne were in full force; and it was not without a sigh that he made known his confined position.

Unaccustomed to control his inclinations himself, or to submit to their control from circumstances, expense, or difficulty, Mr. Greville mocked this puny obstacle; and, instantly visiting Dr. Arne in person, demanded his own terms for liberating his Cheshire pupil.

Dr. Arne, at first, would listen to no proposition; protesting that a youth of such promise was beyond all equivalent. But no sooner was a round sum mentioned, than the Doctor, who, in common with all the dupes of extravagance, was evermore needy, could not disguise from himself that he was dolorously out of cash; and the dazzling glare of three hundred pounds could not but play most temptingly in his sight, for one of those immediate, though imaginary wants, that the man of pleasure is always sure to see waving, with decoying allurement, before his longing eyes.

The articles, therefore, were cancelled: and young Burney was received in the house of Mr. Greville as a desired inmate, a talented professor, and a youth of genius: to which appellations, from his pleasantry, gaiety, reading, and readiness, was soon superadded the title—not of a humble, but of a chosen and confidential companion.

* * * * *

Young Burney now moved in a completely new sphere, and led a completely new life. All his leisure nevertheless was still devoted to improvement in his own art, by practice and by composition. But the hours for such sage pursuits were soon curtailed from half the day to its quarter; and again from that to merely the early morning that preceded any communication with his gay host: for so partial grew Mr. Greville to his new favourite, that, speedily, there was no remission of claim upon his time or his talents, whether for music or discourse.

Nor even here ended the requisition for his presence; his company had a charm that gave a zest to whatever went forward: his opinions were so ingenious, his truth was so inviolate, his spirits were so entertaining, that, shortly, to make him a part of whatever was said or done, seemed necessary to Mr. Greville for either speech or action.

GAMING CLUBS.

The consequence of this taste for his society carried young Burney into every scene of high dissipation which, at that period, made the round of the existence of a buckish fine gentleman; and he was continually of the party at White's, at Brookes's, and at every other superfine club house, whether public or private, to which the dangerous allurement of gaming, or the scarcely less so of being *à la mode,* tempted his fashionable patron.

As Mr. Greville uniformly, whether at cards, dice, or betting, played with Honour, his success, of course, was precarious; but as he never was so splendidly prosperous as to suffer himself to be beguiled out of all caution; nor yet so frequently unfortunate as to be rendered desperate, he was rarely distressed, though now and then he might be embarrassed.

At these clubs, the subject of these memoirs witnessed scenes that were ever after rivetted on his memory. Cards, betting, dice, opened every nocturnal orgie with an *éclat* of expectation, hope, ardour, and fire, that seemed to cause a mental inflammation of the feelings and faculties of the whole assembly in a mass.

On the first night of the entrance of young Burney into this set, Mr. Greville amused himself with keeping out of the way, that he might make over the new comer to what was called the humour of the thing; so that, by being unknown, he might be assailed, as a matter of course, for bets, holding stakes, choosing cards, &c. &c., and become initiated in the arcana of a modish gaming house; while watchful, though apart, Mr. Greville enjoyed, with high secret glee, the novelty of the youth's confusion.

But young Burney had the native good sense to have observed already, that a hoax soon loses its power of ridicule where it excites no alarm in its object. He gaily, therefore, treated as a farce every attempt to bring him forward, and covered up his real ignorance upon such subjects by wilful blunders that apparently doubled it; till, by making himself a pretended caricature of newness and inaptness, he got, what in coteries of that sort is always successful, the laugh on his side.

As the evening advanced, the busy hum of common-place chattery subsided; and a general and collected calmness ensued, such as might best dispose the gambling associates to a wily deliberation, how most coolly to penetrate into the mystic obscurities that brought them together.

All, however, was not yet involved in the gaping cauldron of chance, whence so soon was to emerge the brilliant prize, or desolating blank, that was to blazon the lustre, or stamp the destruction, of whoever, with his last trembling mite, came to sound its perilous depths. They as yet played, or prowled around it, lightly and slightly; not more impatient than fearful of hurrying their fate; and seeking to hide from themselves, as well as from their competitors, their anticipating exultation or dread.

Still, therefore, they had some command of the general use of their faculties, and of what was due from them to general social commerce. Still some vivacious sallies called forth passing smiles from those who had been seldomest betrayed, or whose fortunes had least been embezzled; and still such cheeks as were not too dragged or haggard to exhibit them, were able to give graceful symptoms of self-possession, by the pleasing and becoming dimples produced through arch, though silent observance.

But by degrees the fever of doubt and anxiety broke forth all around, and every breath caught its infection. Every look then showed the contagion of lurking suspicion : every eye that fixed a prosperous object, seemed to fix it with the stamp of detection. All was contrast the most discordant, unblended by any gradation ; for wherever the laughing brilliancy of any countenance denoted exulting victory, the glaring vacancy of some other hard by, displayed incipient despair.

Like the awe of death was next the muteness of taciturnity, from the absorption of agonizing attention while the last decisive strokes, upon which hung affluence or beggary, were impending. Every die, then, became a bliss or a blast; every extorted word was an execration ; every fear whispered ruin with dishonour ; every wish was a dagger to some antagonist ! — till, finally, the result was proclaimed, which carried off the winner in a whirl of maddening triumph ; and to the loser left the recovery of his nervous, hoarse, husky, grating voice, only for curses and oaths, louder and more appalling than thunder in its deepest roll.

NEWMARKET.

The next vortex of high dissipation into which, as its season arrived, young Burney was ushered, was that of Newmarket: and there, as far as belonged to the spirit of the race, and the beauty, the form, and the motions of the noble quadrupeds, whose rival swiftness made running seem a flight, and that flight appear an airy game, or gambol, of some fabled animal of elastic grace and celerity, he was enchanted with his sojourn. And the accompanying scenes of gambling, betting, &c., though of the same character and description as those of St. James's-street, he thought less darkly terrible, because the winners or losers seemed to him more generally assorted according to their equality in rank or fortune: though no one, in the long run, however high, or however low, escaped becoming the dupe, or the prey, of whoever was most adroit, —whether plebeian or patrician.

BATH.

The ensuing initiation into this mingled existence of inertness and effort, of luxury and of desolation, was made at Bath. But Bath, from its buildings and its position, had a charm around it for the subject of these memoirs, to soften off the monotony of this wayward taste, and these wilful sufferings; though the seat of dissipation alone he found to be changed; its basis—cards, dice, or betting—being always the same.

Nevertheless, that beautiful city, then little more than a splendid village in comparison with its actual metropolitan size and grandeur, had intrinsic claims to the most vivid admiration, and the strongest incitements to youthful curiosity, from the antiquity of its origin, real as well as fabulous; from its Bladud, its baths, its cathedral; and its countless surrounding glories of military remains; all magically followed up, to vary impression, and stimulate approbation, by its rising excellence in Grecian and Roman architecture.

Born with an enthusiastic passion for rural scenery, the picturesque view of this city offered to the ravished eye of young Burney some new loveliness, or striking effect, with an endless enchantment of variety, at almost every fresh opening of every fresh street into which he sauntered.

And here, not only did he find this perpetual,

yet changeful, prospect of Nature in her most smiling attire, and of Art in her most chaste and elegant constructions; Bath had yet further attraction to its new visitor; another captivation stronger still to a character soaring to intellectual heights, caught him in its chains,—it was that of literary eminence; Bath, at this moment, being illumined by that sparkling but dangerous Meteor of philosophy, politics, history, and metaphysics, St. John, Lord Bolingbroke.

Happily, perhaps, for his safety, it was in vain that young Burney struggled, by every effort of ingenuity he could exert, to bask in the radiance of this Meteor's wit and eloquence. Every attempt at that purpose failed; and merely a glimpse of this extraordinary personage, was all that the utmost vigilance of romantic research ever caught.

Young Burney could not, at that period, have studied the works of Lord Bolingbroke, who was then chiefly known by his political honours and disgraces; his exile and his pardon; and by that most perfect panegyric that ever, perhaps, poet penned, of Pope:

> " Come then, my friend! my Genius!— —
> Oh, master of the poet and the song!"

Fortunately, therefore, the ingenuous youth and inexperience of the subject of these memoirs, escaped the brilliant poison of metaphysical sophistry, that might else have disturbed his peace, and darkened his happiness.

The set to which Mr. Greville belonged, was as little studious to seek, as likely to gain, either for its advantage or its evil, admission to a character so eminently scholastic, or so personally fastidious, as that of Lord Bolingbroke; though, had he been unhampered by such colleagues, Lord Bolingbroke, as a metaphysician, would have been sought with eager, nay, fond alacrity, by Mr. Greville; metaphysics being, in his own conception and opinion, the proper bent of his mind and understanding. But those with whom he now was connected, encompassed him with snares that left little opening to any higher pursuits than their own.

The aim, therefore, of young Burney, was soon limited to obtaining a glance of the still noble, though infirm figure, and still handsome, though aged countenance of this celebrated statesman. And of these, for the most transitory view, he would frequently, with a book in his hand, loiter by the hour opposite to his lordship's windows, which were *vis à vis* to those of Mr. Greville; or run, in circular eddies, from side to side of the sedan chair in which his lordship was carried to the pump-room.

Mr. Greville, though always entertained by the juvenile eagerness of his young favourite, pursued his own modish course with the alternate ardour and apathy, which were then beginning to be what Now is called the order of the day; steering—for he thought that was *the thing*—with whatever was most in vogue, even when it was least to his taste; and making whatever was most expensive the criterion for his choice, even in diversions; because that was what most effectually would exclude plebeian participation.

And to this lofty motive, rather than to any appropriate fondness for its charms, might be attributed, in its origin, his fervour for gaming; though gaming, with that poignant stimulus, self-conceit, which, where calculation tries to battle with chance, goads on, with resistless force, our designs by our presumption, soon left wholly in the back ground every attempt at rivalry by any other species of recreation.

Hunting therefore, shooting, riding, music, drawing, dancing, fencing, tennis, horse-racing, the joys of Bacchus, and numerous other exertions of skill, of strength, of prowess, and of ingenuity, served but, ere long, to fill up the annoying chasms by which these nocturnal orgies were interrupted through the obtrusion of day.

FULK GREVILLE.

Such was the new world into which the subject of these memoirs was thus abruptly let loose; but, happily, his good taste was as much revolted as his morality, against its practices. And his astonishment at the dreadful night-work that has been described; so absorbent, concentrating, and fearful, hung round with such dire prognostics, pursued with so much fury, or brooded over with such despondence; never so thoughtlessly wore away as to deaden his horror of its perils.

Mr. Greville himself, though frequenting these scenes as an expert and favourite member of the coteries in which they were enacted, had too real a sense of right, and too sincere a feeling of humanity, to intend involving an inexperienced youth in a passion for the amusements of hazard; or to excite in him a propensity for the dissolute company of which its followers are composed; who, satiated with every species of pleasure that is innoxious, are alive alone to such as can rescue them from ruin, even though at the fatal price of betraying into its gulph the associates with whom they chiefly herd.

Nevertheless, he gave no warning to young Burney of danger. Aware that there was no fortune to lose, he concluded there was no mischief to apprehend; and, satisfied that the sentiments of the youth were good, to meddle with his principles seemed probably a work of supererogation. Without reflection, therefore, rather than with any project, he was glad of a sprightly participator, with whom he could laugh the next morning, at whatever had been ludicrous over-night; though to utter either caution or counsel, he would have thought moralizing, and, consequently, *fogrum;* a term which he adopted for whatever speech, action, or mode of conduct, he disdainfully believed to be beneath the high *ton* to which he considered himself to be born and bred.

From such *fogrum* sort of work, therefore, he contemptuously recoiled, deeming it fitted exclusively for schoolmasters, or for priests.

WILBURY HOUSE.

Not solely, however, to public places were the pleasures, or the magnificence, of Mr. Greville confined. He visited, with great fondness and great state, his family seat in Wiltshire; and had the highest gratification in receiving company there with splendour, and in awakening their surprise, and surpassing their expectations, by the spirit and the changes of their entertainment.

He travelled in a style that was even princely; not only from his equipages, out-riders, horses, and liveries, but from constantly having two of his attendants skilled in playing the French horn. And these were always stationed to recreate him with marches and warlike movements, on the outside of the windows, where he took any repast.

Wilbury House, the seat of Mr. Greville, situated near Andover, in Wiltshire, was a really pretty place; but it had a recommendation to those who possess wealth and taste with superfluous time, far greater than any actual beauty, by requiring expensive alterations, and being susceptible of lavish improvements.

This enhanced all its merits to Mr. Greville, who,

when out of other employment for his thoughts, devoted them to avenues, plantations, rising hills, sinking dales, and unexpected vistas; to each of which he called upon whatever guests were at his house, during their creation, for as much astonishment as applause.

The call, however, was frequently unanswered; it was so palpable that he was urged to this pursuit by lassitude rather than pleasure; by flourishing ostentation rather than by genuine picturesque taste; so obvious that to draw forth admiration to the beauties of his grounds, was far less his object than to stir up wonder at the recesses of his purse; that the wearied and wary visitor, who had once been entrapped to follow his footsteps, in echoing his exclamations of delight at his growing embellishments, was, ever after, sedulous, when he was with his workmen and his works, to elude them: though all alike were happy to again rejoin him at his sports and at his table; for there he was gay, hospitable, and pleasing, brilliant in raillery, and full of enjoyment.

SAMUEL CRISP, ESQ.

The first entrance of young Burney into Wilbury House was engraven, ever after it took place, in golden characters of sacred friendship upon his mind, for there he first met with Mr. Crisp. And as his acquaintance with Mr. Greville had opened new roads and pursuits in life to his prospects, that of Mr. Crisp opened new sources and new energies to his faculties, for almost every species of improvement.

Mr. Crisp, by birth and education a gentleman, according to the ordinary acceptation of that word, was in mind, manners, and habits yet more truly so, according to the most refined definition of the appellation, as including honour, spirit, elegance, language, and grace.

His person and port were distinguished; his address was even courtly; his face had the embellishment of a strikingly fine outline; bright, hazel, penetrating, yet arch eyes; an open front; a noble Roman nose; and a smile of a thousand varied expressions.

But all that was external, however attractive, however full of promise, however impossible to pass over, was of utterly inferior worth compared with the inward man; for there he was rare indeed. Profound in wisdom; sportive in wit; sound in understanding. A scholar of the highest order; a critic of the clearest acumen; possessing, with equal delicacy of discrimination, a taste for literature and for the arts; and personally excelling, as a *diletante,* both in music and painting.

It was difficult to discuss any classical or political work, that his conversation did not impregnate with more information and more wit than, commonly speaking, their acutest authors had brought forward. And such was his knowledge of mankind, that it was something beyond difficult, it was scarcely even possible, to investigate any subject requiring worldly sagacity, in which he did not dive into the abysses of the minds and the propensities of the principals, through whom the business was to be transacted, with a perspicuity so masterly, that while weighing all that was presented to him, it developed all that was held back; and fathomed at once the intentions and the resources of his opponents.

And with abilities thus grand and uncommon for great and important purposes, if to such he had been called, he was endowed with discursive powers for the social circle, the most varied in matter, the most solid in reasoning, and the most delighting in gaiety—or nearly so—that ever fell to favoured mortal's lot.

The subject of these memoirs was but seventeen

years of age, when first he had the incalculable advantage of being attracted to explore this Mine of wisdom, experience, and accomplishments. His musical talents, and a sympathy of taste in the choice of composers, quickly caught the responsive ears of Mr. Crisp; which vibrated to every passage, every sound, that the young musician embellished by graces intuitively his own, either of expression or execution. And whenever Mr. Crisp could contrive to retreat, and induce his new Orpheus to retreat, from the sports of the field, it was even with ardour that he escaped from the clang of horses and hounds, to devote whole mornings to the charms,

<blockquote>Softly sweet, in Lydian measures,</blockquote>

of harmony. And harmony indeed, in its most enlarged combinations, united here the player and the auditor; for they soon discovered that not in music alone, but in general sentiments, their hearts were tuned to the same key, and expanded to the same "concord of sweet sounds."

The love of music, in Mr. Crisp, amounted to passion; yet that passion could not have differed more from modern enthusiasm in that art, if it had been hatred; since, far from demanding, according to the present mode, every two or three seasons, new compositions and new composers, his musical taste and consistency deviated not from his taste and consistency in literature : and where a composer had hit his fancy, and a composition had filled him with delight, he would call for his favourite pieces of Bach of Berlin, Handel, Scarlatti, or Echard, with the same reiteration of eagerness that he would again and again read, hear, or recite chosen passages from the works of his favourite bards, Shakespeare, Milton, or Pope.

Mr. Greville was sometimes diverted, and sometimes nettled, by this double defection; for in whatever went forward, he loved to be lord of the ascendant : but Mr. Crisp, whose temper was as unruffled as his understanding was firm, only smiled at his friend's diversion; and from his pique looked away. Mr. Greville then sought to combat this musical mania by ridicule, and called upon his companions of the chase to halloo the recreant huntsman to the field; affirming that he courted the pipe and the song, only to avoid clearing a ditch, and elude leaping a five-barred gate.

This was sufficient to raise the cry against the delinquent; for Man without business or employment is always disposed to be a censor of his neighbour; and whenever he thinks his antagonist on the road to defeat, is always alert to start up for a wit. Mr. Crisp, therefore, now, was assailed as a renegado from the chase; as a lounger; a loiterer; scared by the horses; panic-struck by the dogs; and more fearful of the deer, than the deer could be of the hunter.

In the well-poized hope, that the less the sportsmen were answered, the sooner they would be fatigued and depart, Mr. Crisp now and then gave them a nod, but never once a word; even though this forbearance instigated a triumph, loud, merry, and exulting; and sent them off, and brought them back, in the jovial persuasion that, in their own phrase, they had dumb-founded him.

With this self-satisfied enjoyment, Mr. Crisp unresistingly indulged them; though with a single pointed sentence, he could rapidly have descended them from their fancied elevation. But, above all petty pride of superiority in trifles, he never held things of small import to be worth the trouble of an argument. Still less, however, did he choose to be put out of his own way; which he always pursued with placid equanimity whenever it was opposed without irrefragable reason. Good-humouredly, however, he granted to his adversaries, in whose laughs and railing he sometimes heartily joined, the full play of their epigrams; internally conscious that, if seriously provoked, he could retort them by lampoons. Sometimes, nevertheless, when he was hard beset by gibes and jeers at his loss of sport; or by a chorus of mock pitiers shouting out, " Poor Crisp! poor fellow! how consumedly thou art moped!" he would quietly say, with a smile of inexpressible archness, " Go to, my friends, go to! go you your way, and let me go mine! And pray, don't be troubled for me; depend upon it there is nobody will take more care of Samuel Crisp than I will!"

* * * * *

In this manner, and in these sets, rapidly, gaily, uncounted, and untutored, glided on imperceptibly the first youth of the subject of these memoirs: surrounded by temptations to luxury, expense, and dangerous pleasures, that, in weaker intellects, might have sapped for ever the foundations of religion and virtue. But a love of right was the predominant feature of the mind of young Burney. Mr. Greville, also, himself, with whatever mockery he would have sneered away any expression tending either to practice or meditation in piety, instinctively held in esteem whatever was virtuous; and what was vicious in scorn: though his esteem for virtue was never pronounced, lest it should pass for pedantry; and his scorn for vice was studiously disguised, lest he should be set down himself for a Fogrum.

MISS FANNY MACARTNEY.

New scenes, and of deeper interest, presented themselves ere long. A lovely female, in the bloom of youth, equally high in a double celebrity, the most rarely accorded to her sex, of beauty and of wit, and exquisite in her possession of both, made an assault upon the eyes, the understanding, and the heart of Mr. Greville; so potent in its first attack, and so varied in its after stages, that, little as he felt at that time disposed to barter his boundless liberty, his desultory pursuits, and his brilliant, though indefinite expectations, for a bondage so narrow, so derogatory to the swing of his wild will, as that of marriage appeared to him; he was caught by so many charms, entangled in so many inducements, and inflamed by such a whirl of passions, that he soon almost involuntarily surrendered to the besieger; not absolutely at discretion, but very unequivocally from resistless impulse.

This lady was Miss Fanny Macartney, the third daughter of Mr. Macartney, a gentleman of large fortune, and of an ancient Irish family.

In Horace Walpole's Beauties, Miss Fanny Macartney was the Flora.

In Greville's Maxims, Characters, and Reflections, she was also Flora, contrasted with Camilla, who was meant for Mrs. Garrick.

Miss Fanny Macartney was of a character which, at least in its latter stages, seems to demand two pencils to delineate; so diversely was it understood, or appreciated.

To many she passed for being pedantic, sarcastic, and supercilious: as such, she affrighted the timid, who shrunk into silence; and braved the bold, to whom she allowed no quarter. The latter, in truth, seemed to stimulate exertions which brought her faculties into play; and which—besides creating admiration in all who escaped her shafts—appeared to offer to herself a mental exercise, useful to her health, and agreeable to her spirits.

Her understanding was truly masculine; not from being harsh or rough, but from depth, soundness, and capacity; yet her fine small features, and the whole style of her beauty, looked as if meant by Nature for the most feminine delicacy: but her voice, which had something in it of a croak; and her manner, latterly at least, of sitting, which was that of lounging completely at her ease, in such curves as she found most commodious, with her head alone upright; and her eyes commonly fixed, with an expression rather alarming than flattering, in examination of some object that caught her attention; probably caused, as they naturally excited, the hard general notion to her disadvantage above mentioned.

This notion, nevertheless, though almost universally harboured in the circle of her public acquaintance, was nearly reversed in the smaller circles that came more in contact with her feelings. By this last must be understood, solely, the few who were happy enough to possess her favour; and to them she was a treasure of ideas and of variety. The keenness of her satire yielded its asperity to the zest of her good-humour, and the kindness of her heart. Her noble indifference to superior rank, if placed in opposition to superior merit; and her delight in comparing notes with those with whom she desired to balance opinions, established her, in her own elected set, as one of the first of women. And though the fame of her beauty must pass away in the same oblivious rotation which has withered that of her rival contemporaries, the fame of her intellect must ever live, while sensibility may be linked with poetry, and the Ode to Indifference shall remain to shew their union.

The various incidents that incited and led to the connexion that resulted from this impassioned opening, appertain to the history of Mr. Greville; but, in its solemn ratification, young Burney took a part so essential, as to produce a striking and pleasing consequence to much of his after life.

The wedding, though no one but the bride and bridegroom themselves knew why, was a stolen one; and kept profoundly secret; which, notwithstanding the bride was under age, was by no means, at that time, difficult, the marriage act having not yet passed. Young Burney, though the most juvenile of the party, was fixed upon to give the lady away;* which evinced a trust and a partiality in the bridegroom, that were immediately adopted by his fair

---

* The bride's sisters, the Misses Macartney, were privately present at this clandestine ceremony.

partner; and by her unremittingly sustained, with the frankest confidence, and the sincerest esteem, through the whole of a long and varied life. With sense and taste such as hers, it was not, indeed, likely she should be slack to discern and develop a merit so formed to meet their perceptions.

When the new married pair went through the customary routine of matrimonial elopers, namely, that of returning home to demand pardon and a blessing, Mr. Macartney coolly said: "Mr. Greville has chosen to take a wife out of the window, whom he might just as well have taken out of the door."

The immediate concurrence of the lovely new mistress of Wilbury House, in desiring the society, even more than enjoying the talents, of her lord and master's favourite, occasioned his residence there to be nearly as unbroken as their own. And the whole extensive neighbourhood so completely joined in this kindly partiality, that no engagement, no assemblage whatsoever took place, from the most selectly private, to the most gorgeously public, to which the Grevilles were invited, in which he was not included: and he formed at that period many connections of lasting and honourable intimacy; particularly with Dr. Hawkesworth, Mr. Boone, and Mr. Cox.

They acted, also, sundry proverbs, interludes, and farces, in which young Burney was always a principal personage. In one, amongst others, he played his part with a humour so entertaining, that its nick-name was fastened upon him for many years after its appropriate representation. It would be difficult, indeed, not to accord him theatrical talents, when he could perform with success a character so little congenial with his own, as that of a finical, conceited coxcomb, a paltry and illiterate poltroon; namely, Will Fribble, Esq., in Garrick's farce of Miss in her Teens. Mr. Greville himself was Captain Flash, and the beautiful Mrs. Greville was Miss Biddy Bellair; by which three names, from the great diversion their adoption had afforded, they corresponded with one another during several years.

The more serious honour that had been conferred upon young Burney, of personating the part of father to Mrs. Greville, was succeeded, in due season after these gay espousals, by that of personating the part of god-father to her daughter; in standing, as the representative of the Duke of Beaufort, at the baptism of Miss Greville, afterwards the all-admired, and indescribably beautiful Lady Crewe.

Little could he then foresee, that he was bringing

into the christian community a permanent blessing for his own after-life, in one of the most cordial, confidential, open-hearted, and unalterable of his friends.

ESTHER.

But not to Mr. Greville alone was flung one of those blissful or baneful darts, that sometimes fix in a moment, and irreversibly, the domestic fate of man; just such another, as potent, as pointed, as piercing, yet as delicious, penetrated, a short time afterwards, the breast of young Burney; and from eyes perhaps as lovely, though not as celebrated; and from a mind perhaps as highly gifted, though not as renowned.

Esther Sleepe — this memorialist's mother — of whom she must now with reverence, with fear — yet with pride and delight — offer the tribute of a description — was small and delicate, but not diminutive, in person. Her face had that sculptural oval form which gives to the air of the head something like the ideal perfection of the poet's imagination. Her fair complexion was embellished by a rosy hue upon her cheeks of Hebe freshness. Her eyes were of the finest azure, and beaming with the brightest intelligence; though they owed to the softness of their lustre a still more resistless fascination: and they were set in her head with such a peculiarity of elegance in shape and proportion, that they imparted a nobleness of expression to her brow and to her forehead, that, whether she were beheld when attired for society; or surprised under the negligence of domestic avocation; she could be viewed by no stranger whom she did not strike with admiration; she could be broken in upon by no old friend who did not look at her with new pleasure.

It was at a dance that she first was seen by young Burney, at the house of his elder brother, in Hatton Garden; and that first sight was to him decisive, for he was not more charmed by her beauty than enchanted by her conversation.

So extraordinary, indeed, were the endowments of her mind, that, her small opportunity for their attainment considered, they are credible only from having been known upon proof.

Born in the midst of the city—but not in one of those mansions where, formerly,* luxury and

---

* The rich citizens, at present, generally migrate to the west; leaving their eastern dwelling, with its current business-control, to their partners or dependents.

riches revelled with a lavish preponderance of magnificence, that left many of those of the nobles of the west plain or old-fashioned in comparison: not in one of those dwellings of the hospitable English merchant of early days, whose boundless liberality brought tributary under his roof the arts and sciences, in the persons of their professors; and who rivalled the nobles in the accomplishments of their progeny, till, by mingling in acquirements, they mingled in blood:—the birth of the lovely Esther had nothing to boast from parental dignity, parental opulence, nor—strange, and stranger yet to tell—parental worth.

Alone stood the lovely Esther, unsustained by ancestry, unsupported by wealth, unimpelled by family virtue——

Yet no!—in this last article there was a partnership that redeemed the defection, since the Male parent was not more wanting in goodness, probity, and conduct, than the Female was perfect in all—if perfect were a word that, without presumption, might ever be applied to a human being.

With no advantage, therefore, of education, save the simple one of early learning, or, rather, imbibing the French language, from her maternal grandfather, who was a native of France, but had been forced from his country by the edict of Nantz; this gifted young creature was one of the most pleasing, well-mannered, well-read, elegant, and even cultivated, of her sex: and wherever she appeared in a social circle, and was drawn forth—which the attraction of her beauty made commonly one and the same thing—she was generally distinguished as the first female of the party for sense, literature, and, rarer still, for judgment; a pre-eminence, however, not more justly, than, by herself, unsuspectedly her due; for, more than unassuming, she was ignorant of her singular superiority.*

To excel in music, or in painting, so as to rival even professors, save the highest, in those arts, had not then been regarded as the mere ordinary progress of female education: nor had the sciences yet become playthings for the nursery. These new roads of ambition for juvenile eminence are un-

---

* This resistless filial tribute to such extraordinary *independent* and *individual* merit, must now be offenceless; as the family of its honoured object has for very many years, in its every Male branch, been, in this world, utterly extinct.— And, for another world,— of what avail were disguise?

doubtedly improvements, where they leave not out more essential acquirements. Yet, perhaps, those who were born before this elevation was the mode; whose calls, therefore, were not so multitudinous for demonstrative embellishments, may be presumed to have risen to more solid advantages in mental attainments, and in the knowledge and practice of domestic duties, than the super-accomplished aspirants at excellence in a mass, of the present moment.

A middle course might, perhaps, be more intellectually salubrious, because more simple and natural: and foremost herself, if she may be judged by analogy, foremost herself, had stood this lovely Esther, in amalgamating the two systems in her own studies and pursuits, had they equally, at that time, been within the scope of her consciousness: for straight-forward as was her design in all that she deemed right, whatever was presented to even a glimpse of her perceptions that was new and ingenious, rapidly opened to her lively understanding a fresh avenue to something curious, useful, or amusing, that she felt herself irresistibly invited to explore.

Botany, then, was no familiar accomplishment; but flowers and plants she cultivated with assiduous care; sowing, planting, pruning, grafting, and rearing them, to all the purposes of sight and scent that belong to their fragrant enjoyment; though untutored in their nomenclature, and unlearned in their classification.

Astronomy, though beyond her grasp as a science, she passionately caught at in its elementary visibility, loving it for its intrinsic glory, and enamoured of it yet more fondly from her own favourite idea, that the soul of the righteous, upon the decease of the body, may be wafted to realms of light, and permitted thence to look down, as guardian angel, on those most precious to it left behind.

Yet so strict was her sense of duty, that she never suffered this vivid imagination to put it out of its bias; and the clearness of her judgment regulated so scrupulously the disposition of her hours, that, without neglecting any real devoir, she made leisure, by skilful arrangements and quickness of execution, for nearly every favourite object that hit her fancy; holding almost as sacred the employment of her spare moments, as most others hold the fulfilment of their stated occupations.

And, indeed, so only could she, thus self-taught by self-investigation, study, and labour, have risen to those various excellences that struck all who saw, and impressed all who knew her, with admiration mingled with wonder.

Critical was the first instant of meeting between two young persons thus similarly self-modelled, and thus singularly demonstrating, that Education, with all her rules, her skill, her experienced knowledge, and her warning wisdom, may so be supplied, be superseded, by Genius, when allied to Industry, as to raise beings who merit to be pointed out as examples, even to those who have not a difficulty to combat, who are spurred by encouragement, and instructed by able teachers; to all which advantages young Burney and Esther—though as far removed from distress as from affluence—were equally strangers.

Who shall be surprised that two such beings, thus opening into life and distinction through intellectual vigour, and thus instinctively sustaining unaided conflicts against the darkness of ignorance, the intricacies of new doctrines, and all the annoying obstructions of early prejudices,— who shall be surprised, that two such beings, where, on one side, there was so much beauty to attract, and on the other so much discernment to perceive the value of her votary, upon meeting each other at the susceptible age of ardent youth, should have emitted, spontaneously, and at first sight, from heart to heart, sparks so bright and pure that they might be called electric, save that their flame was exempt from any shock?

Young Burney at this time had no power to sue for the hand, though he had still less to forbear suing for the heart, of this fair creature: not only he had no fortune to lay at her feet, no home to which he could take her, no prosperity which he could invite her to share; another barrier, which seemed to him still more formidable, stood imperviously in his way—his peculiar position with Mr. Greville.

That gentleman, in freeing the subject of these memoirs from his engagements with Dr. Arne, meant to act with as much kindness as munificence; for, casting aside all ostentatious parade, he had shown himself as desirous to gain, as to become, a friend. Yet was there no reason to suppose he purposed to rear a vine, of which he would not touch the grapes.

To be liberal, suited at once the real good taste of his character, and his opinion of what was due to his rank in life; and in procuring to himself the double pleasure of the society and the talents of young Burney, he thought his largess to Dr. Arne well bestowed; but it escaped his reflections, that the youth whom he made his companion in London, at Wilbury House, at Newmarket, and at Bath, in quitting the regular pursuit of his destined profession, risked forfeiting the most certain guarantee to prosperity in business, progressive perseverance.

Nevertheless, those drawbacks to this splendid connection occurred not at its beginning, nor yet for many a day after, to the young votary of Apollo. The flattering brilliancy of the change, and the sort of romance that hung upon its origin, kept aloof all calculations of its relative mischiefs; which only distantly to have contemplated, in the sparkling novelty that mingled such gay pleasure with his gratitude, would have appeared to him ungenerous, if not sordid. Youth is rarely enlightened by foresight upon prudential prospects; and the mental optic of young Burney was not quickened to this perception, till the desire of independence to his fortune was excited by the loss of it to his heart; for never had he missed his liberty, till he sighed to make it a fresh sacrifice to a more lasting bondage.

It was then he first felt the torment of uncertain situation; it was then he appreciated the high male value of self-dependence; it was then he first conceived, that, though gaiety may be found, and followed, and met, and enjoyed abroad, not there, but at home, is happiness! Yet, from the moment a bosom whisper softly murmured to him the name of Esther, he had no difficulty to believe in the distinct existence of happiness from pleasure; and—still less to devise where—for him—it must be sought.

When he made known to his fair enslaver his singular position, and entreated her counsel to disentangle him from a net, of which, till now, the soft texture had impeded all discernment of the confinement, the early wisdom with which she preached to him patience and forbearance, rather diminished than augmented his power of practising either, by an increase of admiration that doubled the eagerness of his passion.

Nevertheless, he was fain to comply with her counsel, though less from acquiescence than from helplessness how to devise stronger measures, while under this nameless species of obligation to Mr. Greville, which he could not satisfy his delicacy in breaking; nor yet, in adhering to, justify his sense of his own rights.

He could consent, however, to be passive only

while awaiting some happy turn for propitiating his efforts to escape from the sumptuous scenes, which, with his heart away from them, he now looked upon as obscuring, not illuminating, his existence; since they promoted not the means of arrriving at all he began to hold worth pursuit, "Home, sweet home!" which he now severely saw could be reached only by regular assiduity in his profession.

From this time it was with difficulty he could assume spirit sufficient for sustaining his intercourse, hitherto so happy, so lively, with the Grevilles; not alone from the sufferings of absence, but from hard secret conflicts, whether or not to reveal his distress. Mr. Greville, who, a short time back would quickly have discerned his latent uneasiness, was now so occupied by his own new happiness, conjugal and paternal, that though he welcomed young Burney with unabated kindness, his own thoughts, and his observations, were all centered in his two Fannys.

During the first fair breathings of early wedded love, the scoff of the tender passion, the sneer against romance, the contempt of refined reciprocations of sentiment, are done away, even from the most sarcastic, by a newly imbibed consciousness of the felicity of virtuous tenderness; which were its permanence more frequently equal to its enjoyment, would irresistibly convert the scorn of its deriders into envy. But constancy in affection from long dissipated characters, must always, whether in friendship or in love, be as rare as it is right; for constancy requires virtue to be leagued with the passions.

Unmarked, therefore, young Burney kept to himself his unhappiness; though he was not now impeded from communication by fears of the raillery with which, previously to his marriage, Mr. Greville would have held up to mockery a tale of love in a cottage, as a proper pendant to a tale of love in bedlam. But still he was withheld from all genial confidence, by apprehensions of remonstrances which he now considered as mercenary, if not derogatory, against imprudent connexions; and of representations of his own claims to higher views; which he now, from his belief that his incomparable choice would out-balance in excellence all vain attempts at competition, deemed profane if not insane.

Mrs. Greville, having no clew to his secret feelings, was not aware of their disturbance; she might else easily, and she would willingly, have drawn forth his confidence, from the kindly disposition that subsisted, on both sides, to trust and to friendship.

But a discovery the most painful of the perturbed state of his mind, was soon afterwards impelled by a change of affairs in the Grevilles, which they believed would enchant him with pleasure; but which they found, to their unspeakable astonishment, overpowered him with affliction.

This was no other than a plan of going abroad for some years, and of including him in their party.

Concealment was instantly at an end. The sudden dismay of his ingenuous countenance, though it told not the cause, betrayed past recal his repugnance to the scheme.

With parts so lively, powers of observation so ready, and a spirit so delighting in whatever was uncommon and curious, they had expected that such a prospect of visiting new countries, surveying new scenes, mingling with new characters; and traversing the foreign world, under their auspices, in all its splendour, would have raised in him a buoyant transport, exhilarating to behold. But the sudden paleness that overspread his face; his downcast eye; the quiver of his lips; and the unintelligible stammer of his vainly attempted reply, excited interrogatories so anxious and so vehement, that they soon induced an avowal that a secret power had gotten possession of his mind, and sturdily exiled from it all ambition, curiosity, or pleasure, that came not in the form of an offering to its all-absorbing shrine.

Every objection and admonition which he had anticipated, were immediately brought forward by this confession ; but they were presented with a lenity that showed his advisers to be fully capable of conceiving, though persuaded that they ought to oppose, his feelings.

Disconcerted, as well as dejected, because dissatisfied as well as unhappy in his situation, from mental incertitudes what were its real calls ; and whether or not the ties of interest and obligation were here of sufficient strength to demand the sacrifice of those of love ; he attempted not to vindicate, unreflectingly, his wishes ; and still less did he permit himself to treat them as his intentions. With faint smiles, therefore, but stifled sighs, he heard, with civil attention, their opinions; though, determined not to involve himself in any embarrassing conditions, he would risk no reply ; and soon afterwards, curbing his emotion, he started abruptly another subject.

"They thought him wise, and followed as he led."

All the anguish, however, that was here suppressed, found vent with redoubled force at the feet of the fair partner in his disappointment; who, while unaffectedly sharing it, resolutely declined receiving clandestinely his hand, though tenderly she clung to his heart. She would listen to no project that might lead him to relinquish such solid friends, at the very moment that they were preparing to give him the strongest proof of their fondness for his society, and of their zeal in his benefit and improvement.

Young Burney was not the less unhappy at this decision from being sensible of its justice, since his judgment could not but thank her, in secret, for pronouncing the hard dictates of his own.

All that he now solicited was her picture, that he might wear her resemblance next his heart, till that heart should beat to its responsive original.

With this request she gracefully complied; and she sate for him to Spencer, one of the most famous miniature painters of that day.

Of striking likeness was this performance, of which the head and unornamented hair were executed with the most chaste simplicity; and young Burney reaped from this possession all that had power to afford him consolation; since he now could soften off the pangs of separation, by gliding from company, public places or assemblages, to commune by himself with the countenance of all he held most dear.

Thus solaced, he resigned himself with more courage to his approaching misfortune.

The Grevilles, it is probable, from seeing him apparently revived, imagined that, awakened from his flights of fancy, he was recovering his senses: but when, from this idea, they started, with light raillery, the tender subject, they found their utter mistake. The most distant hint of abandoning such excellence, save for the moment, and from the moment's necessity, nearly convulsed him with inward disturbance; and so changed his whole appearance, that, concerned as well as amazed, they were themselves glad to hasten from so piercing a topic.

Too much moved, however, to regain his equilibrium, he could not be drawn from a disturbed taciturnity, till shame, conquering his agitation, enabled him to call back his self-command. He forced, then, a laugh at his own emotion; but, presently afterwards seized with an irresistible desire of shewing what he thought its vindication, he took from his bosom the cherished miniature, and placed it, fearfully, almost awfully, upon a table.

It was instantly and eagerly snatched from hand to hand by the gay couple; and young Burney had the unspeakable relief of perceiving that this impulsive trial was successful. With expansive smiles they examined and discussed the charm of the complexion, the beauty of the features, and the sensibility and sweetness conveyed by their expression: and what was then the joy, the pride of heart, the soul's delight of the subject of these memoirs, when those fastidious judges, and superior self-possessors of personal attractions, voluntarily and generously united in avowing that they could no longer wonder at his captivation.

As a statue he stood fixed before them; a smiling one, indeed; a happy one; but as breathless, as speechless, as motionless.

Mr. Greville then, with a laugh, exclaimed, "But why, Burney, why don't you marry her?"

Whether this were uttered sportively, inadvertently, or seriously, young Burney took neither time nor reflection to weigh; but, starting forward with ingenuous transport, called out, "May I?"

No negative could immediately follow an interrogatory that had thus been invited ; and to have pronounced one in another minute would have been too late; for the enraptured and ardent young lover, hastily construing a short pause into an affirmative, blithely left them to the enjoyment of their palpable amusement at his precipitancy; and flew, with extatic celerity, to proclaim himself liberated from all mundane shackles, to her with whom he thought eternal bondage would be a state celestial.

From this period, to that of their exquisitely happy union,

"Gallopp'd apace the fiery-footed steeds,"

that urged on Time with as much gay delight as prancing rapidity ; for if they had not, in their matrimonial preparations, the luxuries of wealth, neither had they its fatiguing ceremonies; if they had not the security of future advantage, they avoided the torment of present procrastination ; and if they had but little to bestow upon one another, they were saved, at least, the impatiency of waiting for the seals, signatures, and etiquettes of lawyers, to bind down a lucrative prosperity to survivorship.

To the mother of the bride, alone of her family, was confided, on the instant, this spontaneous, this sudden felicity. Little formality was requisite, before the passing of the marriage act, for presenting at the hymeneal altar its detined votaries ; and contracts the most sacred could be rendered indissoluble almost at the very moment of their projection: a strange dearth of foresight in those legislators who could so little weigh the chances of a minor's judgment upon what, eventually, may either suit his taste or form his happiness, for the larger portion of existence that commonly follows his majority.

This mother of the bride was of a nature so free from stain, so elementally white, that it would scarcely seem an hyperbole to denominate her an angel upon earth—if purity of mind that breathed to late old age the innocence of infancy, and sustained the whole intervening period in the constant practice of self-sacrificing virtue, with piety for its sole stimulus, and holy hope for its sole reward, can make pardonable the hazard of such an anticipating appellation,—from which, however, she, her humble self, would have shrunk as from sacrilege.

She was originally of French extraction, from a family of the name of Dubois; but though her father was one of the conscientious victims of the Edict of Nantz, she, from some unknown cause—

probably of maternal education—had been brought up a Roman Catholic. The inborn religion of her mind, however, counteracted all that was hostile to her fellow-creatures, in the doctrine of the religion of her ancestors; and her gentle hopes and fervent prayers were offered up as devoutly for those whom she feared were wrong, as they were vented enthusiastically for those whom she was bred to believe were right.

Her bridal daughter, who had been educated a Protestant, and who to that faith adhered steadily and piously through life, loved her with that devoted love which could not but emanate from sympathy of excellence. She was the first pride of her mother,—or, rather, the first delight; for pride, under any form, or through any avenue, direct or collateral, by which that subtle passion works or swells its way to the human breast, her mother knew not; though she was endued with an innate sense of dignity that seemed to exhale around her a sentiment of reverence that, notwithstanding her genuine and invariable humility, guarded her from every species and every approach of disrespect.

She could not but be gratified by an alliance so productive, rather than promising, of happiness to her favourite child; and Mr. Burney—as the married man must now be called—soon imbibed the filial veneration felt by his wife, and loved his mother-in-law as sincerely as if she had been his mother-in-blood.

All plan of going abroad was now, of course, at an end; and the Grevilles, and their beautiful infant daughter, leaving behind them Benedict the married man, set out, a family trio, upon their tour.

The customary compliments of introduction on one hand, and of congratulation on the other, passed, in their usual forms upon such occasions, between the bridegroom and his own family.

* * * * * * *

Rarely can the highest zest of pleasure awaken, in its most active votary, a sprightliness of pursuit more gay or more spirited, than Mr. Burney now experienced and exhibited in the commonly grave and sober career of business, from the ardour of his desire to obtain self-dependence.

He worked not, indeed, with the fiery excitement of expectation; his reward was already in his hands; but from the nobler impulse he worked of meriting his fair lot; while she, his stimulus, deemed her own the highest prize from that matrimonial wheel whence issue bliss or bane to the remnant life of a sensitive female.

THE CITY.

It was in the city, in consequence of his wife's connexions, that Mr. Burney made his first essay as a housekeeper; and with a prosperity that left not a doubt of his ultimate success. Scholars, in his musical art, poured in upon him from all quarters of that British meridian; and he mounted so rapidly into the good graces of those who were most opulent and most influential, that it was no sooner known that there was a vacancy for an organist professor, in one of the fine old fabrics of devotion which decorate religion in the city and reflect credit on our commercial ancestors, than the Fullers, Hankeys, and all other great houses of the day to which he had yet been introduced, exerted themselves in his service with an activity and a warmth that were speedily successful; and that he constantly recounted with pleasure.

Anxious to improve as well as to prosper in his profession, he also elaborately studied composition, and brought forth several musical pieces; all of which that are authenticated, will be enumerated in a general list of his musical works.

And thus, with a felicity that made toil delicious, through labour repaid by prosperity; exertions, by comfort; fatigue, by soothing tenderness; and all the fond passions of juvenile elasticity, by the charm of happiest sympathy,—began, and were rolling on, equally blissful and busy, the first wedded years of this animated young couple;—when a storm suddenly broke over their heads, which menaced one of those deadly catastrophes, that, by engulphing one loved object in that "bourne whence no traveller returns," tears up for ever by the root all genial, spontaneous, unsophisticated happiness, from the survivor.

Mr. Burney, whether from overstrained efforts in business; or from an application exceeding his physical powers in composition; or from the changed atmosphere of Cheshire, Shropshire, and Wiltshire, for the confined air of our great and crowded city; which had not then, as now, by a vast mass of improvement, been made nearly as sane as it is populous; suddenly fell, from a state of the most vigorous health, to one the most alarming, of premature decay. And to this defalcation of strength was shortly added the seizure of a violent and dangerous fever that threatened his life.

The sufferings of the young wife, who was now also a young mother, can only be conceived by contrasting them with her so recent happiness. Yet never did she permit grief to absorb her faculties, nor to vanquish her fortitude. She acted with the same spirited force of mind, as if she had been a stranger to the timid terrors of the heart. She superintended all that was ordered; she executed, where it was possible, all that was performed; she was sedulously careful that no business should be neglected; and her firmness in all that belonged to the interests of her husband, seemed as invulnerable as if that had been her sole occupation; though never, for a moment, was grief away from her side, and though perpetually, irresistibly she wept,—for sorrow with the youthful is always tearful. Yet she strove to disallow herself that indulgence; refusing time even for gently wiping from her cheeks the big drops of liquid anguish which coursed their way; and only, and hastily, almost with displeasure, brushing them off with her hand; while resolutely continuing, or renewing, some useful operation, as if she were but mechanically engaged.

All this was recorded by her adoring husband in an elegy of after-times.

The excellent and able Dr. Armstrong, already the friend of the invalid, was now sent to his aid by the Hon. and Rev. Mr. Home, who had conceived the warmest esteem for the subject of these memoirs. The very sight of this eminent physician was medicinal; though the torture he inflicted by the blister after blister with which he deemed it necessary to almost cover, and almost flay alive, his poor patient, required all the high opinion in which that patient held the doctor's skill for endurance.

The unsparing, but well-poised, prescriptions of this poetical Æsculapius, succeeded, however, in dethroning and extirpating the raging fever, that, perhaps, with milder means, had undermined the sufferer's existence. But a consumptive menace ensued, with all its fearful train of cough, night perspiration, weakness, glassy eyes, and hectic complexion; and Dr. Armstrong, foreseeing an evil beyond the remedies of medicine, strenuously urged an adoption of their most efficient successor, change of air.

The patient, therefore, was removed to Canonbury-house; whence, ere long, by the further advice, nay, injunction, of Dr. Armstrong, he was compelled to retire wholly from London; after an illness by which, for thirteen weeks, he had been confined to his bed.

Most fortunately, Mr. Burney, at this time, had proposals made to him by a Norfolk baronet, Sir John Turner, who was member for Lynn Regis, of the place of organist of that royal borough; of which, for a young man of talents and character, the Mayor and Corporation offered to raise the salary from twenty to one hundred pounds a year; with an engagement for procuring to him the most respectable pupils from all the best families in the town and its neighbourhood.

Though greatly chagrined and mortified to quit a situation in which he now was surrounded by cordial friends, who were zealously preparing for him all the harmonical honours which the city holds within its patronage; the declining health of the invalid, and the forcibly pronounced opinion of his scientific medical counsellor, decided the acceptance of this proposal; and Mr. Burney, with his first restored strength, set out for his new destination.

LYNN REGIS.

Mr. Burney was compelled to make his first essay of the air, situation, and promised advantages of Lynn, without the companion to whom he owed the re-establishment of health that enabled him to try the experiment: his Esther, as exemplary in her maternal as in her conjugal duties, was now indispensably detained in town by the most endearing of all ties to female tenderness, the first offsprings of a union of mutual love; of which the elder could but just go alone, and the younger was still in her arms.

Mr. Burney was received at Lynn with every mark of favour, that could demonstrate the desire of its inhabitants to attach and fix him to that spot. He was introduced by Sir John Turner to the mayor, aldermen, recorder, clergy, physicians, lawyers, and principal merchants, who formed the higher population of the town; and who in their traffic, the wine trade, were equally eminent for the goodness of their merchandize and the integrity of their dealings.

All were gratified by an acquisition to their distant and quiet town, that seemed as propitious to society as to the arts; the men with respect gave their approbation to his sense and knowledge; the women with smiles bestowed theirs upon his manners and appearance. His air was so lively, and his figure was so youthful, that the most elegant as well as beautiful woman of the place, Mrs. Stephen Allen, took him for a Cambridge student, who, at that time, was expected at Lynn.

He was not insensible to such a welcome; yet the change was so great from the splendid or elegant, the classical or amusing circles, into which he had been initiated in the metropolis, that, in looking, he said, around him, he seemed to see but a void.

The following energetic lament to his Esther, written about a week after his Lynn residence, will best explain his tormented sensations at this altered scene of life. He was but in his twenty-fourth year, when he gave way to this quick burst of chagrin.

"To Mrs. Burney.

"*Lynn Regis, Monday.*

"Now, my amiable friend, let me unbosom myself to thee, as if I were to enjoy the incomparable felicity of thy presence. And first—let me exclaim at the unreasonableness of man's desires; at his unbounded ambition and avarice, and at the inconstancy of his temper, which impels him, the moment he is in the possession of the thing that once employed all his thoughts and wishes, to relinquish it, and to fix his "mind's eye" on some bauble that next becomes his point of view, and that, if attained, he would wish as much to change for still another toy, of still less consequence to his interest and quiet. Oh thou constant tenant of my heart! to apply the above to myself,—thou art the only good I have been constant to! the only blessing I have been thankful to Providence for! the only one, I feel, I shall ever continue to have a true sense of! Ought I not to blush at this character's suiting me? Indeed I ought, and I do. Not that I think it one peculiar to myself; I believe it would fit more than half mankind. But it shames me to think how little I knew myself, when I fancied I should be happy in this place. Oh God! I find it impossible I should ever be so. Would you believe it, that I have more than a hundred times wished I had never heard its name? Nothing but the hope of acquiring an independent fortune in a short space of time will keep me here; though I am too deeply entered to retreat without great loss. But happiness cannot be too dearly purchased. In short, I would gladly change again for London, at any rate.

*   *   *   *   *

"The organ is execrably bad; and, add to that, a total ignorance of the most known and common musical merits runs through the whole body of people I have yet conversed with. Even Sir J. T., who is the oracle of Apollo in this country, is, in these matters, extremely shallow. Now the bad organ, with the ignorance of my auditors, must totally extinguish the few sparks of genius for composition that I may have, and entirely discourage practice; for where would any pains I may take to execute the most difficult piece of music be repaid, if, like poor Orpheus, I am to perform to stocks and stones?"

Ere long, however, Mr. Burney saw his prospects in a fairer point of view. He found himself surrounded by some very worthy and amiable persons, perfectly disposed to be his friends; and he became attached to their kindness. The unfixed state of his health made London a perilous place of abode for him; and his Esther pleaded for his accommodating himself to his new situation.

He took, therefore, a pretty and convenient house, and sent for what, next to his lovely wife, he most valued, his books; and when they came, and when she herself was coming, he revived in his hopes and spirits, and hastened her approach by the following affectionate rhymes — they must not, in these fastidious days, be called verses. The austere critic is besought, therefore, not to fall on the fair fame of the writer, by considering them as produced for public inspection; nor as assuming the high present character of poetry. They are inserted only biographically, from a dearth of any further prose document, by which might be conveyed, in the simplicity of his own veracious diction, some idea of the sympathy and the purity of his marriage happiness, by the rare picture which these lines present of an intellectual lover in a tender husband.

" To Mrs. Burney.
" *Lynn Regis.*

" Come, my darling !—quit the town ;
Come !—and me with rapture crown.

* * * *

If 'tis meet to fee or bribe
A leech of th' Æsculapius tribe,
We Hepburn have, who's wise as Socrates,
And deep in physic as Hippocrates.
Or, if 'tis meet to take the air,
You borne shall be on horse or mare ;
And, 'gainst all chances to provide,
I'll be your faithful 'squire and guide.
If unadulterate wine be good
To glad the heart, and mend the blood,
We that in plenty boast at Lynn,
Would make with pleasure Bacchus grin.
Should nerves auricular demand
A head profound, and cunning hand,
The charms of music to display,
Pray,—cannot *I* compose and play ?
And strains to your each humour suit
On organ, violin, or flute ?

If these delights you deem too transient,
We modern authors have, or antient,
Which, while I've lungs from phthisicks freed,
To thee with rapture, sweet, I'll read.

If Homer's bold, inventive fire,
Or Virgil's art, you most admire;
If Pliny's eloquence and ease,
Or Ovid's flowery fancy please;
In fair array they marshall'd stand,
Most humbly waiting your command.

To humanize and mend the heart,
Our serious hours we'll set apart.

* * * *

We'll learn to separate right from wrong,
Through Pope's mellifluous moral song.

If wit and humour be our drift,
We'll laugh at knaves and fools with Swift.

To know the world, its follies see,
Ourselves from ridicule to free,
To whom for lessons shall we run,
But to the pleasing Addison?

Great Bacon's learning; Congreve's wit,
By turns thy humour well may hit.

How sweet, original, and strong,
How high the flights of Dryden's song!
He, though so often careless found,
Lifts us so high above the ground
That we disdain terrestrial things,
And scale Olympus while he sings.

Among the bards who mount the skies
Whoe'er to such a height could rise

As Milton? he, to whom 'twas given
To plunge to Hell, and mount to Heaven.
How few like thee—my soul's delight!
Can follow him in every flight?

  La Mancha's knight, on gloomy day,
Shall teach our muscles how to play,
And at the black fanatic class,
We'll sometimes laugh with Hudibras.

  When human passions all subside,
Where shall we find so sure a guide
Through metaphysics' mazy ground
As Locke—scrutator most profound?

  One bard there still remains in store,
And who has him need little more:
A bard above my feeble lay;
Above what wiser scribes can say.
He would the secret thoughts reveal
Of all the human mind can feel:
None e'er like him in every feature
So fair a likeness drew of Nature.
No passion swells the mortal breast
But what his pencil has exprest:
Nor need I tell my heart's sole queen
That Shakespeare is the bard I mean.

  May heaven, all bounteous in its care,
These blessings, and our offspring spare!
And while our lives are thus employ'd,
No earthly bliss left unenjoy'd,
May we—without a sigh or tear—
Together finish our career!

>   Together gain another station
>   Without the pangs of separation!
>   And when our souls have travelled far
>   Beyond this little dirty star,
>   Beyond the reach of strife, or noise,
>   To taste celestial, stable joys—
>   O may we still together keep—
>   Or may our death be endless sleep!
>   "*Lynn Regis,* 19*th Dec.* 1751."

The wife and the babies were soon now in his arms; and this generous appreciator of the various charms of the one, and kind protector of the infantile feebleness of the other, cast away every remnant of discontent; and devoted himself to his family and profession, with an ardour that left nothing unattempted that seemed within the grasp of industry, and nothing unaccomplished that came within the reach of perseverance.

He had immediately for his pupils the daughters of every house in Lynn, whose chief had the smallest pretensions to belonging to the upper classes of the town; while almost all persons of rank in its vicinity, eagerly sought the assistance of the new professor for polishing the education of their females: and all alike coveted his society for their own information or entertainment.

First amongst those with whom these latter advantages might be reciprocated, stood, as usual, in towns far off from the metropolis, the physicians; who, for general education, learning, science, and politeness, are as frequently the leaders in literature as they are the oracles in health; and who, with the confraternity of the vicar, and the superior lawyer, are commonly the allowed despots of erudition and the belles lettres in provincial circles.

But while amongst the male inhabitants of the town, Mr. Burney associated with many whose understandings, and some few whose tastes, met his own; his wife, amongst the females, was less happy, though not more fastidious. She found them occupied almost exclusively, in seeking who should be earliest in importing from London what was newest and most fashionable in attire; or in vying with each other in giving and receiving splendid repasts; and in struggling to make their every rotation become more and more luxurious.

By no means was this love of frippery, or feebleness of character among the females, peculiar to Lynn: such, ALMOST* universally, is the inheritance

---

* The word *almost* must here stand to acknowledge the several exceptions that may be offered to this paragraph; but which, nevertheless, seem to make, not annul, a general rule.

bequeathed from mother to daughter in small towns at a distance from the metropolis; where there are few suspensive subjects or pursuits of interest, ambition, or literature, that can enlist either imagination or instruction into conversation.

That men, when equally removed from the busy turmoils of cities, or the meditative studies of retirement, to such circumscribed spheres, should manifest more vigour of mind, may not always be owing to possessing it; but rather to their escaping, through the calls of business, that inertness which casts the females upon themselves: for though many are the calls more refined than those of business, there are few that more completely do away with insignificancy.

In the state, however, in which Lynn then was found, Lynn will be found no longer. The tide of ignorance is turned; and not there alone, nor alone in any other small town, but in every village, every hamlet, nay, every cottage in the kingdom; and though mental cultivation is as slowly gradual, and as precarious of circulation, as Genius, o'erleaping all barriers, and disdaining all auxiliaries, is rapid and decisive, still the work of general improvement is advancing so universally, that the dark ages which are rolling away, would soon be lost even to man's joy at their extirpation, but for the retrospective and noble services of the press, through which their memory—if only to be blasted—must live for ever.

There were two exceptions, nevertheless, to this stagnation of female merit, that were flowing with pellucid clearness.

The first, Mrs. Stephen Allen, has already been mentioned. She was the wife of a wine-merchant of considerable fortune, and of a very worthy character. She was the most celebrated beauty of Lynn, and might have been so of a much larger district, for her beauty was high, commanding, and truly uncommon: and her understanding bore the same description. She had wit at will; spirits the most vivacious and entertaining; and, from a passionate fondness for reading, she had collected stores of knowledge which she was always able, and "nothing loath" to display; and which raised her to as marked a pre-eminence over her townswomen in literary acquirements, as she was raised to exterior superiority from her personal charms.

The other exception, Miss Dorothy Young, was of a different description. She was not only denied beauty either of face or person, but in the first she had various unhappy defects, and in the second she was extremely deformed.

Here, however, ends all that can be said in her disfavour; for her mind was the seat of every virtue that occasion could call into use; and her disposition had a patience that no provocation could even momentarily subdue; though her feelings were so sensitive, that tears started into her eyes at every thing she either saw or heard of mortal sufferings, or of mortal unkindness—to any human creature but herself.

It may easily be imagined that this amiable Dorothy Young, and the elegant and intellectual Mrs. Allen, were peculiar and deeply attached friends.

When a professional call brought Mr. Burney and his wife to this town, that accomplished couple gave a new zest to rational, as well as a new spring to musical, society. Mr. Burney, between business and conviviality, immediately visited almost every house in the county; but his wife, less easily known, because necessarily more domestic, began her Lynn career almost exclusively with Mrs. Allen and Dolly Young, and proved to both an inestimable treasure; Mrs. Allen generously avowing that she set up Mrs.

Burney as a model for her own mental improvement; and Dolly Young becoming instinctively the most affectionate, as well as most cultivated of Mrs. Burney's friends; and with an attachment so fervent and so sincere, that she took charge of the little family upon every occasion of its increase during the nine or ten years of the Lynn residence.*

With regard to the extensive neighbourhood, Mr. Burney had soon nothing left to desire in hospitality, friendship, or politeness; and here, as heretofore, he scarcely ever entered a house upon terms of business, without leaving it upon those of intimacy.

The first mansions to which, naturally, his curiosity pointed, and at which his ambition aimed, were those two magnificent structures which stood loftily pre-eminent over all others in the county of Norfolk, Holcomb and Haughton; though neither the nobleness of their architecture, the grandeur of their dimensions, nor the vast expense of their erection, bore any sway in their celebrity, that could compare with what, at that period, they owed to the arts of sculpture and of painting.

---

* Miss Young's were the kind arms that first welcomed to this nether sphere the writer of these memoirs.

HOLCOMB.

At Holcomb, the superb collection of statues, as well as of pictures, could not fail to soon draw thither persons of such strong native taste for all the arts as Mr. Burney and his wife; though, as there were, at that time, which preceded the possession of that fine mansion by the Cokes, neither pupils nor a Male chief, no intercourse beyond that of the civilities of reception on a public day, took place with Mr. Burney and the last very ancient lady of the house of Leicester, to whom Holcomb then belonged.

HAUGHTON HALL

boasted, at that period, a collection of pictures that not only every lover of painting, but every British patriot in the arts, must lament that it can boast no longer.*

It had, however, in the heir and grandson of its

---

* The whole of this finest gallery of pictures that, then, had been formed in England, was sold, during some pecuniary difficulties, by its owner, George, Earl of Orford, for £40,000, to Catherine the Great, Empress of Russia.

founder, Sir Robert Walpole, first Earl of Orford, a possessor of the most liberal cast; a patron of arts and artists; munificent in promoting the prosperity of the first, and blending pleasure with recompence to the second, by the frank equality with which he treated all his guests; and the ease and freedom with which his unaffected good humour and good sense cheered, to all about him, his festal board.

Far, nevertheless, from meriting unqualified praise was this noble peer; and his moral defects, both in practice and example, were as dangerous to the neighbourhood, of which he ought to have been the guide and protector, as the political corruption of his famous progenitor, the statesman, had been hurtful to probity and virtue, in the courtly circles of his day, by proclaiming, and striving to bring to proof, his nefarious maxim, "that every man has his price."

At the head of Lord Orford's table was placed, for the reception of his visitors, a person whom he denominated simply "Patty;" and that so unceremoniously, that all the most intimate of his associates addressed her by the same free appellation.

Those, however, if such there were, who might

conclude from this degrading familiarity, that the Patty of Lord Orford was " every body's Patty," must soon have been undeceived, if tempted to make any experiment upon such a belief. The peer knew whom he trusted, though he rewarded not the fidelity in which he confided; but the fond, faulty Patty loved him with a blindness of passion, that hid alike from her weak perceptions, her own frailties, and his seductions.

In all, save that blot, which, on earth, must to a female be ever indelible, Patty was good, faithful, kind, friendly, and praise-worthy.

The table of Lord Orford, then commonly called Arthur's Round Table, assembled in its circle all of peculiar merit that its neighbourhood, or rather that the county produced, to meet there the great, the renowned, and the splendid, who, from their various villas, or the metropolis, visited Haughton Hall.

Mr. Burney was soon one of those whom the penetrating peer selected for a general invitation to his repasts; and who here, as at Wilbury House, formed sundry intimacies, some of which were enjoyed by him nearly through life. Particularly must be mentioned

Mr. Hayes, who was a scholar, a man of sense,

and a passionate lover of books and of prints. He had a great and pleasant turn for humour, and a fondness and facility for rhyming so insatiable and irrepressible, that it seemed, like Strife in Spencer's Faerie Queene, to be always seeking occasion.

Yet, save in speaking of that propensity, Strife and John Hayes ought never to come within the same sentence; for in character, disposition, and conduct, he was a compound of benevolence and liberality.

There was a frankness of so unusual a cast, and a warmth of affection, that seemed so glowing from the heart, in Mr. Hayes for Lord Orford; joined to so strong a resemblance in face and feature, that a belief, if not something beyond, prevailed, that Mr. Hayes was a natural son of Sir Robert Walpole, the first Earl of Orford, and, consequently, a natural uncle of his Lordship's grandson.

RAINHAM.

To name the several mansions that called for, or welcomed, Mr. Burney, would almost be to make a Norfolk Register. At Rainham Castle he was full as well received by its master, General Lord

Townshend, as a guest, as by its lady, the Baroness de Frerrars in her own right, for an instructor; the lady being natively cold and quiet, though well bred and sensible; while the General was warm-hearted, witty, and agreeable; and conceived a liking for Mr. Burney, that was sustained, with only added regard, through all his lordship's various elevations.

FELBRIG.

But there was no villa to which he resorted with more certainty of finding congenial pleasure, than to Felbrig, where he began an acquaintance of highest esteem and respect with Mr. Windham, father of the Right Honourable Privy Counsellor and orator; with whom, also, long afterwards, he became still more closely connected; and who proved himself just the son that so erudite and elegant a parent would have joyed to have reared, had he lived to behold the distinguished rank in the political and in the learned world to which that son rose; and the admiration which he excited, and the pleasure which he expanded in select society.

WILLIAM BEWLEY.

A name next comes forward that must not briefly be glided by; that of William Bewley; a man for whom Mr. Burney felt the most enlightened friendship that the sympathetic magnetism of similar tastes, humours, and feelings, could inspire.

Mr. Bewley was truly a philosopher, according to the simplest, though highest, acceptation of that word; for his love of wisdom was of that unsophisticated species, that regards learning, science, and knowledge, with whatever delight they may be pursued abstractedly, to be wholly subservient, collectively, to the duties and practice of benevolence.

To this nobleness of soul, which made the basis of his character, he superadded a fund of wit equally rare, equally extraordinary: it was a wit that sparkled from the vivid tints of an imagination as pure as it was bright; untarnished by malice, uninfluenced by spleen, uninstigated by satire. It was playful, original, eccentric: but the depth with which it could have cut, and slashed, and pierced around him, would never have been even surmised, from the urbanity with which he forbore making that missile use of its power, had he not frequently darted out its keenest edge in ridicule against himself.

And not alone in this personal severity did he resemble the self-unsparing Scarron; his outside, though not deformed, was peculiarly unfortunate; and his eyes, though announcing, upon examination, something of his mind, were ill-shaped, and ill set in his head, and singularly small; and no other feature parried this local disproportion; for his mouth, and his under-jaw, which commonly hung open, were displeasing to behold.

The first sight, however, which of so many is the best, was of Mr. Bewley, not only the worst, but the only bad; for no sooner, in the most squeamish, was the revolted eye turned away, than the attracted ear, even of the most fastidious, brought it back, to listen to genuine instruction conveyed through unexpected pleasantry.

This original and high character, was that of an obscure surgeon of Massingham, a small town in the neighbourhood of Haughton Hall. He had been brought up with no advantages, but what laborious toil had worked out of native abilities; and he only subsisted by the ordinary process of rigidly following up the multifarious calls to which, in its provincial practice, his widely diversified profession is amenable.

Yet not wholly in "the desert air," were his talents doomed to be wasted : they were no sooner spoken of at Haughton Hall, than the gates of that superb mansion were spontaneously flung open, and its Chief proved at once, and permanently remained, his noble patron and kind friend.

LYNN REGIS.

The visits of Mr. Burney to Massingham, and his attachment to its philosopher, contributed, more than any other connection, to stimulate that love and pursuit of knowledge, that urge its votaries to snatch from waste or dissipation those fragments of time, which, by the general herd of mankind, are made over to Lethe, for reading ; learning languages ; composing music ; studying sciences ; fathoming the theoretical and mathematical depths of his own art ; and seeking at large every species of intelligence to which either chance or design afforded him any clew.

As he could wait upon his country pupils only

on horseback, he purchased a mare that so exactly suited his convenience and his wishes, in sure-footedness, gentleness and sagacity, that she soon seemed to him a part of his family: and the welfare and comfort of Peggy became, ere long, a matter of kind interest to all his house.

On this mare he studied Italian; for, obliged to go leisurely over the cross roads with which Norfolk then abounded, and which were tiresome from dragging sands, or dangerous from deep ruts in clay, half his valuable time would have been lost in nothingness, but for his trust in Peggy; who was as careful in safely picking her way, as she was adroit in remembering from week to week whither she was meant to go.

Her master, at various odd moments, and from various opportunities, had compressed, from the best Italian Dictionaries, every word of the Italian language into a small octavo volume; and from this in one pocket, and a volume of Dante, Petrarch, Tasso, Ariosto, or Metastasio, in another, he made himself completely at home in that language of elegance and poetry.

His common-place book, at this period, rather merits the appellation of *un*common, from the assiduous research it manifests, to illustrate every sort of information, by extracts, abstracts, strictures, or descriptions, upon the almost universality of subject-matter which it contains.

It is without system or method; he had no leisure to put it into order; yet it is possible, he might owe to his familiar recurrence to that desultory assemblage of unconcocted materials, the general and striking readiness with which he met at once almost every topic of discourse.

This manuscript of scraps, drawn from reading and observation, was, like his Italian Dictionary, always in his great coat pocket, when he travelled; so that if unusually rugged roads, or busied haste, impeded more regular study, he was sure, in opening promiscuously his pocket collection of *odds and ends*, to come upon some remark worth weighing; some point of science on which to ruminate; some point of knowledge to fix in his memory; or something amusing, grotesque, or little known, that might recreate his fancy.

THE GREVILLES.

Meanwhile, he had made too real an impression on the affections of his first friends, to let absence of sight produce absence of mind. With Mr. and Mrs. Greville he was always in correspondence; though, of course, neither frequently nor punctually, now that his engagements were so numerous, his obligations to fulfil them so serious, and that his own fireside was so bewitchingly in harmony with his feelings, as to make every moment he passed away from it a sacrifice.

He expounds his new situation and new devoirs, in reply to a letter that had long been unanswered, of Mr. Greville's, from the Continent, with a sincerity so ingenuous that, though it is in rhyme, it is here inserted biographically.

"TO FULK GREVILLE, ESQ., AT PARIS.

"Hence, ' loathed business,' which so long
Has plunged me in the toiling throng.
Forgive, dear Sir! and gentle Madam!
A drudging younger son of Adam,
Who's forc'd from morn to night to labor
Or at the pipe, or at the tabor:
Nor has he hope 'twill e'er be o'er
Till landed on some kinder shore;
Some more propitious star, whose rays
Benign, may cheer his future days.
  Ah, think for rest how he must pant
Whose life's the summer of an ant!

With grief o'erwhelm'd, the wretched Abel*
Is dumb as architect of Babel.
—Three months of sullen silence—seem
With black ingratitude to teem;
As if my heart were made of stone
Which kindness could not work upon;
Or benefits e'er sit enshrin'd
Within the precincts of my mind.

But think not so, dear Sir! my crime
Proceeds alone from want of time.
No more a giddy youth, and idle,
Without a curb, without a bridle,
Who frisk'd about like colt unbroke,
And life regarded as a joke.—
No!—different duties now are mine;
Nor do I at my cares repine:
With naught to think of but myself
I little heeded worldly pelf;
But now, alert I act and move
For others whom I better love.

Should you refuse me absolution,
Condemning my new institution,
'Twould chill at once my heart and zeal
For this my little commonweal.—
O give my peace not such a stab!
Nor slay—as Cain did—name-sake Nab.

* * * * *

---

* This name alludes to that which young Burney had acquired from imitating Garrick in Abel Drugger, during the theatricals at Wilbury House.

> This prologue first premis'd, in hopes
> Such figures, metaphors, and tropes
> For pardon will not plead in vain,
> We'll now proceed in lighter strain.
>
> *   *   *   *   *

The epistle then goes on to strictures frank and honest, though softened off by courteous praise and becoming diffidence, on a manuscript poem of Mr. Greville's, that had been confidentially transmitted to Lynn, for the private opinion and critical judgment of Mr. Burney.

Mr. Greville, now, was assuming a new character—that of an author; and he printed a work which he had long had in agitation, entitled "Maxims, Characters, and Reflections, Moral, Serious, and Entertaining;" a title that seemed to announce that England, in its turn, was now to produce, in a man of family and fashion, a La Bruyere, or a La Rochefaucault. And Mr. Greville, in fact, waited for a similar fame with dignity rather than anxiety, because with expectation unclogged by doubt.

With Mrs. Greville, also, Mr. Burney kept up an equal, or more than equal, intercourse, for their minds were invariably in unison.

The following copy remains of a burlesque rhyming *billet-doux*, written by Mr. Burney in his old dramatic character of Will Fribble, and addressed to Mrs. Greville in that of Miss Biddy Bellair, upon her going abroad.

" WILLIAM FRIBBLE, ESQ.
" TO HER WHO WAS ONCE MISS BIDDY BELLAIR.
" *Greeting*.

" No boisterous hackney coachman clown,
No frisky fair nymph of the town
E'er wore so insolent a brow
As Captain Flash, since Hymen's vow
To him in silken bonds has tied
So sweet, so fair, so kind a bride.
 Well! curse me, now, if I can bear it!—
Though to his face I'd not declare it—
To think that you should take a dance
With such a roister into France;
And leave poor Will in torturing anguish
To sigh and pine, to grieve and languish.
 'Twas—let me tell you, Ma'am—quite cruel!
Though Jack and I shall fight a duel
If ever he to England come
And does not skulk behind a drum.
 But— apropos to coming over,
I hope you soon will land at Dover
That I may fly, more swift than hawk,
With you to have some *serus* talk.

>   The while, how great will be my bliss
>   Should you but deign to let me kiss—
>   O may these ardent vows prevail!—
>   Your little finger's vermeil nail!
>   Who am,
>   Till direful death to dust shall crumble,
>   My dearest *cretur!* yours,
>   most humble,
>   " WILL FRIBBLE."

Mrs. Greville, too, had commenced being an author; but without either the throes of pain or the joys of hope. It was, in fact, a burst of genius emanating from a burst of sorrow, which found an alleviating vent in a supplication to Indifference.

This celebrated ode was no sooner seen than it was hailed with a blaze of admiration, that passed first from friend to friend; next from newspapers to magazines; and next to every collection of fugitive pieces of poetry in the English language.*

---

* It is written with a flow of tender but harassed sensations, so natural, so unstrained, that it seems to have been penned merely because felt; though clearly to have been incited by acute disappointment to heart-dear expectations.

>   I ask no kind return in love;
>   No melting power to please;

The constant friendship that subsisted between this lady and Mr. Burney had been cemented after his marriage, by the grateful pleasure with which he saw his chosen partner almost instantly included in it by a triple bond. The quick-sighted, and quick-feeling author of that sensitive ode, needed nor time nor circumstance for animating her perception of such merit as deserved a place in her heart; which had not, at that early period, become a suppliant for the stoical composure with which her wounded sensibility sought afterwards to close its passage.

She had first seen the fair Esther in the dawning bloom of youthful wedded love, while new-born happiness enlivened her courage, embellished her beauty, and enabled her to do honour to the choice of her happy husband; who stood so high in the favour of Mrs. Greville, that the sole aim of that lady, in the opening of the acquaintance, had been his gratification; aided, perhaps, by a natural curi-

---

> Far from the heart such gifts remove
> That sighs for peace and ease!
> Nor peace nor ease the heart can know
> That, like the needle true,
> Turns at the touch of joy and woe—
> But, turning—trembles too!

osity, which attaches itself to the sight of any object who has inspired an extraordinary passion.

Far easier to conceive than to delineate was the rapture of the young bridegroom when, upon a meeting that, unavoidably, must have been somewhat tremendous, he saw the exertions of his lovely bride to substitute serenity for bashfulness; and read, in the piercing eyes of Mrs. Greville, the fullest approbation of such native self-possession.

From that time all inferiority of worldly situation was counteracted by intellectual equality.*

But the intercourse had for several years been interrupted from the Grevilles living abroad. It was renewed, however, upon their return to England; and the Burneys, with their eldest daughter,† visited Wilbury House upon every vacation that allowed time to Mr. Burney for the excursion. And every fresh meeting increased the zest for another. They fell into the same train of observation upon characters, things, and books; and enjoyed, with the same gaiety of remark, all humorous incidents,

---

* And subsequently, through this partial regard, the writer of these memoirs had the honour of being a god-daughter of Mrs. Greville.

† Afterwards Mrs. Charles Burney, of Bath.

and all traits of characteristic eccentricity. Mrs. Greville began a correspondence with Mrs. Burney the most open and pleasantly communicative. But no letters of Mrs. Burney remain; and two only of Mrs. Greville have been preserved. These two, however, demonstrate all that has been said of the terms and the trust of their sociality.*

DOCTOR JOHNSON.

How singularly Mr. Burney merited encouragement himself, cannot more aptly be exemplified than by portraying the genuine ardour with which he sought to stimulate the exertions of genius in others, and to promote their golden as well as literary laurels.

Mr. Burney was one of the first and most fervent admirers of those luminous periodical essays upon morals, literature, and human nature, that adorned the eighteenth century, and immortalized their author, under the vague and inadequate titles of the Rambler and the Idler. He took them both in; he read them to all his friends; and was the first to bring them to a bookish little coterie that assembled

---

* See correspondence.

weekly at Mrs. Stephen Allen's. And the charm expanded over these meetings, by the original lecture of these refined and energetic lessons of life, conduct, and opinions, when breathed through the sympathetic lips of one who felt every word with nearly the same force with which every word had been dictated, excited in that small auditory a species of enthusiasm for the author, that exalted him at once in their ideas, to that place which the general voice of his country has since assigned him, of the first writer of the age.

Mr. Bewley more than joined in this literary idolatry; and the works, the character, and the name of Dr. Johnson, were held by him in a reverence nearly enthusiastic.

At Haughton, at Felbrig, at Rainham, at Sir A. Wodehouse's, at Major Mackenzie's, and wherever his judgment had weight, Mr. Burney introduced and recommended these papers. And when, in 1755, the plan of Dr. Johnson's Dictionary reached Norfolk, Mr. Burney, by the zeal with which he spread the fame of that lasting monument of the Doctor's matchless abilities, was enabled to collect orders for a Norfolk packet of half a dozen copies of that noble work.

This empowered him to give some vent to his admiration; and the following letter made the opening to a connection that he always considered as one of the greatest honours of his life.*

MR. BURNEY TO MR. JOHNSON.

"Sir,

"Though I have never had the happiness of a personal knowledge of you, I cannot think myself wholly a stranger to a man with whose sentiments I have so long been acquainted; for it seems to me as if the writer, who was sincere, had effected the plan of that philosopher who wished men had windows at their breasts, through which the affections of their hearts might be viewed.

"It is with great self-denial that I refrain from giving way to panegyric in speaking of the pleasure and instruction I have received from your admirable writings; but knowing that transcendent merit shrinks more at praise, than either vice or dulness at

---

* The letters of Dr. Johnson were made over to Mr. Boswell by Dr. Burney, and have already been published; but the modesty which withheld his own, will not, it is hoped, be thought here to be violated by printing them in his memoirs; as they not only shew his early and generous enthusiasm for genius, but carry with them a striking proof of the genuine urbanity with which Dr. Johnson was open to every act of kindness that was offered to him unaffectedly, even from persons the most obscure and unknown.

censure, I shall compress my encomiums into a short compass, and only tell you that I revere your principles and integrity, in not prostituting your genius, learning, and knowledge of the human heart, in ornamenting vice or folly with those beautiful flowers of language due only to wisdom and virtue. I must add, that your periodical productions seem to me models of true genius, useful learning, and elegant diction, employed in the service of the purest precepts of religion, and the most inviting morality.

" I shall waive any further gratification of my wish to tell you, Sir, how much I have been delighted by your productions, and proceed to the *business* of this letter; which is no other than to beg the favour of you to inform me, by the way that will give you the least trouble, when, and in what manner, your admirably planned, and long wished-for Dictionary will be published? If it should be by subscription, or you should have any books at your own disposal, I shall beg of you to favour me with six copies for myself and friends, for which I will send you a draft.

" I ought to beg pardon of the public as well as yourself, Sir, for detaining you thus long from your useful labours; but it is the fate of men of eminence to be persecuted by insignificant friends as well as enemies; and the simple cur who barks through fondness and affection, is no less troublesome than if stimulated by anger and aversion.

" I hope, however, that your philosophy will incline you to forgive the intemperance of my zeal and impatience in making these inquiries; as well as my ambition to subscribe myself, with very great regard,

" Sir, your sincere admirer, and most humble servant,

" CHARLES BURNEY."

" *Lynn Regis*, 16*th Feb.* 1755."

Within two months of the date of this letter, its writer was honoured with the following answer.

"*To Mr. Burney, in Lynn Regis, Norfolk.*

"Sir,

"If you imagine that by delaying my answer I intended to shew any neglect of the notice with which you have favoured me, you will neither think justly of yourself nor of me. Your civilities were offered with too much elegance not to engage attention; and I have too much pleasure in pleasing men like you, not to feel very sensibly the distinction which you have bestowed upon me.

"Few consequences of my endeavours to please or to benefit mankind, have delighted me more than your friendship thus voluntarily offered; which, now I have it, I hope to keep, because I hope to continue to deserve it.

"I have no Dictionaries to dispose of for myself; but shall be glad to have you direct your friends to Mr. Dodsley, because it was by his recommendation that I was employed in the work.

"When you have leisure to think again upon me, let me be favoured with another letter, and another yet, when you have looked into my Dictionary. If you find faults, I shall endeavour to mend them: if you find none, I shall think you blinded by kind partiality: but to have made you partial in his favour will very much gratify the ambition of,

"Sir,

"Your most obliged

"And most humble servant,

"*Gough-square, Fleet-street,*   "Sam. Johnson."

"*April* 8, 1755."

A reply so singularly encouraging, demanding "another letter," and yet "another," raised the spirits, and flattered the hopes—it might almost be said the foresight—of Mr. Burney, with a prospect of future intimacy, that instigated the following unaffected answer.

"Sir,

"That you should think my letter worthy of notice was what I began to despair of; and, indeed, I had framed and admitted several reasons for your silence, more than sufficient for your exculpation. But so highly has your politeness over-rated my intentions, that I find it impossible for me to resist accepting the invitation with which you have honoured me, of writing to you again, though conscious that I have nothing to offer that can by any means merit your attention.

"It is with the utmost impatience that I await the possession of your great work, in which every literary difficulty will be solved, and curiosity gratified, at least as far as English literature is concerned: nor am I fearful of letting expectation rise to the highest summit in which she can accompany reason.

"From what you are pleased to say concerning Mr. Dodsley, I shall ever think myself much his debtor; but yet I cannot help suspecting that you intended him a compliment when you talked of *recommendation*. Is it possible that the world should be so blind, or booksellers so stupid, as to need other recommendation than your own? Indeed, I shall honour *both*, world and booksellers, so far as to substitute *solicitation* in the place of the above humiliating term.

" Perhaps you will smile when I inform you, that since first the rumour of your Dictionary's coming abroad this winter was spread, I have been supposed to be marvellously deep in politics: not a sun has set since the above time without previously lighting me to the coffee-house; nor risen, without renewing my curiosity. But time, the great revealer of secrets, has at length put an end to my solicitude; for, if there be truth in book men, I can now, by cunning calculation, foretell the day and hour when it will arrive at Lynn.

" If, which is probable, I should fix my future abode in London, I cannot help rejoicing that I shall then be an inhabitant of the same town, and exulting that I shall then be a fellow citizen with Mr. Johnson; and were it possible I could be honoured with a small share of his esteem, I should regard it as the most grateful circumstance of my life. And—shall I add, that I have a female companion, whose intellects are sufficiently masculine to enter into the true spirit of your writings, and, consequently, to have an enthusiastic zeal for them and their author? How happy would your presence make us over our tea, so often meliorated by your productions!

" If, in the mean time, your avocations would permit you to bestow a line or two upon me, without greatly incommoding yourself, it would communicate the highest delight to

" Sir,

" Your most obedient,

" And most humble servant,

" CHA^s. BURNEY."

" Have you, Sir, ever met with a little French book, entitled, ' Synonimes François, par M. l'Abbé Girard?' I am inclined to imagine, if you have not seen it, that it would afford you, as a philologer, some pleasure, it being written with great spirit, and, I think, accuracy : but I should rejoice to have my opinion either confirmed or corrected by yours. If you should find any difficulty in procuring the book, mine is wholly at your service."

"*Lynn Regis, April* 14*th*, 1755."

To this letter there was little chance of any answer, the demanded "another," relative to the Dictionary, being still due.

That splendid, and probably, from any single intellect, unequalled work, for vigour of imagination and knowledge amidst the depths of erudition, came out in 1756. And, early in 1757, Mr. Burney paid his faithful homage to its author.

"*To Mr. Johnson, Gough-square.*

"Sir,

"Without exercising the greatest self-denial, I should not have been able thus long to withhold from you my grateful acknowledgments for the delight and instruction you have afforded me by means of your admirable Dictionary—a work, I believe, not yet equalled in any language; for, not to mention the accuracy, precision, and elegance of the definitions, the illustrations of words are so judiciously and happily selected as to render it a repository, and, I had almost said, universal register of whatever is sublime or beautiful in English literature. In looking for words, we constantly find things. The road, indeed, to the former, is so flowery as not to be travelled with speed, at least by me, who find it impossible to arrive at the intelligence I want, without bating by the way, and revelling in collateral entertainment. Were I to express all that I think upon this subject, your Dictionary would be stript of a great part of its furniture: but as praise is never gratefully received by the justly deserving till a deduction is first made of the ignorance or partiality of him who bestows it, I shall support my opinion by a passage from a work of reputation among our neighbours, which, if it have not yet reached you, I shall rejoice at being the first to communicate, in hopes of augmenting the satisfaction arising from honest fame, and a conviction of having conferred benefits on mankind: well knowing with how parsimonious and niggard a hand men administer comfort of the kind to modest merit.

"'Le savant et ingenieux M. Samuel Johnson, qui, dans l'incomparable feuille periodique intitulée le Rambler, apprenoit à ses compatriotes à penser avec justesse sur les matières les plus interessantes, vient de leur fournir des secours pour bien parler, et pour écrire correctement ; talens que personne, peut être, ne possede dans un degré plus eminent que lui. Il n'y a qu'une voix sur le succès de l'auteur pour epurer, fixer, et enricher une langue dont son Rambler montre si admirablement l'abondance et la force, l'elegance et l'harmonie.'

"*Bibliotheque des Savans.* Tom. iii. p. 482.

" Though I had constantly in my remembrance the encouragement with which you flattered me in your reply to my first letter, yet knowing that civility and politeness seem often to countenance actions which they would not perform, I could hardly think myself entitled to the permission you gave me of writing to you again, had I not lately been apprised of your intention to oblige the admirers of Shakespeare with a new edition of his works by subscription. But, shall I venture to tell you, notwithstanding my veneration for you and Shakespeare, that I do not partake of the joy which the selfish public seem to feel on this occasion?—so far from it, I could not but be afflicted at reflecting, that so exalted, so refined a genius as the author of the Rambler, should submit to a task so unworthy of him as that of a mere editor: for who would not grieve to see a Palladio, or a Jones, undergo the dull drudgery of carrying rubbish from an old building, when he should be tracing the model of a new one? But I detain you too long from the main subject of this letter, which is to beg a place in the subscription for,

 The Right Hon. the Earl of Brigs Carey, Esq.
  Orford,   Archdale Wilson, Esq.
 Miss Mason,   Richard Fuller, Esq.

    " And for, Sir,
 " Your most humble, and extremely devoted servant,
        " CHARLES BURNEY."

" *Lynn Regis*,
28*th March*, 1757."

It was yet some years later than this last date of correspondence, before Mr. Burney found an opportunity of paying his personal respects to Dr. Johnson; who then, in 1760, resided in chambers at the Temple. No account, unfortunately, remains of this first interview, except an anecdote that relates to Mr. Bewley.

While awaiting the appearance of his revered host, Mr. Burney recollected a supplication from the philosopher of Massingham, to be indulged with some token, however trifling or common, of his friend's admission to the habitation of this great man. Vainly, however, Mr. Burney looked around the apartment for something that he might innoxiously purloin. Nothing but coarse and necessary furniture was in view; nothing portable—not even a wafer, the cover of a letter, or a split pen, was to be caught; till, at length, he had the happiness to espie an old hearth broom in the chimney corner. From this, with hasty glee, he cut off a bristly wisp, which he hurried into his pocket-book; and afterwards formally folded in silver paper, and forwarded, in a frank, to Lord Orford, for Mr. Bewley; by whom the burlesque offering was hailed with good-humoured acclamation, and preserved through life.

LYNN REGIS.

In this manner passed on, quick though occupied, and happy though toilsome, nine or ten years in Norfolk; when the health of Mr. Burney being re-established, and his rising reputation demanding a wider field for expansion, a sort of cry was raised amongst his early friends to spur his return to the metropolis.

Fully, however, as he felt the flattery of that cry, and ill as, in its origin, he had been satisfied with his Lynn residence, he had now experienced from that town and its vicinity, so much true kindness, and cordial hospitality, that his reluctance to quit them was verging upon renouncing such a measure; when he received the following admonition upon the subject from his first friend, and earliest guide, Mr. Crisp.

"To Mr. Burney.

*   *   *

"I have no more to say, my dear Burney, about harpsichords: and if you remain amongst your foggy aldermen, I shall be the more indifferent whether I have one or not. But really, among friends, is not settling at Lynn, planting your youth, genius, hopes, fortune, &c., against a north wall? Can you ever expect ripe, high-flavoured fruit, from such an aspect? Your underrate prices in the town, and galloping about the country for higher, especially in the winter—are they worthy of your talents? In all professions, do you not see every thing that has the least pretence to genius, fly up to the capital—the centre of riches, luxury, taste, pride, extravagance,—all that ingenuity is to fatten upon? Take, then, your spare person, your pretty mate, and your brats, to that propitious mart, and,

'Seize the glorious, golden opportunity,'

while yet you have youth, spirits, and vigour to give fair play to your abilities, for placing them and yourself in a proper point of view. And so I give you my blessing.

"SAMUEL CRISP."

Mr. Crisp, almost immediately after this letter, visited, and for some years, the continent.

This exhortation, in common with whatever emanated from Mr. Crisp, proved decisive; and Mr. Burney fixed at once his resolve upon returning to the capital; though some years still passed ere he could put it in execution.

The following are his reflections, written at a much later period, upon this determination.

After enumerating, with warm regard, the many to whom he owed kindness in the county of Norfolk, he adds:

"All of these, for nearly thirty miles round, had their houses and tables pressingly open to me: and, in the town of Lynn, my wife, to all evening parties, though herself no card player, never failed to be equally invited; for she had a most delightful turn in conversation, seasoned with agreeable wit, and pleasing manners ; and great powers of entering into the humours of her company ; which, with the beauty of her person, occasioned her to receive more invitations than she wished; as she was truly domestic, had a young family on her hands, and, generally, one of them at her breast. But whenever we could spend an evening at home, without disappointing our almost too kind inviters, we had a course of reading so various and entertaining, in history, voyages, poetry, and, as far as Chambers' Dictionary, the Philosophical Transactions, and the French Encyclopedia, to the first edition of which I was a subscriber, could carry us, in science, that those *tête à tête* seclusions were what we enjoyed the most completely.

" This, of course, raised my wife far above all the females of Lynn, who were, then, no readers, with the exception of Mrs. Stephen Allen and Dolly Young. And this congeniality of taste brought on an intimacy of friendship in these three females, that lasted during their several lives.

" My wife was the delight of all her acquaintance ; excellent mother—zealous friend—of highly superior intellects.

" We enjoyed at Lynn tranquillity and social happiness—"

*　　*　　*　　*　　*

Here again must be inserted another poetical epistle, written, during a short separation, while still at Lynn; which shews that, with whatever fervour of passion he married, he himself was "that other happy man," in the words of Lord Lyttleton, who had found " How much the wife is dearer than the bride."

"To Mrs. Burney.

"To thee, henceforth, my matchless mate,
My leisure hours I'll dedicate ;
To thee my inmost thoughts transmit,
Whene'er the busy scene I quit.

For thee, companion dear! I feel
An unextinguishable zeal ;
A love implanted in the mind,
From all the grosser dregs refined.
Ah! tell me, must not love like mine
Be planted by a hand divine,
Which, when creation's work was done,
Our heart-strings tuned in unison ?

If business, or domestic care
The vigour of my mind impair;
If forc'd by toil from thee to rove,
'Till wearied limbs forget to move,
At night, reclin'd upon thy breast,
Thy converse lulls my soul to rest.

If sickness her distemper'd brood
Let loose,—to burn, or freeze my blood,
Thy tender vigilance and care,
My feeble frame can soon repair.

When in some doubtful maze I stray,
'Tis thou point'st out the unerring way ;
If judgment float on wavering wings,
In notions vague of men and things;
If different views my mind divide,
Thy nod instructs me to decide.

My pliant soul 'tis thou can'st bend,
My help! companion! wife! and friend!
   When, in the irksome day of trouble
The mental eye sees evils double,
Sweet partner of my hopes and fears!
'Tis thou alone can'st dry my tears.
'Tis thou alone can'st bring relief,
Partner of every joy and grief!
E'en when encompass'd with distress,
Thy smile can every ill redress.
   On thee, my lovely, faithful friend,
My worldly blessings all depend:
But if a cloud thy visage low'r,
Not all the wealth in Plutus' power,
Could buy my heart one peaceful hour.
Then, lodg'd within that aching heart,
Is sorrow's sympathetic dart.

      *   *   *   *

   But when upon that brow, the seat
Of sense refin'd, and beauty sweet,
The graces and the loves are seen,
And Venus sits by Wisdom's queen;
Pale sadness takes her heavy flight,
And, envious, shuns the blissful sight.
   So when the sun has long endur'd
His radiant face to be obscur'd
By baleful mists and vapours dense,
All nature mourns with grief intense:
But the refulgent God of Day
Soon shews himself in bright array;

And as his glorious visage clears,
The globe itself in smiles appears."

"*Lynn*, 1753."

The last act of Mr. Burney in relinquishing his residence in Norfolk, was drawing up a petition to Lord Orford to allow park-room in the Haughton grounds, for the rest of its life, to his excellent, faithful mare, the intelligent Peggy; whose truly useful services he could not bear to requite, according to the unfeeling usage of the many, by selling her to hard labour in the decline of her existence.

Lord Orford good-humouredly complied with the request; and the justly-prized Peggy, after enjoying for several years the most perfect ease and freedom, died the death of old age, in Haughton Park.

LONDON.

In 1760, Mr. Burney, with his wife and young family, returned to London; but no longer to the city, which has the peculiar fate, whilst praised and reverenced by the many who to its noble encouragement owe their first dawn of prosperity, of being almost always set aside and relinquished, when that prosperity is effected. Is it that Fortune, like the sun, while it rises, cold, though of fairest promise, in the East, must ever, in its more luxuriant splendour, set in the West?

The new establishment was in Poland-street; which was not then, as it is now, a sort of street that, like the rest of its neighbourhood, appears to be left in the lurch. House-fanciers were not yet as fastidious as they are become at present, from the endless variety of new habitations. Oxford-road, as, at that time, Oxford-street was called, into which Poland-street terminated, had little on its further side but fields, gardeners' grounds, or uncultivated suburbs. Portman, Manchester, Russel, Belgrave squares, Portland-place, &c. &c., had not yet a single stone or brick laid, in signal of intended erection: while in plain Poland-street, Mr. Burney, then, had successively for his neighbours, the Duke of Chandos, Lady Augusta Bridges, the Hon. John Smith and the Miss Barrys, Sir Willoughby and the Miss Astons; and, well noted by Mr. Burney's little family, on the visit of his black majesty to England, sojourned, almost immediately opposite to it, the Cherokee King.

The opening of this new plan of life, was as successful to Mr. Burney as its projection had been promising. Pupils of rank, wealth, and talents, were continually proposed to him; and, in a very short time, he had hardly an hour unappropriated to some fair disciple.

Lady Tankerville, amongst the rest, resumed her lessons with her early master, obligingly submitting her time to his convenience, be it what it might, rather than change her first favourite instructor. Ere long, however, she resided almost wholly abroad, having attached herself with enthusiastic fervour to the Princess Amelia, sister to Frederick the Great of Prussia. The Countess even accepted the place of Dame d'Atour to that accomplished princess; whose charms, according to poetical record, banished for a while their too daring admirer, Voltaire, from the Court of Berlin.

This enterprising Countess retained her spirit of whim, singularity, and activity, through a long life; for when, many years later, she returned to her own country, quite old, while Dr. Burney had not yet reached the zenith of his fame, she again applied to him for musical tuition; and when he told her, with regret, that his day was completely filled up, from eight o'clock in the morning; "Come to me, then," cried she, with vivacity, "at seven!" which appointment literally, and twice a week, took place.

All the first friends of Mr. Burney were happy to renew with him their social intercourse. Mrs. Greville, when in town, was foremost in eagerly seeking his Esther; and Mr. Greville met again his early favourite with all his original impetuosity of regard: while their joint newer friends of Norfolk, Mrs. Stephen Allen and Miss Dorothy Young in particular, warmly sustained an unremitting communication by letters: and Lords Orford, Eglinton, and March, General Lord Townshend, Charles Boone, and many others, sought this enlivening couple, with an unabating sense of their worth, upon every occasion that either music or conversation offered, for accepting, or desiring, admission to their small parties: for so uncommon were the powers of pleasing which they possessed, that all idea of condescension in their worldly superiors seemed superseded, if not annihilated, by personal eagerness to enjoy their rare society.

ESTHER.

Thus glided away, in peace, domestic joys, improvement, and prosperity, this first—and last! happy year of the new London residence. In the course of the second, a cough, with alarming symptoms, menaced the breast of the life and soul of the little circle; consisting now of six children, clinging with equal affection around each parent chief.

She rapidly grew weaker and worse. Her tender husband hastened her to Bristol Hotwells, whither he followed her upon his first possible vacation; and where, in a short time, he had the extasy to believe that he saw her recover, and to bring her back to her fond little family.

But though hope was brightened, expectation was deceived! stability of strength was restored no more; and, in the ensuing autumn, she was seized with an inflammatory disorder with which her delicate and shaken frame had not force to combat. No means were left unessayed to stop the progress of danger; but all were fruitless! and, after less than a week of pain the most terrific, the deadly ease of mortification suddenly, awfully succeeded to the most excruciating torture.

Twelve stated hours of morbid bodily repose became, from that tremendous moment of baleful relief, the counted boundary of her earthly existence.

The wretchedness of her idolizing husband at the development of such a predestined termination to her sufferings, when pronounced by the celebrated Dr. Hunter, was only not distraction. But she herself, though completely aware that her hours now were told, met the irrevocable doom with open, religious, and even cheerful composure—sustained, no doubt, by the blessed aspirations of mediatory salvation; and calmly declaring that she quitted the world with perfect tranquillity, save for leaving her tender husband and helpless children. And, in the arms of that nearly frantic husband, who, till that fatal epoch, had literally believed her existence and his own, in this mortal journey, to be indispensably one—she expired.

When the fatal scene was finally closed, the disconsolate survivor immured himself almost from light and life, through inability to speak or act, or yet to bear witnesses to his misery.

He was soon, however, direfully called from this concentrated anguish, by the last awful summons to the last awful rites to human memory, the funeral; which he attended in a frame of mind that nothing, probably, could have rescued from unrestrained despair, save a pious invocation to submission that had been ejaculated by his Esther, when she perceived his rising agony, in an impressive " Oh, Charles ! " — almost at the very moment she was expiring : an appeal that could not but still vibrate in his penetrated ears, and control his tragic passions.

The character, and its rare, resplendent worth, of this inestimable person, is best committed to the pen of him to whom it best was known ; as will appear by the subsequent letter, copied from his own hand-writing. It was found amongst his posthumous papers, so ill-written and so blotted by his tears, that he must have felt himself obliged to re-write it for the post.

It may be proper to again mention, that though Esther was maternally of French extraction, and though her revered mother was a Roman Catholic, she herself was a confirmed Protestant. But that angelic mother had brought her up with a love and a practice of genuine piety which undeviatingly intermingled in every action, and, probably, in every thought of her virtuous life, so religiously, so deeply, that neither pain nor calamity could make her impatient of existence ; nor yet could felicity the most perfect make her reluctant to die.

To paint the despairing grief produced by this deadly blow must be cast, like the portrait of its object, upon the sufferer ; and the inartificial pathos, the ingenuous humility, with which both are marked in the affecting detail of her death, written in answer to a letter of sympathizing condolence from the tenderest friend of the deceased, Miss Dorothy Young, so strongly speak a language of virtue as well as of sorrow, that, unconsciously, they exhibit his own fair unsophisticated character in delineating that of his lost love. A more touching description of happiness in conjugal life, or of wretchedness in its dissolution, is rarely, perhaps, with equal simplicity of truth, to be found upon record.

" To Miss Dorothy Young.

" I had not thought it possible that any thing could urge me to write in the present deplorable disposition of my mind; but my dear Miss Young's letter haunts me ! Neither did I think it possible for any thing to add to my affliction, borne down and broken-hearted as I am. But the current of your woes and sympathetic sorrows meeting mine, has overpowered all bounds which religion, philosophy, reason, or even despair, may have been likely to set to my grief. Oh Miss Young! you knew her worth—you were one of the few people capable of seeing and feeling it. Good God! that she should be snatched from me at a time when I thought her health re-establishing, and fixing for a long old age! when our plans began to succeed, and we flattered ourselves with enjoying each other's society ere long, in a peaceable and quiet retirement from the bustling frivolousness of a capital, to which our niggard stars had compelled us to fly for the prospect of establishing our children.

" Amongst the numberless losses I sustain, there are none that unman me so much as the total deprivation of domestic comfort and converse—that converse from which I tore myself with such difficulty in a morning, and to which I flew back with such celerity at night! She was the source of all I could ever project or perform that was praise-worthy--all that I could do that was laudable had an eye to her approbation. There was a rectitude in her mind and judgment, that rendered her approbation so animating, so rational, so satisfactory! I have lost the spur, the stimulus to all exertions, all warrantable pursuits,—except those of another world. From an ambitious, active, enterprizing Being, I am become a torpid drone, a listless, desponding wretch!—I know you will bear with my weakness, nay, in part, participate in it; but this is a kind of dotage unfit for common eyes, or even for common friends, to be entrusted with.

" You kindly, and truly, my dear Miss Young, styled her one of the greatest ornaments of society; but, apart from the ornamental, in which she shone in a superior degree, think, oh think, of her high merit as a daughter, mother, wife, sister, friend! I always, from the first moment I saw her to the last, had an ardent passion for her person, to which time had added true friendship and rational regard. Perhaps it is honouring myself too much to say, few people were more suited to each other; but, at least, I always endeavoured to render myself more worthy of her than nature, perhaps, had formed me. But she could mould me to what she pleased! A distant hint—a remote wish from her was enough to inspire me with courage for any undertaking. But all is lost and gone in losing her—the whole world is a desert to me! nor does its whole circumference afford the least hope of succour—not a single ray of that fortitude She so fully possessed!

" You, and all who knew her, respected and admired her understanding while she was living. Judge, then, with what awe and veneration I must be struck to hear her counsel when dying!— to see her meet that tremendous spectre, death, with that calmness, resignation, and true religious fortitude, that no stoic philosopher, nor scarcely christian, could surpass; for it was all in privacy and simplicity. Socrates and Seneca called their friends around them to give them that courage that perhaps solitude might have robbed them of, and to spread abroad their fame to posterity; but she, dear pattern of humility! had no such vain view; no parade, no grimace! When she was aware that all was over—when she had herself pronounced the dread sentence, that she felt she should not outlive the coming night, she composedly gave herself up to religion, and begged that she might not be interrupted in her prayers and meditations.

" Afterwards she called me to her, and then tranquilly talked about our family and affairs, in a manner quite oracular.

" Sometime later she desired to see Hetty,* who, till that day, had spent the miserable week almost constantly at her bed-side,

---

* The eldest daughter.

or at the foot of the bed. Fanny, Susan, and Charley, had been sent, some days before, to the kind care of Mrs. Sheeles in Queen Square, to be out of the way; and little Charlotte was taken to the house of her nurse.

" To poor Hetty she then discoursed in so kind, so feeling, so tender a manner, that I am sure her words will never be forgotten. And, this over, she talked of her own death—her funeral—her place of burial,—with as much composure as if talking of a journey to Lynn! Think of this, my dear Miss Young, and see the impossibility of supporting such a loss—such an adieu, with calmness! I hovered over her till she sighed, not groaned, her last—placidly sighed it—just after midnight.

" Her disorder was an inflammation of the stomach, with which she was seized on the 19th of September, after being on that day, and for some days previously, remarkably in health and spirits. She suffered the most excruciating torments for eight days, with a patience, a resignation, nearly quite silent. Her malady baffled all medical skill from the beginning. I called in Dr. Hunter.

" On the 28th, the last day! she suffered, I suppose, less, perhaps nothing! as mortification must have taken place, which must have afforded that sort of ease, that those who have escaped such previous agony shudder to think of! On that ever memorable, that dreadful day, she talked more than she had done throughout her whole illness. She forgot nothing, nor threw one word away! always hoping we should meet and know each other hereafter!—She told poor Hetty how sweet it would be if she could see her constantly from whence she was going, and begged she would invariably suppose that that would be the case. What a lesson to leave to a daughter!—She exhorted her to remember how much her example might influence the poor younger ones;

and bid her write little letters, and fancies, to her in the other world, to say how they all went on; adding, that she felt as if she should surely know something of them.

"Afterwards, feeling probably her end fast approaching, she serenely said, with one hand on the head of Hetty, and the other grasped in mine: " Now this is dying pleasantly! in the arms of one's friends! " I burst into an unrestrained agony of grief, when, with a superiority of wisdom, resignation, and true religion,— though awaiting, consciously, from instant to instant awaiting the shaft of death,—she mildly uttered, in a faint, faint voice, but penetratingly tender, " Oh Charles!—"

" I checked myself instantaneously, over-awed and stilled as by a voice from one above. I felt she meant to beg me not to agitate her last moments!—I entreated her forgiveness, and told her it was but human nature. "And so it is!" said she, gently; and presently added, " Nay, it is worse for the living than the dying,—though a moment sets us even!—life is but a paltry business—yet

> " ' Who, to dumb forgetfulness a prey
> This pleasing—anxious being e'er resign'd?
> Left the warm precincts of the cheerful day,
> Nor cast one longing, lingering look behind?' "

" She had still muscular strength left to softly press both our hands as she pronounced these affecting lines.

" Other fine passages, also, both from holy writ, and from what is most religious in our best poets, she from time to time recited, with fervent prayers; in which most devoutly we joined.

" These, my dear Miss Young, are the outlines of her sublime and edifying exit——— ———What a situation was mine! but for my poor helpless children, how gladly, how most gladly should I have wished to accompany her hence on the very instant, to that other world to which she so divinely passed!—for what in this remains for me?"

Part of a letter, also, to Mrs. Stephen Allen, the friend to whom, next to Miss Dorothy Young, the departed had been most attached, seems to belong to this place. Its style, as it was written at a later period, is more composed; but it evinces in the wretched mourner the same devotion to his Esther's excellences, and the same hopelessness of earthly happiness.

"To Mrs. Stephen Allen.

*   *   *   *   *

"Even prosperity is insipid without participation with those we love; for me, therefore, heaven knows, all is at an end—all is accumulated wretchedness! I have lost a soul congenial with my own;—a companion, who in outward appurtenances and internal conceptions, condescended to assimilate her ideas and manners with mine. Yet believe not that all my feelings are for myself; my poor girls have sustained a loss far more extensive than they, poor innocents! are at present sensible of. Unprovided as I should have left them with respect to fortune, had it been my fate to resign her and life first, I should have been under no great apprehension for the welfare of my children, in leaving them to a mother who had such inexhaustible resources in her mind and intellects. It would have grieved me, indeed, to have quitted her oppressed by such a load of care; but I could have had no doubt of her supporting it with fortitude and abilities, as long as life and health had been allowed her. Fortitude and abilities she possessed, indeed, to a degree that, without hyperbole, no human being can conceive but myself, who have seen her under such severe trials as alone can manifest, unquestionably, true parts and greatness of mind. I am thoroughly convinced she was fitted for any situation, either exalted or humble, which this life can furnish. And with all her nice discernment, quickness of perception, and delicacy, she could submit, if occasion seemed to require it, to such drudgery and toil as are suited to the meanest domestic; and that, with a liveliness and alacrity that, in general, are to be found in those only who have never known a better state. Yet with a strength of reason the most solid, and a capacity for literature the most intelligent, she never for a moment relinquished the female and amiable softness of her sex with which, above every other attribute, men are most charmed and captivated."

Such, in their early effervescence, was the vent which this man of affliction found to his sorrows, in the sympathy of his affectionate friends.

At other times, they were beguiled from their deadly heaviness by the expansion of fond description in melancholy verse. To this he was less led by poetical enthusiasm—for all of fire, fancy, and imagery, that light up the poet's flame, was now extinct, or smothered—than by a gentle request of his Esther, uttered in her last days, that he would address to her some poetry; a request intended, there can be no doubt, as a stimulus to some endearing occupation that might tear him from his first despondence, by an idea that he had still a wish of hers to execute.

Not as poetry, in an era fastidious as the present in metrical criticism, does the editor presume to offer the verses now about to be selected and copied from a vast mass of elegiac laments found amongst the posthumous papers of Dr. Burney: it is biographically alone, like those that have preceded them, that they are brought forward. They are testimonies of the purity of his love, as well as of the acuteness of his bereavement; and, as such, they certainly belong to his memoirs. The reader, therefore, is again entreated to remember that they were not designed for the press, though they were committed, unshackled, to the discretion of the editor. If that be in fault, the motive will probably prove a palliative that will make the heart, not the head, of the reader, the seat of his judgment.

> " She's gone!—the all-pervading soul is fled
> T' explore the unknown mansions of the dead,
> Where, free from earthly clay, the immortal mind
> Casts many a pitying glance on those behind;

Sees us deplore the wife--the mother—friend—
Sees fell despair our wretched bosoms rend!

   Oh death!—thy dire inexorable dart
Of every blessing has bereft my heart!
Better to have died like her, in hope of rest,
Than live forlorn, and life and light detest.—

   In hope of rest? ah no! her fervent pray'r
Was that her soul, when once dissolv'd in air
Might, conscious of its pre-existent state,
On those she lov'd alive, benignly wait,—
Our genius, and our guardian angel be
Till fate unite us in eternity!

   But—the bless'd shade to me no hope bequeaths
Till death his faulchion in my bosom sheaths!
Sorrowing, I close my eyes in restless sleep;
Sorrowing, I wake the live-long day to weep.
No future comfort can this world bestow,
'Tis blank and cold, as overwhelm'd with snow.

   *   *   *   *   *

   When dying in my arms, she softly said:
" Write me some verses!"—and shall be obey'd.
The sacred mandate vibrates in my ears,
And fills my eyes with reverential tears.
For ever on her virtues let me dwell,
A Patriarch's life too short her worth to tell.
Such manly sense to female softness join'd,
Her person grac'd, and dignified her mind,
That she in beauty, while she trod life's stage,
A Venus seem'd—in intellect, a sage.

Before I her beheld, the untutor'd mind
Still vacant lay, to mental beauty blind:
But when her angel form my sight had bless'd
The flame of passion instant fill'd my breast;
Through every vein the fire electric stole,
And took dominion of my inmost soul.
    By her.... possess'd of every pow'r to please,
Each toilsome task was exercis'd with ease.

    *   *   *   *   *

For me, comprising every charm of life,
Friend—Mistress—Counsellor—Companion—Wife—
Wife!—wife!—oh honour'd name! for ever dear,
Alike enchanting to the eye and ear!
    Let the corrupt, licentious, and profane
Rail, scoff, and murmur at the sacred chain:
It suits not them. Few but the wise and good
It's blessings e'er have priz'd or understood.
Matur'd in virtue first the heart must glow,
Ere happiness can vegetate and grow.
    From her I learnt to feel the holy flame,
And found that she and virtue were the same.
From dissipation, though I might receive—
Ere yet I knew I had a heart to give—
An evanescent joy, untouch'd the mind
Still torpid lay, to mental beauty blind;
Till by example more than precept taught
From her, to act aright, the flame I caught.
    How chang'd the face of nature now is grown!

    *   *   *   *   *

Illusive hope no more her charms displays;
Her flattering schemes no more my spirits raise;
Each airy vision which her pencil drew
Inexorable death has banish'd from my view.
Each gentle solace is withheld by fate
Till death conduct me through his awful gate.
　　Come then, Oh Death! let kindred souls be join'd!
Oh thou, so often cruel—once be kind!"

A total chasm ensues of all account of events belonging to the period of this irreparable earthly blast. Not a personal memorandum of the unhappy survivor is left; not a single document in his hand-writing, except of verses to her idea, or to her memory; or of imitations, adapted to his loss, and to her excellences, from some selected sonnets of Petrarch, whom he considered to have loved, entombed, and bewailed another Esther in his Laura.

When this similitude, which soothed his spirit and flattered his feelings, had been studied and paralleled in every possible line of comparison, he had recourse to the works of Dante, which, ere long, beguiled from him some attention; because, through the difficulty of idiom, he had not, as of nearly all other favourite authors, lost all zest of the beauties of Dante in solitude, from having tasted the sweetness of his numbers with a pleasure exalted by participation: for, during the last two years that his Esther was spared to him, her increased maternal claims from a new baby;* and augmented domestic cares from a new residence, had checked the daily mutuality of their progress in the pursuit of improvement; and to Esther this great poet was scarcely known.

To Dante, therefore, he first delivered over what he could yet summon from his grief-worn faculties; and to initiate himself into the works, and nearly obsolete style, of that hardest, but most sublime of Italian poets, became the occupation to which, with the least repugnance, he was capable of recurring.

A sedulous, yet energetic, though prose translation of the Inferno, remains amongst his posthumous relics, to demonstrate the sincere struggles with which, even amidst this overwhelming calamity, he strove to combat that most dangerously consuming of all canker-worms upon life and virtue, utter inertness.

Of his children, James,† his eldest son, had

---

* Charlotte.   † Afterwards Rear-Admiral James Burney.

already, at ten years of age, been sent to sea, a nominal midshipman, in the ship of Admiral Montagu.

The second son, Charles,* who was placed, several years later, in the Charterhouse, by Mr. Burney's first and constant patron, the Earl of Holdernesse, was then but a child.

The eldest daughter was still a little girl; and the last born of her three sisters could scarcely walk alone. But all, save the seaman, who was then aboard his ship, were now called back to the paternal roof of the unhappy father.

None of them, however, were of an age to be companionable; his fondness for them, therefore, full of care and trouble, procured no mitigation to his grief by the pleasure of society: and the heavy march of time, where no solace is accepted from abroad, or attainable at home, gave a species of stagnation to his existence, that made him take, in the words of Young,

> "No note of time,
> Save by its loss!"

His tenderness, however, as a father; his situation

---

* Afterwards the celebrated Greek scholar.

as a man; and his duties as a Christian, drew, tore him, at length, from this retreat of lonely woe; and, in the manuscript already quoted from, which was written many years after the period of which it speaks, he says: " I was forced, ere long, to plunge into business; and then found, that having my time occupied by my affairs was a useful dissipation of my sorrows, as it compelled me to a temporary inattention to myself, and to the irreparable loss I had sustained."

Still, however, all mitigation to his grief that was not imposed upon him by necessity, he avoided even with aversion; and even the sight of those who most had loved and esteemed the departed, was the sight most painful to him in sharpening his regrets, " which, therefore, no meeting whatsoever," he says; " could blunt; since to love and admire her, had been universally the consequence of seeing and knowing her."

From this mournful monotony of life, he was especially, however, called, by reflecting that his eldest daughter was fast advancing to that age when education is most requisite to improvement; and that, at such a period, the loss of her mother and instructress might be permanently hurtful to her, if no measure should be taken to avert the possible consequences of neglect.

Yet the idea of a governess, who, to him, unless his children were wholly confined to the nursery, must indispensably be a species of companion, was not, in his present desolate state of mind, even tolerable. Nevertheless masters without superintendence, and lessons without practice, he well knew to be nugatory. Projects how to remedy this evil, as fruitless as they were numberless, crossed his mind; till a plan occurred to him, that, by combining economy with novelty, and change of scene for himself, with various modes of advantage to his daughters, ripened into an exertion that brought him, about a month after its formation, to the gates of Paris.

The design of Mr. Burney was to place two of his daughters in some convent, or boarding-house, where their education might be forwarded by his own directions.

Sundry reasons decided him to make his third daughter, Susanna, take place, in this expedition, of his second, Frances; but, amongst them, the principal and most serious motive, was a fearful tendency to a consumptive habit in that most delicate of his young plants, that seemed to require the balsamic qualities of a warmer and clearer atmosphere.

Another reason, which he acknowledged, in after times, to have had great weight with him for this arrangement, was the tender veneration with which Frances was impressed for her maternal grandmother; whose angelic piety, and captivating softness, had won her young heart with such reverential affection, that he apprehended there might be danger of her being led to follow, even enthusiastically, the religion of so pure a votary, if she should fall so early, within the influence of any zealot in the work of conversion. He determined, therefore, as he could part with two of them only at a time, that Fanny and Charlotte should follow their sisters in succession, at a later period.

PARIS.

Immediately upon his arrival at Paris, Mr. Burney, by singular good fortune, had the honour to be introduced to Lady Clifford, a Roman Catholic dowager, of a character the most benevolent, who resided entirely in France, for the pious purpose of enjoying with facility the rites of her religion, which could not, at that period, be followed in England without peril of persecution.

This lady took the children of Mr. Burney into her kindest favour, and invited their father to consult with her unreservedly upon his projects and wishes; and, through such honourable auspices, scarcely ten days elapsed, ere Esther and Susan were placed under the care of Madame St. Mart, a woman of perfect goodness of heart, and of a disposition the most affectionate.

Madame St. Mart was accustomed to the charge of *des jeunes Anglaises,* two daughters of Sir Willoughby Aston, Selina and Belinda, being then under her roof.

Highly satisfied with this arrangement, Mr. Burney now visited the delightful capital of France; made himself acquainted with its antiquities, curiosities, public buildings, public places, general laws, and peculiar customs; its politics, its resources, its festivities, its arts and its artists; as well as with the arbitrary tyrannies, and degrading oppressions towards the lower classes, which, at that epoch, were, to an English looker-on, incomprehensibly combined, not with murmurs nor discontent, but with the most lively animal spirits, and the freshest glee of national gaiety.

But his chosen haunts were the Public Libraries, to which an easiness of access, at that time deplorably unknown in England, encouraged, nay, excited, the intelligent visitor, who might be mentally inclined to any literary project, to hit upon some subject congenial to his taste; by rousing in him that spirit of emulation, which ultimately animates the humbly instructed, to soar to the heights that distinguish the luminous instructor.

Collections of books, even the most multitudinous and the most rare, may hold, to the common runner through life, but an ordinary niche in places of general resort; nevertheless, the Public Libraries, those Patrons of the Mind, must always be entered with a glow of grateful pleasure, by those who, instinctively, meditate upon the vast mass of thought that they contain.

To wander amidst those stores, that commit talents to posterity as indubitably as the Herald's Register transmits names and titles; to develop as accurately the systems of nations, the conditions of communities, the progress of knowledge, and the turn of men's minds, two or three thousand years ago, as in this our living minute; to visit, in fact, the Brains of our fellow creatures,—not alone with the harrowing knife to dissect physical conformation, but, with the piercing eye of penetration to dive into the recesses of human intelligence, the sources of imagination, and the springs of genius; and there, in those sacred receptacles of mental remains, to survey, in clear, indestructible evidence, all of the soul that man is able to bequeath to man— —

Views such as these of the powers of his gifted, though gone fellow-creatures, seen thus abstractedly through their intellectual attributes; purified equally from the frailties and selfishness of active life, and the sickly humours and baleful infirmities of age; seen through the medium of learned, useful, or fanciful productions; and beheld in so insulated a moment of vacuity of any positive plan of life, instinctively roused the dormant faculties of the subject of these memoirs, by setting before him a comprehensive chart of human capabilities, which involuntarily incited a conscious inquiry: what, peradventure, might be his own share, if sought for, in such heavenly gifts?

And it was now that, vaguely, yet powerfully, he first fell into that stream of ideas, or visions, that seemed to hail him to that class indefinable and indescribable, from its mingled elevation and abjectness, which, by joining the publicity of the press to the secret intercourse of the mind with the pen, insensibly allures its adventurous votaries to make the world at large the judge of their abilities, or their deficiences—namely, the class of authors.

For this was the real, though not yet the ostensible epoch, whence may be traced the opening of his passion for literary pursuits.

And from this period, to the very close of his long mortal career, this late, though newly chosen occupation, became all that was most consoling to his sorrows, most diversifying to his ideas, and most animating to his faculties.

Some new stimulus had been eminently wanting to draw a man of his natively ardent and aspiring character from the torpid blight of availless misery; which, in despoiling him of all bosom felicity, had left only to an attempt at some untried project and purpose, any chance for the restoration of his energies.

He did not immediately fix on a subject for any work, though he had the wisdom, at once, and the modesty, to resolve, since so tardily he entered such lists, to adopt no plan that might wean him from his profession—for his profession was his whole estate! but rather to seek one that might amalgamate his rising desire of fame in literature, with his original labours to be distinguished as a follower of Orpheus.

He took notes innumerable in the public libraries, which he meant to revisit on returning to Paris for his daughters, of the books, subjects, passages, and authors which invited re-perusal; and which, hereafter, might happily conduct to some curious investigation, or elucidating commentary.

He made himself master of a beautiful collection of what then was esteemed to be most select of the French classics.

He completed, by adding to what already he possessed, all that recently had been published of that noblest work that had yet appeared in the republic of letters, the original Encyclopedia.

He opened an account with the reigning bookseller of the day, whose reputation in his mind-enlightening business still sustains its renown, M. Guy, whom he commissioned to send over to England the principal works then suspending over the heights of the French Parnassus; where resplendently were grouped all that was most attract-tive in Wit, Poetry, Eloquence, Science, Pathos, and Entertainment; from Rousseau, Voltaire, D'Alembert, Marmontel, Destouches, Marivaux, Gilbert, Diderot, Fontenelle, de Jaucourt; and many others.

It will easily be conceived how wistfully Mr. Burney must have coveted to make acquaintance with this brilliant set; his high veneration for genius having always led him to consider the first sight of an eminent author to form a data in his life.

But he had neither leisure, nor recommendatory letters; nor, perhaps, courage for such an attempt; the diffidence of his nature by no means anticipating the honourable place he himself was destined to hold in similar circles.

Not small, however, was his solace, while missing every ray of living light from this foreign constellation, when he found himself shone upon by a fixed star of the first magnitude belonging to his own system; for at the house of the English ambassador, the Earl of Hertford, he became acquainted with the celebrated secretary of his lordship, the justly admired, and justly censured DAVID HUME; who, with the skilful discernment that waited neither name nor fame for its stimulus, took Mr. Burney immediately and warmly into his favour.

Had this powerful and popular author, in his erudite, spirited, and intellectual researches and reflections, given to mankind his luminous talents, and his moral philosophy, for fair, open, and useful purposes, suited to the high character which he bore, not alone for genius, but for worth and benevolence; intead of bending, blending, involving them with missive weapons of baneful sarcasm, insidiously at work to undermine our form of faith; he would have been hailed universally, not applauded partially, as, in every point, one of the first of British writers.

To the world no man is accountable for his thoughts and his ruminations; but for their propagation, if they are dangerous or mischievous, the risks which he may allure others to share, seem impelled by wanton lack of feeling; if not by an ignorant yet presumptuous dearth of foresight to the effect he is working to produce: two deficiencies equally impossible to be attributed to a man to whom philanthropy is as unequivocally accorded as philosophy.

Unsolved therefore, perhaps, yet remains, as a problem in the history of human nature, how a being, at once wise and benign, could have refrained from the self-examination of demanding: what—had he been successful in exterminating from the eyes and the hearts of men the lecture and the doctrines of the Holy Scriptures, would have been achieved? Had he any other more perfect religion to offer? More purifying from evil? more fortifying in misfortune? more consoling in woe?—No!—indubitably no!—Nothing fanatical, or mystic, could cope with judgment such as his. To undermine, not to construct, is all the obvious purpose of his efforts—of which he laments the failure as a calamity!* He leaves, therefore, nothing to conjecture of his motives but what least seems to belong to a character of his sedate equanimity; a personal desire to proclaim to mankind their folly in their belief, and his sagacity in his infidelity.

LONDON.

Mr. Burney now, greatly lightened, and somewhat brightened in spirits, returned to his country and his home. His mind seemed no longer left in desolating inertness to prey upon itself. Nutriment

---

* In his letters.

of an invigorating nature was in view, though not yet of a consistence to afford spontaneous refreshment. On the contrary, it required taste for selection, labour for culture, and skill for appropriation. But such nutriment, if attainable, was precisely that which best could re-inforce the poor " tenement of clay," * which the lassitude of unbraced nerves had nearly " fretted to decay."

Sketches, hints, notes, and scattered ideas of all sorts, began to open the way to some original composition; though the timidity of his Muse, not the dearth of his fancy, long kept back the force of mind for meeting the public eye, that now, in these more easy, dauntless times, urges almost every stripling to present his mental powers to the world, nearly ere his physical ones have emerged from leading-strings in the nursery.

The first, because the least responsible, method of facing the critic eye, that occurred to him, was that of translation; and he began with acutely studying d'Alembert's *Elémens de Musique théorique et pratique, selon les principes de Rameau;* in which he was assiduously engaged, when the appearance of the celebrated musical *Dictionaire* of the

---

* Dryden.

still more celebrated Rousseau, from its far nearer congeniality to his taste, surprised him into inconstancy.

Yet this also, from circumstances that intervened, was laid aside; and his first actual essay was a trifle, though a pleasing one, from which no real fame could either accrue, or be marred; it was translating, and adapting to the stage, the little pastoral afterpiece of Rousseau, *Le Divan du Village.*

GARRICK.

To this he was urged by Garrick; and the execution was appropriate, and full of merit. But though the music, from its simplicity and the sweetness of its melody, was peculiarly fitted to refine the public taste amongst the middle classes; while it could not fail to give passing pleasure even to the highest; the drama was too denuded of intricacy or variety for the amusement of John Bull; and the appearance of only three interlocuters caused a gaping expectation of some followers, that made every new scene begin by inflicting disapment.

Mr. Garrick, and his accomplished, high-bred,

and engaging wife, La Violetta, had been amongst the earliest of the pristine connexions of Mr. Burney, who had sought him, with compassionate kindness, as soon after his heart-breaking loss as he could admit any friends to his sight. The ensuing paragraph on his warm sentiments of this talented and bewitching pair, is copied from one of his manuscript memorandums.

"My acquaintance, at this time, with Mrs. as well as Mr. Garrick, was improved into a real friendship; and frequently, on the Saturday night, when Mr. Garrick did not act, he carried me to his villa at Hampton, whence he brought me to my home early on Monday morning. I seldom was more happy than in these visits. His wit, humour, and constant gaiety at home; and Mrs. Garrick's good sense, good breeding, and obliging desire to please, rendered their Hampton villa, on these occasions, a terrestrial paradise.

"Mrs. Garrick had every faculty of social judgment, good taste, and steadiness of character, which he wanted. She was an excellent appreciator of the fine arts; and attended all the last rehearsals of new or of revived plays, to give her opinion of effects, dresses, scenery, and machinery. She seemed to be his real other half; and he, by his intelligence and accomplishments, seemed to complete the Hydroggynus."

This eminent couple paid their court to Mr. Burney in the manner that was most sure to be successful, namely, by their endearing and good-natured attentions to his young family; frequently giving them, with some chaperon of their father's appointing, the lightsome pleasure of possessing Mrs. Garrick's private box at Drury Lane Theatre; and that, from time to time, even when the incomparable Roscius acted himself; which so enchanted their gratitude, that they nearly—as Mr. Burney laughingly quoted to Garrick from Hudibras—

> " Did,—as was their duty,
> Worship the shadow of his shoe-tie."

Garrick, who was passionately fond of children, never withheld his visits from Poland-street on account of the absence of the master of the house; for though it was the master he came to seek, he was too susceptible to his own lively gift of bestowing pleasure, to resist witnessing the ecstacy he was sure to excite, when he burst in unexpectedly upon the younger branches: for so playfully he individualised his attentions, by an endless variety of comic badinage,—now exhibited in lofty bombast; now in ludicrous obsequiousness; now by a sarcasm skilfully implying a compliment; now by a compliment archly conveying a sarcasm; that every happy day that gave them but a glimpse of this idol of their juvenile fancy, was exhilarated to its close by reciprocating anecdotes of the look, the smile, the bow, the shrug, the start, that, after his departure, each enraptured admirer could describe.

A circumstance of no small weight at that time, contributed to allure Mr. Garrick to granting these joyous scenes to the young Burney tribe. When he made the tour of Italy, for the recovery of his health, and the refreshment of his popularity, he committed to the care of Mr. Burney and his young family his own and Mrs. Garrick's favourite little dog, Phill, a beautiful black and white spaniel, of King Charles's breed, luxuriant in tail and mane, with the whitest breast, and spotted with perfect symmetry.

The fondness of Mr. Garrick for this little spaniel was so great, that one of his first visits on his return from the continent was to see, caress, and reclaim him. Phill was necessarily resigned, though with the most dismal reluctance, by his new friends: but if parting with the favoured little quadruped was a disaster, how was that annoyance overpaid, when, two or three days afterwards, Phill re-appeared! and when the pleasure of his welcome to the young folks was increased by a message, that the little animal had seemed so moping, so unsettled, and so forlorn, that Mr. and Mrs. Garrick had not the heart to break his new engagements, and requested his entire acceptance and adoption in Poland-street.

During the life of this favourite, all the juvenile group were sought and visited together, by the gay-hearted Roscius; and with as much glee as he himself was received by these happy young creatures, whether two-footed or four.

On the first coming-out of the "Cunning Man," Mr. Garrick, who undoubtedly owed his unequalled varieties in delineating every species of comic character, to an inquisitive observance of Nature in all her workings, amused himself in watching from the orchestra, where he frequently sat on the first night of new pieces, the young auditory in Mrs. Garrick's box; and he imitatingly described to Mr. Burney the innocent confidence of success with which they all openly bent forward, to look exultingly at the audience, when a loud clapping followed the overture: and their smiles, or nods; or chuckling and laughter, according to their more or less advanced years, during the unmingled approbation that was bestowed upon about half the piece—contrasted with, first the amazement; next, the indignation; and, lastly, the affright and disappointment, that were brought forth by the beginning buzz of hissing, and followed by the shrill horrors of the catcall: and then the return—joyous, but no longer dauntless!—of hope, when again the applause prevailed.

In these various changes, Mr. Garrick altered the expression of his features, and almost his features themselves, by apparent transformations—which, however less poetical, were at least more natural than those of Ovid.

Mr. Garrick possessed not only every possible inflexion of voice, save for singing, but also of countenance; varying his looks into young, old, sick, vigorous, downcast, or frolicsome, at his personal volition; as if his face, and even his form, had been put into his own hands to be worked upon like Man a Machine.

Mr. Garrick, about this time, warmly urged the subject of these memoirs to set to music an English opera called Orpheus; but while, for that purpose, Mr. Burney was examining the drama, he was informed that it had been put into the hands of Mr. Barthelemon, who was preparing it for the stage.

Astonished, and very much hurt, Mr. Burney

hastily returned the copy with which he had been entrusted, to Mr. Johnstone, the prompter; dryly, and without letter or comment, directing him to deliver it to Mr. Garrick.

Mr. Garrick, with the utmost animation, instantly wrote to Johnstone an apology rather than a justification; desiring that the opera should be withdrawn from Mr. Barthelemon, and consigned wholly to the subject of these memoirs; for whom Mr. Garrick declared himself to entertain a friendship that nothing should dissolve.*

But Mr. Burney, conceiving that Barthelemon, who had offended no one, and who bore a most amiable character, might justly resent so abrupt a discharge, declined setting the opera: and never afterwards composed for the theatres.

This trait, however trifling, cannot but be considered as biographical, at least for Mr. Garrick; as it so strongly authenticates the veracity of the two principal lines of the epitaph designed for Roscius, many years afterwards, by that acute observer of every character—save his own!—Dr. Goldsmith.

"He cast off his friends as a huntsman his pack,
For he knew, when he would, he could whistle them back."

---

* See Correspondence.

Whether negligence, mistake, or caprice, had occasioned this double nomination to the same office, is not clear; but Garrick, who loved Mr. Burney with real affection, lost no time, and spared no blandishment, to re-instate himself in the confidence which this untoward accident had somewhat shaken. And he had full success, to the great satisfaction of Mr. Burney, and joy of his family; who all rapturously delighted in the talents and society of the immortal Roscius.

MR. CRISP.

While this revival of intercourse with the Garricks, and partial return to public life and affairs, necessarily banished the outward and obvious marks of the change of existence, and lost happiness of Mr. Burney, they operated also, gently, but effectively, in gradually diminishing his sufferings, by forcing him from their contemplation: for in that dilapidated state of sorrow's absorption, where the mind is wholly abandoned to its secret sensations, all that innately recurs to it can spring only from its own concentrated sources; and these, though they may vary the evil by palliatives, offer nothing curative. New scenes and objects alone can open to new ideas; and, happily, a circumstance now occurred that brought on a revival of intercourse with the only man who, at that time, could recal the mourner's faculties to genial feelings, and expand them to confidential sociality.

His earliest favourite, guide, philosopher, and friend, Mr. Crisp, he now, after a separation of very many years, accidentally met at the house of Mr Vincent, a mutual acquaintance.

Their satisfaction at the sight of each other was truly reciprocal; though that of Mr. Burney was tinctured with dejection, that he could no longer present to his dearest friend the partner whom, by such a judge, he had felt would have been instantly and reverentially appreciated.

Mr. Crisp joined in this regret; but was not the less desirous to see and to know all that remained of her; and he hastened the following day to Poland-street; where, from his very first entrance amidst the juvenile group, he became instinctively honoured as a counsellor for his wisdom and judgment, and loved and liked as a companion for his gaiety, his good humour, and his delight in their rising affections; which led him unremittingly, though never obtrusively, to mingle instruction with their most sportive intercourse.

As Mr. Crisp was the earliest and dearest friend of the subject of these memoirs, the reader will not, it is probable, be sorry to be apprised of the circumstances which, since their separation, had turned him from a brilliant man of the world to a decided recluse.

The life of Mr. Crisp had been exposed to much vicissitude. Part of it had been spent in Italy, particularly at Rome, where he took up his residence for some years; and where, from his passion for music, painting, and sculpture, he amassed, for the rest of his existence, recollections of never-dying pleasure. And not alone for his solitary contemplations, but for the delight that the vivacity of his delineations imparted to his friends, when he could be induced to unfold his reminiscences; whether upon the sacred and soul-pervading harmony of the music of the Pope's chapel; or upon the tones, mellifluously melting or elevating, of Sinesino, Custini, or Farinelli: or by bringing to view through glowing images, the seraphic forms and expressions of Raphael and Correggio; and the sculptural sublimity of Michael Angelo. Or when, animated to the climax of his homage for the fine arts, he flitted by all else to concentrate the whole force of his energies, in describing that electrifying wonder, the Apollo Belvedere.

On this he dwelt with a vivacity of language that made his hearers wish to fasten upon every word that he uttered; so vividly he portrayed the commanding port, the chaste symmetry, and the magic form—for which not a tint was requisite, and colouring would have been superfluous—of that unrivalled production, of which the peerless grace, looking softer, though of marble, than the feathered snow; and brightly radiant, though, like the sun, simply white, strike upon the mind rather than the eye, as an ideal representative of ethereal beauty.*

And while such were his favourite topics for his gifted participators, there was a charm for all around in his more general conversation, that illumined with instruction, or gladdened with entertainment, even the most current and desultory subjects of the passing hour.

Thus rarely at once endowed and cultivated, there can be little surprise that Mr. Crisp should be distinguished, speedily and forcibly, by what is

---

* And such it appeared to this memorialist when it was exhibited at the Louvre in 1812.

denominated the Great World; where his striking talents, embellished by his noble countenance and elegant manners, made him so much the mode with the great, and the chosen with the difficult, that time, not friends, was all he wanted for social enjoyment.

High, perhaps highest in this noble class, stood Margaret Cavendish Harley, Duchess Dowager of Portland, *The Friend of Mrs. Delany;* by whom that venerable and exemplary personage, who was styled by Mr. Burke, "The pattern of a real fine lady of times that were past," had been herself made known to Mr. Crisp.

Mrs. Montagu, also, who then, Mr. Crisp was wont to say, was peering at fame, and gradually rising to its temple, was of the same coterie. But most familiarly he resided with Christopher Hamilton of Chesington Hall, and with the Earl of Coventry.

With this last he was intimately connected, at the time of that Earl's marriage with the acknowledged nonpareil of female beauty, the youngest Miss Gunning.

Mr. Crisp had already written his tragedy of Virginia; but Garrick, though he was the author's personal friend, thought it so little equal to the expectations that might await it, that he postponed, season after season, bringing it out; even though Lord Coventry, who admired it with the warmth of partial regard, engaged the first Mr. Pitt * to read it, and to pronounce in its favour. Roscius still was adverse, and still delayed the trial; nor could he be prevailed upon to prepare it for the stage, till Mr. Crisp had won that Venus of her day, the exquisite Lady Coventry, through his influence with her lord, to present a copy of the manuscript, with her own almost sculptured hand, to the Then conquered manager.

The play neither succeeded nor failed. A catastrophe of so yea and nay a character was ill suited to the energies and hopes of its high-minded author, who was bitterly disappointed; and thought the performers had been negligent, Mr. Garrick unfriendly, and the public precipitate.

The zealous Lord Coventry, himself a man of letters, advised sundry changes, and a new trial. Mr. Crisp shut himself up, and worked indefatigably at these suggestions: but when his alterations were

---

* The first Earl of Chatham.

finished, there was no longer a radiant Countess of Coventry to bewitch Mr. Garrick, by " the soft serenity of her smile," to make a further attempt. Lady Coventry, whose brief, dazzling race, was rapidly run, was now already fast fading in the grasping arms of withering consumption : and Mr. Garrick, though, from unwillingness to disoblige, he seemed wavering, was not the less inexorable.

Mr. Crisp then, disgusted with the stage, the manager, and the theatrical public, gave up not alone that point, but every other by which he might have emerged from private life to celebrity. He almost wholly retired from London, and resided at Hampton ; where he fitted up a small house with paintings, prints, sculpture, and musical instruments, arranged with the most classical elegance.

But the vicinity of the metropolis caused allurements such as these, with such a chief to bring them into play, to accord but ill with the small, though unincumbered fortune of their master; and the grace with which, instinctively, he received his visitors, made his habitation so pleasant, as soon to produce a call upon his income that shattered its stability.

His alarm now was such as might be expected from his sense of honour, and his love of independence. Yet the delicacy of his pride forbade any complaint to his friends, that might seem to implicate their discretion in his distress, or to invite their aid ; though his desire to smooth, without publishing, his difficulties, urged him to commune with those of his connexions who were in actual power, and to confess his wishes for some honourable place, or occupation, that might draw forth his faculties to the amelioration of his fortune.

Kind words, and enlivening promises, now raised his hopes to a favourable change in his affairs; and, brightly looking forward, he continued to welcome his friends ; who, enchanted by his society, poured in upon him with a thoughtless frequency, which caused an increase of expenditure that startled him, ere long, with a prospect, sudden and frightful, of the road to ruin.

Shocked, wounded, dismayed, he perceived two ways only by which he could be extricated from the labyrinth into which he had been betrayed by premature expectation; either vigorously to urge his suit for some appointment, and persecute, pester his friends to quicken his advancement; or cut off approaching worldly destruction by an immediate sacrifice of worldly luxury.

A severe fit of the gout, that now, for the first time — hastened, probably, by chagrin — assailed him, decided his resolution. He sold his house at Hampton, his books, prints, pictures, and instruments; with a fixed determination of relinquishing the world, and retiring from mankind.

Within a few miles of Hampton stood Chesington Hall, his chosen retreat; and thither, with what little of his property he had rescued from the auctioneer and the appraiser, he transplanted his person; and there buried every temporal prospect.

Chesington Hall was placed upon a considerable, though not rapid eminence, whence two tall, antique trees, growing upon an old rustic structure called The Mount, were discernible at sixteen miles distance. The Hall had been built upon a large, lone, and nearly desolate common; and no regular road, or even track to the mansion from Epsom, the nearest town, had, for many years, been spared from its encircling ploughed fields, or fallow ground.

This old mansion had fallen into the hands of the Hamiltons from those of the Hattons, by whom its erection had been begun in the same year upon which Cardinal Wolsey had commenced raising, in its vicinity, the magnificent palace of Hampton Court.

Every thing around Chesington Hall was now falling to decay; and its hereditary owner, Christopher Hamilton, the last male of his immediate branch of the Hamilton family, was, at this time, utterly ruined, and sinking in person as well as property in the general desolation.

This was precisely a sojourn to meet the secluding desire of Mr. Crisp; he adopted some pic-nic plan with Mr. Hamilton; and Chesington Hall became his decided residence; it might almost be said, his fugitive sanctuary. He acquainted no one with his intentions, and communicated to no one his place of abode. Firm to resist the kindness, he determined to escape the tediousness, of persuasion: and, however often, in after life, when renovated health gave him a consciousness of renovated faculties, he might have regretted this intellectual interment, he was immoveable never more to emerge from a tranquillity, which now, to his sickened mind, made the pursuits of ambition seem as oppressively troublesome in their manœuvres, as they were morbidly bitter in their disappointments.

His fondness, however, for the arts, was less subordinate to the casualties of life than his love of the world. It was too much an integral part of his composition to be annihilated in the same gulph in which were sunk his mundane expectations. Regularly, therefore, every spring, he came up to the metropolis, where, in keeping pace with the times, he enjoyed every modern improvement in music and painting.

Rarely can a re-union of early associates have dispensed brighter felicity with more solid advantages, than were produced by the accidental re-meeting of these long separated friends. To Mr. Burney it brought back a congeniality of feeling and intelligence, that re-invigorated his social virtues; and to Mr. Crisp it gave not only a friend, but a family.

It operated, however, no further. To Mr. Burney alone was confided the clue for a safe route across the wild common to Chesington Hall; from all others it was stedfastly withheld; and from Mr. Greville it was studiously and peculiarly concealed.

That gentleman now was greatly altered, from the large and larger strides which he had made, and was making, into the dangerous purlieus of horse racing and of play; into whose precincts, from the delusive difference of their surface from their foundation, no incursions can be hazarded without as perilous a shake to character and disposition, as to fortune and conduct. And Mr. Greville, who, always honourable, was almost necessarily a frequent loser, was evidently on the high road to turn from a man of pleasure to a man of spleen; venting his wrath at his failures upon the turf and at the clubs, by growing fastidious and cavilling in general society. Mr. Crisp, therefore, bent to maintain the dear bought quiet of his worldly sacrifices as unmingled with the turbulent agitations of querulous debate, as with the restless solicitudes of active life, shunned the now pertinacious disputant almost with dread.

Yet Mr. Greville, about this period, was rescued, for a while, from this hovering deterioration, through the exertions of his friends in the government, by whom he was named minister plenipotentiary to the court of Bavaria; in the hope that such an appointment, with its probable consequences, might re-establish his affairs.

No change, however, of situation, caused any change in Mr. Greville to his early *protegé* and attached and attaching friend, Mr. Burney, to whom he still shewed himself equally eager to communicate his opinions, and reveal his proceedings. A letter from Munich, written when his Excellency was first installed in his new dignity, will display the pleasant openness of their correspondence; at the same time that it depicts the humours and expenses of the official ceremonials then in use, with a frankness that makes them both curious and entertaining.*

* * * * *

A letter to the Earl of Eglinton from the celebrated David Hume, written also about this time, gave Mr. Burney very peculiar satisfaction, from the sincere disposition to esteem and to serve him, which it manifested in that dangerously renowned philosopher; whose judgment of men was as skilfully inviting, as his sophistry in theology was fearfully repelling.

Yet upon the circumstances of this letter hung a cutting disappointment, which, in the midst of his rising prospects, severely pierced the hopes of Mr. Burney; and, from the sharpness of its injury, and its future aggravating repetitions, would permanently

---

* See correspondence.

have festered them, had their composition been of less elastic quality.

To be Master of the King's Band, as the highest professional honour to be obtained, had been the earliest aim of Mr. Burney; and, through the medium of warm friends, joined to his now well approved and obvious merit, the promise of the then Lord Chamberlain had been procured for the first vacancy. This arrived in 1765; but when the consequent claim was made, how great, how confounding to Mr. Burney was the intelligence, that the place was disposed of already.

He hastened with a relation of this grievance, as unexpected as it was undeserved, to the celebrated historian, to whom his rights had been well known at Paris. And Mr. Hume, whose sense of justice—one fatal warp excepted—was as luminous as it was profound, shocked by such a breach of its simplest and most unchangeable statutes, instantly undertook, with the courage imbibed by his great abilities and high moral character, to make a representation on the subject to Lord Hertford.

Failing, however, of meeting with an immediate opportunity, and well aware of the importance of expedition in such applications, he addressed himself to the Countess; and from her he learnt, and with expressions of benevolent concern, that it was the Duke of York* who had demanded the nomination to the place.

It now occurred to Mr. Hume that the present applicant might possibly be himself the object for whom his Royal Highness had interfered, as Mr. Burney had frequently been seen, and treated with marked kindness, by the Royal Duke at private concerts; which were then often, at the sudden request of that prince, formed by the Earl of Eglinton; and at which Mr. Burney, when in London, was always a principal and favoured assistant. With this in his recollection, and naturally concluding Lord Eglinton, who always shewed an animated partiality for Mr. Burney, to be chief in the application to the Lord Chamberlain, Mr. Hume wrote the following letter.

To the Earl of Eglinton.

"My Lord,

"Not finding an opportunity of speaking yesterday to Lord Hertford, in favour of Mr. Burney, I spoke to my lady, and told her the whole case. She already knows Mr. Burney, and has an esteem for him. She said it gave her great uneasiness, and was

---

* Edward, brother to his Majesty George III.

sure it would do so to my lord, that he was already engaged, and, she believed, to the Duke of York.

"It occurred to me, that his Royal Highness's application might, also, be in favour of Mr. Burney; in which case the matter is easy. If not, it is probable your Lordship may engage his Royal Highness to depart from his application; for really Mr. Burney's case, independently of his merit, is very hard and cruel.

"I have the honour to be,

"My Lord, your Lordship's

"Most humble and most obedient servant,

"DAVID HUME."

"P. S. If your Lordship honour me with an answer in the forenoon, please send it to General Conway's, in Little Warwick Street; if in the afternoon, at Miss Elliot's, Brewer Street, Golden Square."

A reclamation such as this, from a man who was then almost universally held to be at the head of British literature, could not be read unmoved; and an opinion so positive of the justice and merits of the case, manifested by two directions for an immediate reply, both given for the same day, and without any apology for such precipitancy, shewed a warmth of personal zeal and interest for the welfare of Mr. Burney, that was equally refreshing to his spirits, and stimulating to his hopes.

The place, however, was decidedly gone. The first word from the Duke had fixed its fate; though, from the real amenity of the character of the prince, joined to the previous favour he had shewn to Mr. Burney, there cannot be a doubt that, had the history of the affair reached the ear of his Royal Highness, he would have been foremost himself, as Mr. Hume suggested, to have nominated Mr. Burney.

Here the matter dropped; and the expressed regret and civilities of the Countess, with the implied ones of the Earl, somewhat softened the infliction: but the active services, and manly appeal of David Hume, conduced far more to awaken and to fortify the philosophy that so unexpected a mortification required.

*   *   *   *   *

In mingling again with the world upon its common terms of cultivating what was good, and supporting what was evil, Mr. Burney now, no longer bewitched by beauty, nor absorbed by social sympathies, found literature and its pursuits without rival in his estimation; yet, in missing those vanished delights, he deemed that he had the world to re-begin: for though prosperity met his professional toils with heightened reputation and reward, they were joyless, however essential, since participation was gone!

The time had arrived, and now was passed, for the long-settled project of Mr. Burney of conveying to

Paris his second and, then, youngest daughters, Frances and Charlotte, to replace his eldest and his third, Esther and Susanna; now both returned thence, with every improvement that a kind parent could reasonably desire.

The time had arrived—and was passed.—But if no man can with certainty pronounce what at any stated period he will perform, how much less is he gifted with fore-knowledge of what, at any stated period, he may wish!

Six heartless, nearly desolate, years of lonely conjugal chasm, had succeeded to double their number of nearly unparalleled conjugal enjoyment—and the void was still fallow and hopeless!—when the yet very handsome, though no longer in her bloom, Mrs. Stephen Allen, of Lynn, now become a widow, decided, for promoting the education of her eldest daughter, to make London her winter residence.

Mr. Burney was, of course, applied to for assistance in the musical line; and not less called upon as the most capable judge and counsellor in every other.

The loss that had been sustained by Mrs. Allen was that of a very worthy man, whom she esteemed, but to whom she had been married by her parents early in life, without either choice or aversion. In her situation, therefore, and that of Mr. Burney, there was no other affinity than that each had been widowed by the hand of death.

Highly intellectual, and fond even to passion of books, Mrs. Allen delighted in the conversation of Mr. Burney; and the hour for his instructions to Miss Allen was fixed to be that of tea-time; to the end that, when he was liberated from the daughter, he might be engaged with the mother.

The superior grief of Mr. Burney, as deep as it was acute, was not more prominent than the feeling admiration that it inspired in Mrs. Allen: and if moved by his sorrows, while charmed by his merit, Mrs. Allen saw him with daily increasing interest, Mr. Burney was not less moved by her commiseration, nor less penetrated by her sympathy; and insensibly he became solaced, while involuntarily she grew grateful, upon observing her rising influence over his spirits.

To the tender sentiments of the heart, the avenues are as infinite for entrance as they are difficult for escape; but there are none so direct, and, consequently, none so common, as those through whose gentle mazes soft pity encounters soothing sensibility.

The task of consoling the sorrower seems, to its participator, nearly a devout one; and the sorrower, most especially where beauty and spirit meet in that participator, would think resistance to such benevolence might savour of ingratitude.

Those who judge of the sincerity of pristine connubial tenderness merely by its abhorrence of succession, take a very unenlightened, if not false, view of human grief; unless they limit their stigma to an eager or a facile repetition of those rites which, on their first inauguration, had seemed inviolable and irreplaceable.

So still, in fact, they may faithfully, though silently continue, even under a subsequent new connexion. The secret breast, alive to memory though deprived of sympathy, may still internally adhere to its own choice and fondness; notwithstanding the various and imperious calls of current existence may urge a second alliance: and urge it, from feelings and from affections as clear of inconstancy as of hypocrisy; urge it, from the best of motives, that of accommodating ourselves to our lot, with all its piercing privations; since our lot is dependent upon causes we have no means to either evade or fathom; and as remote from our direction as from our wishes.

If, by any exertion of which mortal man is capable, or any suffering which mortal man can sustain, Mr. Burney could have called back his vanished

Esther to his ecstatic consciousness, labour, even to decrepitude, endurance even to torture, he would have borne, would have sought, would have blessed, for the most transient sight of her adored form. But she was taken away from him by that decree against which there is no appeal.

He who loses a parent, a brother, a sister, a friend, however deeply and deservedly they may be lamented, is never branded with want of feeling if he seek another counsellor and guide, if he accept another companion and favourite. It is but considered to be meeting his destiny as a man who knows he must not choose it; it is but consenting to receive such good as is attainable, while bowing down submissively to such evil as is unavoidable.

Succession is the law of nature; and, as far as her laws are obvious, it is that which stands foremost.

The angel whom Mr. Burney had lost—for an angel both without and within she had seemed to him—had the generous disinterestedness, on the bed of death, to recommend to her miserable husband that he would marry again; well knowing that the tenderness of female friendship would come nearest,—however distant,—to the softness of consolation: and, maternally weighing, no doubt, that a well-chosen partner might prove a benediction to her poor children. And this injunction, though heard at the time with agony scarcely supportable, might probably, and strongly, influence his future conduct, when the desperation of hopelessness was somewhat worn away by all-subduing time, joined to forced exertions in business.

His Esther had even named to him the lady whom she thought most capable to suit him as a companion, and most tenderly disposed to becoming a mother to his children,—Miss Dorothy Young, who was her most valued friend. Mrs. Allen, Dorothy's nearest competitor, was not then a widow. But Mr. Burney, sacred as he held the opinions and the wishes of his Esther, was too ardent an admirer of beauty to dispense, in totality, with that attractive embellishment of the female frame. He honoured and esteemed, with a brother's affection, the excellent Dorothy Young: but those charms which awaken softer sensations, were utterly and unhappily denied to that estimable woman, through her peculiarly unfortunate personal defects.

Not early, and not easily, did Mr. Burney and Mrs. Allen reveal their mutual partiality. The wounded heart of Mr. Burney recoiled from such anodyne as demanded new vows to a new object: and Mrs. Allen, at that period, lived in a state of affluence that made such a marriage require severe worldly sacrifices. Only, however transiently; for by an unfortunate trust in an unfortunate, though honourable speculatist, Dr. King, she completely lost all that, independently, was at her own disposal of fortune. And the noble disinterestedness of Mr. Burney upon this occasion, rivetted to him her affections, with the highest esteem.

Yet even when these scruples were mutually overwhelmed by increasing force of regard, so many unlooked for obstacles stood in the way of their union, that, wearied by delays that seemed at once captious and interminable, Mr. Burney earnestly entreated that an immediate private marriage might avert, at least, a final breach of their engagement: solemnly promising, at the same time, that they should keep the alliance secret, and still live apart, till all prudential exactions should be satisfied.

As they were each wholly independent, save from the influence of opinion,—which, however, is frequently more difficult to subdue than that of authority,—Mrs. Allen saw no objection of sufficient force to counteract her pleasure in compliance.

Their plan was confided to four persons, indispensably requisite for its execution; Mrs., afterwards Lady Strange, Miss Young, Mr. Crisp, and the Rev. Mr. Pugh, curate of St. James's church.

Mr. Pugh, who was of very long standing a friend of Mr. Burney, aided personally in promoting such measures as secured secresy with success; and in St. James's church, Mr. Pugh tied that indissoluble knot, which, however fairly promising, is inevitably rigorous, since it can be loosened only by Crime or by Death: but which, where it binds the destinies of those whose hearts are already knit together by reciprocated regard, gives a charm to captivity that robs liberty of regret.

At the porch of St. James's church, Mrs. Strange and Mr. Pugh whispered their congratulations to the new married couple, as they entered a prepared post-chaise; which, in a very few hours, galloped them to the obscure skirts of the then pathless, and nearly uninhabited, Chesington common; where Mr. Crisp had engaged for them a rural and fragrant retreat, at a small farm-house in a little hamlet, a mile or two from Chesington Hall.

The secret, as usual in matrimonial concealments, was faithfully preserved, for a certain time, by scrupulous discretion in the parties, and watchful circumspection in the witnesses: but, as usual also, error and accident were soon at work to develop the transaction; and the loss of a letter, through some carelessness of conveyance, revealed suddenly but irrevocably the state of the connexion.

This circumstance, however, though, at the time, cruelly distressing, served ultimately but to hasten their own views; as the discovery was necessarily followed by the personal union for which their hands had been joined.

Mrs. Burney,—now no longer Mrs. Stephen Allen—came openly to town to inhabit, for a while, a house in Poland-street, a few doors from that of her husband; while alterations, paintings, and embellishments were progressively preparing the way for her better reception at his home.

The two families, however, awaited not the completion of these improvements for a junction. The younger branches, who already, and from their birth, were well known to one another, were as eager as their parents for a general union; and the very amiable Miss Allen,* the most important personage

---

* Afterwards Mrs. Rishton.

in the juvenile group, conducted herself upon the disclosure of the marriage, with a generous warmth of kindness that quickened the new establishment. And her example would forcibly have weighed with her deserving brother, Stephen Allen,* had such example been wanting; but he entertained so true and affectionate a respect for Mr. Burney, that he required neither duty nor influence to reconcile him to the match.

The four daughters of Mr. Burney,—Esther, Frances, Susan, and Charlotte,—were all earnest to contribute their small mites to the happiness of one of the most beloved of parents, by receiving, with the most respectful alacrity, the lady on whom he had cast his future hopes of regaining domestic comfort.

The Paris scheme for the two daughters, who were to have followed the route of their sisters, long remitted, from the fluctuating affairs and feelings of Mr. Burney, was now finally abandoned. The youngest daughter, Charlotte, was sent to a school in Norfolk. The second, Frances, was the only one of Mr. Burney's family who never was placed in any seminary, and never was put under

---

* Now Rector of Lynn Regis.

any governess or instructor whatsoever. Merely and literally self-educated, her sole emulation for improvement, and sole spur for exertion, were her unbounded veneration for the character, and affection for the person, of her father; who, nevertheless, had not, at the time, a moment to spare for giving her any personal lessons; or even for directing her pursuits.*

POLAND STREET.

The friends of Mr. Burney were not slack in paying their devoirs to his new partner, whose vivacious society, set off by far more than remains of uncommon beauty, failed not to attract various visitors to the house; and whose love, or rather passion, for conversation and argument, were of that gay and brilliant sort, that offers too much enter-

---

* No truth can be more simply exact than that which is conveyed in four lines of the stanzas which she addressed to him in the secret dedication of her first work, Evelina, viz.

> If in my heart the love of virtue glows
> 'Twas kindled there by an unerring rule;
> From thy *example* the pure flame arose,
> Thy *life* my precept; thy *good works* my school.

tainment to be ever left in the lurch for want of partakers.

Fortunate was it that such was the success of her social spirit; which success was by no means less flourishing, from her strong bent to displaying the rites of hospitality. She must else have lived the life of a recluse, Mr. Burney, during the whole of the day, being devoted to his profession; with the single exception of one poor hour of repast, to re-fit him for every other of labour.

But the affection and pleasure with which, as

"The curfew toll'd the knell of parting day,"

he finished his toils, were so animated and so genuine, that the sun, in the zenith of its splendour, was never more ardently hailed, than the cool, silent, evening star, whose soft glimmering light restored him to the bosom of his family; not there to murmur at his fatigues, lament his troubles, nor recount his wearisome exertions; but to return, with cheerful kindness, their tender greetings; to enliven them with the news, the anecdotes, and the rumours of the day; to make a spontaneous *catalogue raisonné* of the people he had mixed with or seen; and always to bring home any new publication, political, poetical, or ethical, that was making any noise in the world.

Amongst those of the old friends of Mr. Burney who were the most eager to judge his second choice, Roscius and Violetta, Mr. and Mrs. Garrick, seem entitled to be first mentioned, from the pleasurable remembrance of the delight bestowed upon the whole family by their presence.

THE GREVILLES.

And equally alert with the same congratulatory courtesies, were his long and rootedly attached friends, the Grevilles. Mr. Greville, curious to behold the successor of her whom he had never named, but as one of the prettiest women he had ever seen, hastened to make his marriage visit on the first morning that he heard of the bride's arrival in town : while of Mrs. Greville, the bridal visit was arranged in such form, and with such attention, as she thought would shew most consideration to its object. She came on an appointed day, that Mr. Burney might be certainly at home, to present her to his wife ; and she stayed to spend the whole evening in Poland-street.

Her nearly peerless daughter, then in the first

radiance of her matchless bloom, who had been lately married to Mr. Crewe, of Cheshire, with the same zeal as her parents to manifest esteem and affection for Mr. Burney, joined the party; which consisted but of themselves, and of Mr. Burney's new and original young families.

Mrs. Greville, as was peculiarly in her power, took the lead, and bore the burthen of the conversation; which chiefly turned upon Sterne's Sentimental Journey, at that time the reigning reading in vogue: but when the new Mrs. Burney recited, with animated encomiums, various passages of Sterne's seducing sensibility, Mrs. Greville, shrugging her shoulders, exclaimed: "A feeling heart is certainly a right heart; nobody will contest that: but when a man chooses to walk about the world with a cambrick handkerchief always in his hand, that he may always be ready to weep, either with man or beast,—he only turns me sick."

DR. HAWKESWORTH.

With Dr. Hawkesworth Mr. Burney renewed an acquaintance that he had begun at Wilbury House, where he who could write the Adventurer, was not likely to have wanted the public voice to awaken his attention to a youth of such striking merit. Long before that voice had sounded, Dr. Hawkesworth had formed the most liberal and impartial opinion of the young favourite of Mr. Greville. And when, upon the occasion of the Doctor's writing a hymn for the children of the Foundling Hospital, Mr. Burney, through the medium of Mr. Greville, was applied to for setting it to music, the expressions, incidentally dropt, of genius and judgment, in a letter of thanks from Dr. Hawkesworth, would have been in perfect accord with the attributes of the composer, had they been bestowed after the History of Music had stamped them as his due.

No opportunity was omitted by Mr. Burney for cultivating the already established kindness of Mr. Mason and of Dr. Armstrong.

Mr. Burney had frequent relations also, with that scientific diver into natural history, and whatever was ingenious, quaint, and little known, the Hon. Daines Barrington.

Arthur Young, the afterwards famous agriculturist, who had married a younger sister of Mr. Burney, was, when in London, all but an inmate of the Poland-street family; and the high, nay, at that time, volatile spirits of Arthur Young, though always kept within certain bounds by natively well-bred manners, and instinctive powers of pleasing, made him, to the younger group especially, the most entertaining guest that enlivened the fire side.

Amongst those whom neither literature nor science, but taste and choice, taught to signalise Mr. Burney, foremost in the list of youthful beauty, native talents, and animated softness, appeared Mrs. Pleydell, daughter of Governor Holwell; so highly celebrated for the dreadful sufferings, which he almost miraculously survived to record, of incarceration, in what was denominated the Black Hole of Calcutta.

Mrs. Pleydell, like the first, or Mrs. Linley Sheridan, was encircled with charms that, but for comparison with Mrs. Sheridan, might, at that time, have been called unrivalled; charms at once so personal, yet so mental, that they seemed entwined together by a texture so fine of beauty and sensibility, that her first glance was attraction, and her first speech was captivation.

Nothing could surpass the sweetness with which this lovely East Indian attached herself to Mr. Burney; nor the delicacy of her arrangements for appearing to receive favours in conferring them upon his daughters; who were enamoured of her with an ardour that, happily, he escaped; though his admiration was lively and sincere.

This lady, in taking leave of Mr. Burney, upon her return to India, presented to him a Chinese painting on ivory, which she had inherited from her father; and which he, Governor Holwell, estimated as a sort of treasure. The following is the description of it, drawn up by Mr. Burney, from the account of Mrs. Pleydell.

" It is the representation of a music gallery over a triumphal arch, through which the great Mogul passed at Agra, or Delhi, before his fall. The procession consists of the Emperor, mounted on an elephant, and accompanied by his wives, concubines, and attendants; great officers of state, &c., all exquisitely painted. The heads of the females, Sir Joshua Reynolds and Sir Robert Strange, to whom this painting was shewn, thought sufficiently highly finished to be set in rings."

GEORGE COLMAN, THE ELDER.

With that dramatic genius, man of wit, and elegant scholar, George Colman the elder, Mr. Burney had frequent and pleasant meetings at the mansion of Roscius; for who, at that time, could know Mr. Garrick, and be a stranger to Mr. Colman?*

---

* His son, George Colman the younger, still happily lives and flourishes.

KIT SMART.

Nor amongst the early friends of Mr. Burney must ever be omitted that learned, ingenious, most poetical, but most unfortunate son of Apollo, Kit Smart; whom Mr. Burney always was glad to see, and active to serve; though whatever belonged to that hapless poet seemed to go in constant deterioration; his affairs and his senses annually and palpably darkening together; and nothing, unhappily, flourishing in the attempts made for his relief, save the friendship of Mr. Burney; in speaking of which in a letter, Kit Smart touchingly says: " I bless God for your good nature, which please to take for a receipt."

SIR ROBERT AND LADY STRANGE.

The worthy, as well as eminent, Sir Robert Strange, the first engraver of his day, with his extraordinary wife and agreeable family, were, from the time of the second marriage, amongst the most familiar visitors of the Burney house.

The term extraordinary is not here applied to Lady Strange to denote any singularity of action, conduct, or person ; it is simply limited to her conversational powers; which, for mother wit in brilliancy of native ideas, and readiness of associating analogies, placed her foremost in the rank of understanding females, with whom Mr. Burney delighted to reciprocate sportive, yet deeply reflective, discourse. For though the education of Lady Strange had not been cultivated by scholastic lore, she might have said, with the famous Sarah, Duchess of Marlborough, " My books are men, and I read them very currently." And in that instinctive knowledge of human nature which penetration develops, and observation turns to account, she was a profound adept.

Yet, with these high-seasoned powers of exhilaration for others, she was palpably far from happy herself; and sometimes, when felicitated upon her delightful gaiety, she would smile through a face of woe, and, sorrowfully shaking her head, observe how superficial was judgment upon the surface of things, and how wide from each other might be vivacity and happiness! the one springing only from native animal spirits; the other being always held in subjection by the occurrences that meet, or that mar our feelings. And often, even in the midst of the lively laugh that she had sent around her, there would issue quite aloud, from the inmost recesses of her breast, a sigh so deep it might rather be called a groan.

Very early in life, she had given away her heart and her hand without the sanction of a father whom, while she disobeyed, she ardently loved. And though she was always, and justly, satisfied with her choice, and her deserving mate, she could never so far subdue her retrospective sorrow, as to regain that inward serenity of mind, that has its source in reflections that have never been broken by jarring interests and regrets.

MR. CRISP.

But the social enjoyment that came closest to the bosom of Mr. Burney, and of all his race, sprang spontaneously and unremittingly from the delight of all their hearts, Mr. Crisp; who, from his never abating love of music, of painting, of his early friend, and of that friend's progeny, never failed to make his almost secret visit once a year to town; though still, save for those few weeks, he adhered, with inflexible perseverance, to his retirement and his concealment.

Yet whatever disinclination to general society had been worked upon his temper by disappointment, and fastened to his habits by ill health, the last reproach that could be cast upon his conduct was that of misanthropy; though upon his opinions it might deserve, perhaps, to be the first.

He professed himself to be a complete disciple of Swift, where that satirist, in defending his Yahoos, in Gulliver's Travels, avows that, dearly as he loves John, William, and Thomas, when taken individually, mankind, taken in the lump, he abhors or despises.

Nevertheless, Mr. Crisp had so pitying a humanity for wrongs or misfortunes that were casual, or that appeared to be incurred without vice or crime, that, to serve a fellow creature who called for assistance, whether from his purse or his kindness, was so almost involuntarily his common practice, that it was performed as a thing of course, without emotion or commentary.

Mr. Crisp, at this time, was the chief supporter of Chesington Hall, which had now lost the long dignity of its title, and was sunk into plain Chesington, by the death of its last male descendant, Christopher Hamilton; whose extravagances had exhausted, and whose negligence had dilapidated the old and venerable domain which, for centuries, had belonged to his family.

The mansion, and the estate, fell, by law, into the hands of Mrs. Sarah Hamilton, a maiden sister of Christopher's. But this helpless ancient lady was rescued from the intricacies of so involved a succession, by the skilful counsel of Mr. Crisp; who proposed that she should have the capacious old house parted nearly in halves, between herself and an honest farmer, Master Woodhatch; who hired of her, also, what little remained of grounds, for a farm.

Yet, this done, Mrs. Sarah Hamilton was by no means in a situation to reside in the share left to her disposal: Mr. Crisp, therefore, suggested that she should form a competent establishment for receiving a certain number of boarders; and, to encourage the project, entered his own name the first upon her list; and secured to his own use a favourite apartment, with a light and pleasant closet at the end of a long corridor. This closet, some years afterwards, he devoted to his friend Burney, for whom, and for his pen, while he was writing the History of Music, it was held sacred.

And here, in this long-loved rural abode, during the very few intervals that Mr. Burney could snatch from the toils of his profession, and the cares of his family, he had resorted in his widowhood, with his delighted children, to enjoy the society of this most valued and dearly-loved friend ; whose open arms, open countenance, faithful affection, and enchanting converse, greeted the group with such expansive glee, that here, in this long-loved rural abode, the Burneys and happiness seemed to make a stand.

INSTALLATION ODE.

The first attempt of Mr. Burney, after his recent marriage, to vary, though not to quit his professional occupations, was seeking to set to music the Ode written in the year 1769, by that most delicately perfect, perhaps, of British poets, Gray, for the installation of the Duke of Grafton as Chancellor of the University of Cambridge.

The application to the Duke for this purpose met with no opposition from his Grace ; and the earnest wish of Mr. Burney was to learn, and to gratify, the taste of the exquisite poet whose verses he was musically to harmonize, with regard to the mode of composition that would best accord with the poet's own lyrical ideas.

To this effect, he addressed himself both for counsel and assistance to his early friend, Mr. Mason; from whom he received a trusting and obliging, but not very comfortable answer.*

Not a second did Mr. Burney lose in forwarding every preparation for obviating any disgrace to his melodious muse, Terpsichore, when the poetry of the enchanting bard should come in contact with her lyre. He formed upon a large scale a well chosen band, vocal and instrumental, for the performance; and he engaged, as leader of the orchestra, the celebrated Giardini, who was the acknowledged first violinist of Europe.

But, in the midst of these preliminary measures, he was called upon, by an agent of the Duke, to draw up an estimate of the expense.

This he did, and delivered, with the cheerfulest confidence that his selection fully deserved its appointed retribution, and was elegantly appropriate to the dignity of its purpose.

Such, however, was not the opinion of the advisers of the Duke; and Mr. Burney had the aston-

---

* See Correspondence.

ished chagrin of a note to inform him, that the estimate was so extravagant that it must be reduced to at least one half.

Cruelly disappointed, and, indeed, offended, the charge of every performer being merely what was customary for professors of eminence, Mr. Burney was wholly overset. His own musical fame might be endangered, if his composition should be sung and played by such a band as would accept of terms so disadvantageous; and his sense of his reputation, whether professional or moral, always took place of his interest. He could not, therefore, hesitate to resist so humiliating a proposition; and he wrote, almost on the instant, a cold, though respectful resignation of the office of composer of the Installation Ode.

Not without extreme vexation did he take this decided measure; and he was the more annoyed, as it had been his intention to make use of so favourable an opportunity for taking his degree of Doctor of Music, at the University of Cambridge, for which purpose he had composed an exercise. And, when his disturbance at so unlooked for an extinction of his original project was abated, he still resolved to fulfil that part of his design.

He could not, however, while under the infliction of so recent a rebuff, visit, in this secondary manner, the spot he had thought destined for his greatest professional elevation. He repaired, therefore, to Oxford, where his academic exercise was performed with singular applause, and where he took his degree as Doctor in Music, in the year 1769.

And he then formed many connexions amongst the professors and the learned belonging to that University, that led him to re-visit it with pleasure, from new views and pursuits, in after times.

So warmly was this academic exercise approved, that it was called for at three successive annual choral meetings at Oxford; at the second of which the principal soprano part was sung by the celebrated and most lovely Miss Linley, afterwards the St. Cecilia of Sir Joshua Reynolds, and the wife of the famous Mr. Sheridan; and sung with a sweetness and pathos of voice and expression that, joined to the beauty of her nearly celestial face, almost maddened with admiring enthusiasm, not only the susceptible young students, then in the first glow of the dominion of the passions, but even the gravest and most profound among the learned professors of the University, in whom the "hey-day of the blood" might be presumed, long since, to have been cooled.

From this period, in which the composer and the songstress, in reflecting new credit, raised new plaudits for each other, there arose between them a reciprocation of goodwill and favour, that lasted unbroken, till the retirement of that fairest of syrens from the world.

The Oxonian new lay-dignitary, recruited in health and spirits, from the flattering personal consideration with which his academical degree had been taken, gaily returned to town with his new title of Doctor.

The following little paragraph is copied from a memorandum book of that year.

" I did not, for some time after the honour that had been conferred on me at Oxford, display my title by altering the plate on my street door; for which omission I was attacked by Mr. Steel, author of an essay on the melody of speech. 'Burney,' says he, 'why don't you tip us the Doctor upon your door?' I replied, in provincial dialect, 'I wants dacity!—'I'm ashaeemed!' 'Pho, pho,' says he, 'you had better brazen it.'"

HALLEY'S COMET.

No production had as yet transpired publicly from the pen of Dr. Burney, his new connexion having induced him to consign every interval of leisure to domestic and social circles, whether in London, or at the dowry-house of Mrs. Burney, in Lynn Regis, to which the joint families resorted in the summer.

But when, from peculiar circumstances, Mrs. Burney, and a part of the younger set, remained for a season in Norfolk, the spirit of literary composition resumed its sway; though not in the dignified form in which, afterwards, it fixed its standard.

The long-predicted comet of the immortal Halley, was to make its luminously-calculated appearance this year, 1769; and the Doctor was ardently concurrent with the watchers and awaiters of this prediction.

In the course of this new pursuit, and the researches to which it led, Dr. Burney, no doubt, dwelt even unusually upon the image and the recollection of his Esther; who, with an avidity for knowledge consonant to his own, had found time— made it, rather—in the midst of her conjugal, her maternal, and her domestic devoirs, to translate from the French, the celebrated Letter of Astronomical renown of Maupertuis; not with any prospect of fame; her husband himself was not yet entered upon its annals, nor emerged, save anonymously, from his timid obscurity: it was simply from a love of improvement, and a delight in its acquirement. To view with him the stars, and exchange with him her rising associations of ideas, bounded all the ambition of her exertions.

The recurrence to this manuscript translation, at a moment when astronomy was the nearly universal subject of discourse, was not likely to turn the Doctor aside from this aerial direction of his thoughts; and the little relic, of which even the hand-writing could not but be affecting as well as dear to him, was now read and re-read, till he considered it as too valuable to be lost; and determined, after revising and copying it, to send it to the press.

Whether any tender notion of first, though unsuspectedly, appearing before the public by the side of his Esther, stimulated the production of the Essay that ensued from the revision of this letter; or whether the stimulus of the subject itself led to the publication of the letter, is uncertain; but that they hung upon each other is not without interest, as they unlocked, in concert, the gates through which Doctor Burney first passed to that literary career which, ere long, greeted his more courageous entrance into a publicity that conducted him to celebrity; for it was now that his first prose composition, an Abridged History of Comets, was written; and was printed in a pamphlet that included his Esther's translation of the Letter of Maupertuis.

This opening enterprize cannot but seem extraordinary, the profession, education, and indispensable business of the Doctor considered; and may bear upon its face a character contradictory to what has been said of his prudent resolve, to avoid any attempt that might warp, or wean him from his own settled occupation; till it is made known that this essay was neither then, nor ever after avowed; nor ever printed with his works.

It was the offspring of the moment, springing from the subject of the day; and owing its birth, there scarcely can be a doubt, to a fond, though unacknowledged indulgence of tender recollections.

The title of the little treatise is, "An Essay towards a History of Comets, previous to the reappearance of the Comet whose return had been predicted by Edmund Halley."

In a memorandum upon this subject, by Dr. Burney, are these words:

"The Countess of Pembroke, being reported to have studied astronomy, and to have accustomed herself to telescopical observations, I dedicated, anonymously, this essay to her ladyship, who was much celebrated for her love of the arts and sciences, and many other accomplishments. I had not the honour of being known to her; and I am not certain whether she ever heard by whom the pamphlet was written.*"

This Essay once composed and printed, the Doctor consigned it to its fate, and thought of it no more.

And the public, after the re-invisibility of the meteor, and the declension of the topic, followed the same course.

But not equally passive either with the humility of the author, or with the indifferency of the readers, were the consequences of this little work; which, having been written wholly in moments stolen from repose, though requiring researches and studies that frequently kept him to his pen till four o'clock in the morning, without exempting him from rising at his common hour of seven; terminated in an acute rheumatic fever, that confined him to his bed, or his chamber, during twenty days.

This sharp infliction, however, though it ill re-

---

* Forty-three years after the date of this publication, the Countess Dowager of Pembroke acquainted this memorialist, that she had never known by whom this Essay was dedicated, nor by whom it was written.

compensed his ethereal flights, by no means checked his literary ambition; and the ardour which was cooled for gazing at the stars, soon seemed doubly re-animated for the music of the spheres.

A wish, and a design, energetic, though vague, of composing some considerable work on his own art, had long roved in his thoughts, and flattered his fancy: and he now began seriously to concentrate his meditations, and arrange his schemes to that single point. And the result of these cogitations, when no longer left wild to desultory wanderings, produced his enlightened and scientific plan for a

GENERAL HISTORY OF MUSIC.

This project was no sooner fixed than, transiently, it appeared to him to be executed; so quick was the rush upon his imagination of illuminating and varying ideas; and so vast, so prolific, the material which his immense collection of notes, abridgments, and remarks, had amassed, that it seemed as if he had merely to methodize his manuscripts, and entrust them to a copyist, for completing his purpose.

But how wide from the rapidity of such incipient perceptions were the views by which, progressively, they were superseded! Mightier and mightier appeared the enterprize upon every new investigation; more difficult, more laborious, and more precarious in all its results: yet, also, as is usual where Genius is coupled with Application, more inviting, more inciting, and more alluring to the hope of literary glory. 'Tis only where the springs of Genius are clogged by "the heavy and retarding weight" of Indolence; or where they are relaxed by the nervous and trembling irresolutions of timidity, that difficulties and dangers produce desertion.

Far, however, from the desired goal, as was the measured distance of reality compared with the visionary approaches of imagination, he had nothing to lament from time thrown away by previous labours lost: his long, multifarious, and curious, though hitherto unpointed studies, all, ultimately, turned to account; for he found that his chosen subject involved, circuitously, almost every other.

Thus finally fixed to an enterprize which, in this country, at least, was then new, he gave to it all the undivided energies of his mind; and, urged by the spur of ambition, and glowing with the vivacity of hope, he determined to complete his materials before he consigned them to their ultimate appropriations, by making a scientific musical tour through France and Italy.

A letter,* of which a copy in his own hand-writing remains, containing the opening view of his plan and of his tour, addressed to the Reverend William Mason, will shew how fully he was prepared for what he engaged to perform, before he called for a subscription to aid the publication of so expensive a work.

Through various of his friends amongst persons in power, he procured recommendatory letters to the several ambassadors and ministers from our Court, who were stationed in the countries through which he meant to travel.

And, through the yet more useful services of persons of influence in letters and in the arts, he obtained introductions, the most felicitous for his enterprize, to those who, then, stood highest in learning, in the sciences, and in literature.

None in this latter class so eminently advanced his undertaking as Mr. Garrick; whose solicitations in his favour were written with a warmth of friendship, and an animation of genius, that carried all before them.

---

* See Correspondence.

Here stops, for this period, the pen of the memorialist.

From the month of June, 1770, to that of January, 1771, the life of Doctor Burney is narrated by himself, in his "Tour to France and Italy."

And few who have read, or who may read that Tour, but will regret that the same pen, while in its full fair vigour, had not drawn up what preceded, and what will follow this epoch.

Such, however, not being the case, the memorialist must resume her pen where that of Dr. Burney, in his narrative, drops,—namely, upon his regaining the British shore.

QUEEN'S SQUARE.

With all the soaring feelings of the first sun-beams of hope that irradiate from a bright, though distant glimpse of renown; untamed by difficulties, superior to fatigue, and springing over the hydra-headed monsters of impediment that every where jutted forth their thwarting obstacles to his enterprize, Dr. Burney came back to his country, his friends, his business, and his pursuits, with the vigour of the first youth in spirits, expectations, and activity.

He was received by his longing family, enlivened by the presence of Mr. Crisp, in a new house, purchased in his absence by Mrs. Burney, at the upper end of Queen-square; which was then beautifully open to a picturesque view of Hampstead and Highgate. And no small recommendation to an enthusiastic admirer of the British classics, was a circumstance belonging to this property, of its having been the dwelling of Alderman Barber, a friend of Dean Swift; who might himself, therefore, be presumed to have occasionally made its roof resound with the convivial hilarity, which his strong wit, and stronger humour, excited in every hearer; and which he himself, however soberly holding back, enjoyed, probably, in secret, with still more zest than he inspired.

CHESINGTON.

This new possession, however, Dr. Burney could as yet scarcely even view, from his eagerness to bring out the journal of his tour. No sooner, therefore, had he made arrangements for a prolongation of leisure, that he hastened to Chesington and to Mr. Crisp; where he exchanged his toils and labours for the highest delights of friendship; and a seclusion the most absolute, from the noisy vicissitudes, and unceasing, though often unmeaning persecution, of trivial interruptions.

THE MUSICAL TOURS.

Here he prepared his French and Italian musical tours for the press; omitting all that was miscellaneous of observation or of anecdote, in deference to the opinions of the Earl of Holdernesse, Mr. Mason, and Mr. Garrick; who conjointly believed that books of general travels were already so numerous, and so spread, that their merits were overlooked from their multiplicity.

If such, at that distant period, was the numerical condemnation of this species of writing, which circumscribed the first published tour of Dr. Burney to its own professional subject, what would be now the doom of the endless herd of tourists of all ranks, qualifications, or deficiencies, who, in these later times, have sent forth their divers effusions, without sparing an idea, a recollection, or scarcely a dream, to work their way in the world, through that general master of the ceremonies, the press? whose portals, though guarded by two *vis à vis* sentinels in eternal hostility with each other, Fame and Disgrace, open equally to publicity.

Mr. Crisp, nevertheless, saw in a totally different light the miscellaneous part of the French and Italian tours, and reprehended its rejection with the high and spirited energy that always marked his zeal, whether of censure or approbation, for whatever affected the welfare of his favourites. But Dr. Burney, having first consulted these celebrated critics, who lived in the immediate world, was too timid to resist their representations of the taste of the moment; though in all that belonged not to the modesty of apprehended partiality, he had the firmest persuasion that the judgment of Mr. Crisp was unrivalled.

The work was entitled:

THE PRESENT STATE OF MUSIC

IN FRANCE AND ITALY:

OR THE JOURNAL OF A TOUR THROUGH THOSE COUNTRIES,

UNDERTAKEN TO COLLECT MATERIALS FOR A

GENERAL HISTORY OF MUSIC,

BY CHARLES BURNEY, MUS. D.

Il Canterono allor si dolcemonte
Che la dolcerra ancor destra mi suona.
DANTE.

The motto was thus translated, though not printed, by Dr. Burney.

> "They sung their strains in notes so sweet and clear
> The sound still vibrates on my ravished ear."

The reception of this first acknowledged call for public attention from Dr. Burney, was of the most encouraging description; for though no renown had yet been fastened upon his name, his acquirements and his character, wherever he had been known, had excited a general good-will that prepared the way to kindly approbation for this, and indeed for every work that issued from his pen.

There was, in truth, something so spirited and uncommon, yet of so antique a cast, in the travels, or pilgrimage, that he had undertaken, in search of materials for the history of his art, that curiosity was awakened to the subject, and expectation was earnest for its execution: and it was no sooner published, than orders were received, by most of the great booksellers of the day, for its purchase; and no sooner read, than letters the most flattering, from the deepest theorists of the science, and the best judges of the practice of the art of music, reached the favoured author; who was of too modest a character to have been robbed of the pleasure of praise by presumptuous anticipation; and of too natural a one to lose any of its gratification by an apathetic suppression of its welcome. And the effect, impulsive and unsophisticated, of his success, was so ardent an encouragement to his purpose, that while, mentally, it animated his faculties to a yet more forcible pursuit of their decided object, it darted him, corporeally, into a travelling vehicle, which rapidly wheeled him back again to Dover; where, with new spirit and eagerness, he set sail upon a similar musical tour in the Low Countries and in Germany, to that which he had so lately accomplished in France and Italy.

With respect to the French and Italian tour, the restraint from all but its professional business, was much lamented by the friends to whom the sacrifice of the miscellaneous matter was communicated.

Upon the German tour not a comment will be offered; it is before the public with an approvance that has been stamped by the sanction of time. At the period of its publication, Dr. Burney, somewhat assured, though incapable of being rendered arrogant by favour, ventured to listen only to the voice of his first friend and monitor, who exhorted him to mingle personal anecdotes with his musical information.

The consequence was such as his sage adviser prognosticated; for both the applause and the sale of this second and more diffuse social diary, greatly surpassed those of its more technical predecessor.

Nevertheless, the German tour, though thus successful for narration to the public, terminated for himself in sickness, fatigue, exorbitant expense, and poignant bodily suffering.

While yet far away from his country, and equally distant from accomplishing the purpose of his travels, his solicitude not to leave it incomplete, joined to his anxiety not to break his professional engagements, led him to over-work and over-hurry his mental powers, at the same time that he inflicted a similar harass upon his corporeal strength. And while thus doubly overwhelmed, he was assaulted, during his precipitated return, by the rudest fierceness of wintry elemental strife; through which, with bad accommodations, and innumerable accidents, he became a prey to the merciless pangs of the acutest spasmodic rheumatism; which barely suffered him to reach his home, ere, long and piteously, it confined him, a tortured prisoner, to his bed.

Such was the check that almost instantly curbed, though it could not subdue, the rising pleasure of his hopes of entering upon a new species of existence, that of an approved man of letters; for it was on the bed of sickness, exchanging the light wines of France, Italy, and Germany, for the black and loathsome potions of the Apothecaries' Hall; writhed by darting stitches, and burning with fiery fever; that he felt the full force of that sublunary equipoise, that seems evermore to hang suspended over the attainment of long-sought and uncommon felicity, just as it is ripening to burst forth into enjoyment!

Again he retired to Chesington, to his care-healing, heart-expanding, and head-informing Mr. Crisp: and there, under the auspices of all that could sooth or animate him; and nursed with incessant assiduity by his fondly-attached wife and daughters, he repaired his shattered frame; to fit it, once again, for the exercise of those talents and faculties, which illumine, in their expansive effects, the whole race of mankind; long after the apparent beings whence they have issued, seem faded, dissolved away; leaving not, visibly, a track behind.

In Dr. Burney, disease was no sooner conquered, than the vigour of his character brought back to him pleasure aud activity, through the spirited wisdom with which he dismissed Regret for Anticipation.

There are few things in which his perfect good humour was more playfully demonstrated, than by the looks, arch yet reproachful, and piteous though burlesque, with which he was wont to recount a most provoking and painful little incident that occurred to him in his last voyage home; but of which he was well aware that the relation must excite irresistible risibility in even the most friendly of his auditors.

After travelling by day and by night to expedite his return, over mountains, through marshes, by cross-roads; on horse-back, on mules, in carriages of any and every sort that could but hurry him on, he reached Calais in a December so dreadfully stormy, that not a vessel of any kind could set sail for England. Repeatedly he secured his hammock, and went on board to take possession of it; but as repeatedly was driven back by fresh gales, during the space of nine fatiguing days and tempestuous nights. And when, at last, the passage was effected, so nearly annihilating had been his sufferings from sea-sickness, that it was vainly he was told he might now, at his pleasure, arise, go forth, and touch English ground; he had neither strength nor courage to move, and earnestly desired to be left awhile to himself.

Exhaustion, then, with tranquillity of mind, cast him into a sound sleep.

From this repose, when, much refreshed, he awoke, he called to the man who was in waiting, to help him up, that he might get out of the ship.

"Get out of the ship, sir?" repeated the man. "Good lauk! you'll be drowned!"

"Drowned?—What's to drown me? I want to go ashore."

"Ashore, sir?" again repeated the man; "why you're in the middle of the sea! There ar'nt a bit of ground for your toe nail."

"What do you mean?" cried the Doctor, starting up; "the sea? did you not tell me we were safe in at Dover?"

"O lauk! that's two good hours ago, sir! I could not get you up then, say what I would. You fell downright asleep, like a top. And so I told them. But that's all one. You may go, or you may stay, as you like; but them pilots never stops for nobody."

Filled with alarm, the Doctor now rushed up to the deck, where he had the dismay to discover that he was half-way back to France.

And he was forced to land again at Calais; where again, with the next mail, and a repetition of his sea-sickness, he re-embarked for Dover.

* * * * *

On quitting Chesington, upon his recovery, for re-entering his house in Queen Square, the Doctor compelled himself to abstain from his pen, his papers, his new acquisitions in musical lore, and all that demanded study for the subject that nearly engrossed his thoughts, in order to consecrate the whole of his time to his family and his affairs.

He renewed, therefore, his wonted diurnal course, as if he had never diverged from it; and attended his young pupils as if he had neither ability nor taste for any superior occupation: and he neither rested his body, nor liberated his ideas, till he had re-instated himself in the professional mode of life, upon which his substantial prosperity, and that of his house, depended.

But, this accomplished, his innate propensities sprang again into play, urging him to snatch at every instant he could purloin, without essential mischief, from these sage regulations; with a redundance of vivacity for new movement, new action, and elastic procedure, scarcely conceivable to those who, balancing their projects, their wishes, and their intentions, by the opposing weights of time, of hazard, and of trouble, undertake only what is obviously to their advantage, or indisputably their duty. His Fancy was his dictator; his Spirit was his spur; and whatever the first started, the second pursued to the goal.

ENGLISH CONSERVATORIO.

But neither the pain of his illness, nor the pleasure of his recovery, nor even the loved labours of his History, offered sufficient occupation for the insatiate activity of his mind. No sooner did he breathe again the breath of health, resume his daily business, and return to his nocturnal studies, than a project occurred to him of a new undertaking, which would have seemed to demand the whole time and undivided attention of almost any other man.

This was nothing less than to establish in England a seminary for the education of musical pupils of both sexes, upon a plan of which the idea should be borrowed, though the execution should almost wholly be new-modelled, from the Conservatorios of Naples and Vienna.

As disappointment blighted this scheme just as it

seemed maturing to fruition, it would be to little purpose to enter minutely into its details: and yet, as it is a striking feature of the fervour of Dr. Burney for the advancement of his art, it is not its failure, through the secret workings of undermining prejudice, that ought to induce his biographer to omit recounting so interesting an intention and attempt: and the less, as a plan, in many respects similar, has recently been put into execution, without any reference to the original projector.

The motives that suggested this undertaking to Dr. Burney, with the reasons by which they were influenced and supported, were to this effect.

In England, where more splendid rewards await the favourite votaries of musical excellence than in any other spot on the globe, there was no establishment of any sort for forming such artists as might satisfy the real connoisseur in music; and save English talent from the mortification, and the British purse from the depredations, of seeking a constant annual supply of genius and merit from foreign shores.

An institution, therefore, of this character seemed wanting to the state, for national economy; and to the people, for national encouragement.

Such was the enlarged view which Dr. Burney, while yet in Italy, had taken of such a plan for his own country.

The difficulty of collecting proper subjects to form its members, caused great diversity of opinion and of proposition amongst the advisers with whom Dr. Burney consulted.

It was peculiarly necessary, that these young disciples should be free from every sort of contamination, mental or corporeal, upon entering this musical asylum, that they might spread no dangerous contagion of either sort; but be brought up to the practice of the art, with all its delightful powers of pleasing, chastened from their abuse.

With such a perspective, to take promiscuously the children of the poor, merely where they had an ear for music, or a voice for song, would be running the risk of gathering together a mixed little multitude, which, from intermingling inherent vulgarity, hereditary diseases, or vicious propensities, with the finer qualities requisite for admission, might render the cultivation of their youthful talents, a danger—if not a curse—to the country.

Yet, the length of time that might be required for selecting little subjects, of this unadulterate description, from different quarters; with the next to impossibility of tracing, with any certainty, what might have been their real conduct in times past; or what might be their principles to give any basis of security for the time to come; caused a perplexity of the most serious species: for should a single one of the tribe go astray, the popular cry against teaching the arts to the poor, would stamp the whole little community with a stain indelible; and the institution itself might be branded with infamy.

What, abstractedly, was desirable, was to try this experiment upon youthful beings to whom the world was utterly unknown; and who not only in innocence had breathed their infantine lives, but in complete and unsuspicious ignorance of evil.

Requisites so hard to obtain, and a dilemma so intricate to unravel, led the Doctor to think of the Foundling Hospital; in the neighbourhood of which, in Queen Square, stood his present dwelling.

He communicated, therefore, his project, to Sir Charles Whitworth, the governor of the hospital.

Sir Charles thought it proper, feasible, desirable, and patriotic.

The Doctor, thus seconded, drew up a plan for

forming a Musical Conservatorio in the metropolis of England, and in the bosom of the Foundling Hospital.

The intention was to collect from the whole little corps all who had musical ears, or tuneful voices, to be brought up scientifically, as instrumental or vocal performers.

Those of the group who gave no decided promise of such qualifications, were to go on with their ordinary education, and to abide by its ordinary result, according to the original regulations of the charity.

A meeting of the governors and directors was convened by their chief, Sir Charles Whitworth, for announcing this scheme.

The plan was heard with general approbation; but the discussions to which it gave rise were discursive and perplexing.

It was objected, that music was an art of luxury, by no means requisite to life, or accessary to morality.

These children were all meant to be educated as plain, but essential members of the general community. They were to be trained up to useful purposes, with a singleness that would ward off all ambition for what was higher; and teach them to repay the benefit of their support by cheerful labour. To stimulate them to superior views might mar the religious object of the charity; which was to nullify rather than extinguish, all disposition to pride, vice, or voluptuousness; such as, probably, had demoralized their culpable parents, and thrown these deserted outcasts upon the mercy of the Foundling Hospital.

This representation, the Doctor acknowledged, would be unanswerable, if it were decided to be right, and if it were judged to be possible, wholly to extirpate the art of music in the British empire: or, if the Foundling Hospital were to be considered as a seminary; predestined to menial servitude; and as the only institution of the country where the members were to form a caste, from whose rules and plodden ways no genius could ever emerge.

But such a fiat could never be issued by John Bull; nor so flat a stamp be struck upon any portion of his countrymen. John Bull was at once too liberal and too proud, to seek to adopt the tame ordinances of the immutable Hindoos; with whom ages pass unmarked; generations unchanged; the poor never richer; the simple never wiser; and with whom, family by family, and trade by trade, begin, continue, and terminate, their monotonous existence, by the same pre-determined course, and to the same invariable destiny.

These children, the Doctor answered, are all orphans; they are taken from no family, for by none are they owned; they are drawn from no calling, for to none are they specifically bred. They are all brought up to menial offices, though they are all instructed in reading and writing, and the females in needle-work; but they are all, systematically and indiscriminately, destined to be servants or apprentices, at the age of fifteen; from which period, all their hold upon the benevolent institution to which they are indebted for their infantine rescue from perishing cold and starving want, with their subsequent maintenance and tuition, is rotatorily transferred to new-born claimants; for the Hospital, then, has fulfilled its engagements; and the children must go forth to the world, whether to their benefit or their disgrace.

Were it not better, then, when there are subjects who are success-inviting, to bestow upon them professional improvement, with virtuous education? since, as long as operas, concerts, and theatres, are licensed by government, musical performers, vocal and instrumental, will inevitably be wanted, employed, and remunerated. And every state is surely best served, and the people of every country are surely the most encouraged, when the nation suffices for itself, and no foreign aid is necessarily called in, to share either the fame or the emoluments of public performances.

Stop, then; prohibit, proscribe—if it be possible, —all taste for foreign refinements, and for the exquisite finishing of foreign melody and harmony; or establish a school on our own soil, in which, as in Painting and in Sculpture, the foreign perfection of arts may be taught, transplanted, and culled, till they become indigenous.

And where, if not here, may subjects be found on whom such a national trial may be made with the least danger of injury? subjects who have been brought up with a strictness of regular habits that has warded them from all previous mischief; yet who are too helpless and ignorant, as well as poor, to be able to develop whether or not Nature, in her secret workings, has kindled within their unconscious bosoms, a spark, a single spark of harmonic fire, that might light them, from being hewers of wood, and brushers of spiders, to those regions of vocal and instrumental excellence, that might propitiate the project of drawing from our own culture a school for music, of which the students, under proper moral and religious tutelage, might, in time, supersede the foreign auxiliaries by whom they are now utterly extinguished.

The objectors were charged, also, to weigh well that there was no law, or regulation, and no means whatsoever, that could prevent any of this little association from becoming singers and players, if they had musical powers, and such should be their wish: though, if self-thrown into that walk, singers and players only at the lowest theatres, or at the tea and cake public-gardens; or even in the streets, as fiddlers of country dances, or as ballad squallers: in which degraded exercise of their untaught endowments, not only decent life must necessarily be abandoned, but immorality, licentiousness, and riot, must assimilate with, or, rather, form a prominent part of their exhibitions and performances.

Here the discussion closed. The opponents were silenced, if not convinced, and the trial of the project was decreed.

The hardly-fought battle over, victory, waving her gay banners, that wafted to the Doctor hopes of future renown with present benediction, determined him, for the moment, to relinquish even his history, that he might devote every voluntary thought to consolidating this scheme.

The primary object of his consideration, because the most conscientious, was the preservation of the morals, and fair conduct of the pupils. And here, the exemplary character, and the purity of the principles of Dr. Burney, would have shone forth to national advantage, had the expected prosperity of his design brought his meditated regulations into practice.

Vain would it be to attempt, and useless, if not vain, to describe his indignant consternation, when, while in the full occupation of these arrangements, a letter arrived to him from Sir Charles Whitworth, to make known, with great regret, that the undertaking was suddenly overthrown. The enemies to the attempt, who had seemed quashed, had merely lurked in ambush, to watch for an unsuspected moment to convene a partial committee; in which they voted out the scheme, as an innovation upon the original purpose of the institution; and pleading, also, an old act of parliament against its adoption, they solemnly proscribed it for ever.

Yet a repeal of that act had been fully intended before the plan, which, hitherto, had only been agitating and negociating, should have been put into execution.

All of choice, however, and all of respect, that remained for Dr. Burney, consisted in a personal offer from Sir Charles Whitworth, to re-assemble an opposing meeting amongst those friends who, previously, had carried the day.

But happy as the Doctor would have been to have gained, with the honour of general approbation, a point he had elaborately studied to clear from mystifying objections, and to render desirable, even to patriotism; his pride was justly hurt by so abrupt a defalcation; and he would neither with open hostility, nor under any versatile contest, become the founder, or chief, of so important an enterprize.

He gave up, therefore, the attempt, without further struggle; simply recommending to the mature reflections of the members of the last committee, whether it were not more pious, as well as more rational, to endeavour to ameliorate the character and lives of practical musical noviciates, than to behold the nation, in its highest classes, cherish the art, follow it, embellish it with riches, and make it fashion and pleasure—while, to train to that art, with whatever precautions, its appropriate votaries from the bosom of our own country, seemed to call for opposition, and to deserve condemnation.

Thus died, in its birth, this interesting project, which, but for this brief sketch, might never have been known to have brightened the mind, as one of the projects, or to have mortified it, as one of the failures, of the active and useful life of Dr. Burney.

HISTORY OF MUSIC.

With a spirit greatly hurt through a lively sense of injustice, and a laudable ambition surreptitiously suppressed by misconception and prejudice, all that was left for Dr. Burney in this ungracious business was to lament loss of time, and waste of meditation.

Yet, the matter being without redress, save by struggles which he thought beneath the fair design of the enterprise, he combatted the intrusion of availless discontent, by calling to his aid his well-experienced antidote to inertness and discouragement, a quickened application to changed, or renewed pursuits.

Again, therefore, he returned to his History of Music; and now, indeed, he went to work with all his might. The capacious table of his small but commodious study, exhibited, in what he called his chaos, the countless increasing stores of his materials. Multitudinous, or, rather, innumerous blank books, were severally adapted to concentrating some peculiar portion of the work. Theory, practice; music of the ancients; music in parts; national music; lyric, church, theatrical, warlike music; universal biography of composers and performers, of patrons and of professors; and histories of musical institutions, had all their destined blank volumes.

And he opened a widely circulating correspondence, foreign and domestic, with various musical authors, composers, and students, whether professors or diletante.

And for all this mass of occupation, he neglected no business, he omitted no devoir. The system by which he obtained time that no one missed, yet that gave to him lengthened life, independent of longevity from years, was through the skill with which, indefatigably, he profitted from every fragment of leisure.

Every sick or failing pupil bestowed an hour upon his pen. Every holiday for others, was a day of double labour to his composition. Even illness took activity only from his body, for his mind refused all relaxation. He had constantly, when indisposed, one of his daughters by his side, as an amanuensis; and such was the vigour of his intellect, that even when keeping his bed from acute rheumatism, spasmodic pains, or lurking fever, he caught at every little interval of ease to dictate some illustrative reminiscence; to start some new ideas, or to generalize some old ones; which never failed to while away, partially at least, the pangs of disease, by lessening their greatest torment to a character of such energy, irreparable loss of time.

The plan, with proposals for printing the History by subscription, was no sooner published, than the most honourable lists of orders were sent to his booksellers, from various elegant classic scholars, and from all general patrons or lovers of new enterprises and new works.

But that which deserves most remark, is a letter from two eminent merchants of the city, Messieurs Chandler and Davis, to acquaint the Doctor that a gentleman, who wished to remain concealed, had authorised them to desire, that Dr. Burney would not suffer any failure in the subscription, should any occur, to induce him to drop the work; as this gentleman solemnly undertook to be himself responsible for every set within the five hundred of the Doctor's stipulation, that should remain unsubscribed for on the ensuing Christmas. And Messrs. Davis and Chandler were invested with full powers, to give any security that might be demanded for the fulfilment of this engagement.

Dr. Burney wrote his most grateful thanks to this munificent protector of his project; but declined all sort of tie upon the event. And the subscription filled so voluntarily, that this generous unknown was never called forth. Nor did he ever present himself; nor was he ever discovered. But the incident helped to keep warmly alive the predilection which the Doctor had early imbibed, in favour of the noble spirit of liberality of the city and the citizens of his native land, for whatever seems to have any claim to public character.

MR. HUTTON.

Another letter from another stranger, equally animated by a sincere interest in the undertaking, though producing, for the moment, a sensation as warm of resentment, as that just mentioned had excited of gratitude, was next received by the Doctor.

It was written with the most profuse praise of the Musical Tours; but with a view to admonish the Tourist to revise the account drawn up of the expenses, the bad roads, the bad living, the bad carriages, and other various faults and deficiencies upon which the travels in Germany had expatiated: all which this new correspondent was convinced were related from misinformation, or misconception; as he had himself visited the same spots without witnessing any such imperfections. He conjured the Doctor, therefore, to set right these statements in his next edition; which single amendment would render the journal of his Tour in Germany the most delightful now in print: and, with wishes sincerely fervent for all honour and all success to the business, he signed himself, Dr. Burney's true admirer,

JOHN HUTTON,
Of Lindsey House, Chelsea.

Dr. Burney, who felt that his veracity had that unsullied honour that, like the virtue of the wife of

Cæsar, must not be suspected, read this letter with the amazement, and answered it with the indignation, of offended integrity. He could not, he said, be the dupe of misrepresentation, for he had related only what he had experienced. His narrative was all personal, all individual; and he had documents, through letters, bills, and witnesses in fellow-travellers, and in friends or inhabitants of the several places described, that could easily be produced to verify his assertions: all which he was most able and willing to call forth; not so much, perhaps, for the satisfaction of Mr. Hutton, who so hastily had misjudged him, as for his own; in certifying, upon proof, how little he had deserved the mistrust of his readers, as being capable of giving hearsay intelligence to the public.

Mr. Hutton instantly, and in a tone of mingled alarm and penitence, wrote a humble, yet energetic apology for his letter; earnestly entreating the Doctor's pardon for his officious precipitancy; and appealing to Dr. Hawkesworth, whom he called his excellent friend, to intercede in his favour. He took shame, he added, to himself, for not having weighed the subject more chronologically before he wrote his strictures; as he had now made out that his hasty animadversion was the unreflecting result of the different periods in which the Doctor and himself had travelled; his own German visit having taken place previously to the devastating war between the King of Prussia and the Empress Queen, which had since laid waste the whole country in which, unhappily, it had been waged.

Dr. Burney accepted with pleasure this conceding explanation. The good offices of Dr. Hawkesworth were prompt to accelerate a reconciliation and an interview; and Mr. Hutton, with even tears of eager feelings to repair an unjust accusation, hastened to Queen-square. Dr. Burney, touched by his ingenuous contrition, received him with open arms. And, from that moment, he became one of the Doctor's most reverential and most ardent admirers.

He made frequent visits to the house; conceived the most friendly regard for the whole family; and abruptly, and with great singularity, addressed a letter, that was as original in ideas as in diction, to one of the daughters,* with whom he demanded permission of the Doctor to correspond. And in

---

* This Editor.

a postscript, that was nearly as long as the epistle, to obviate, probably, any ambiguous notions from his zeal—though he was already a grey and wrinkled old man—he acquainted his new young correspondent that he had been married four-and-thirty years.

Mr. Hutton was one of the sect of the Moravians, or Hurnhuters, and resided at Lindsey House, Chelsea, as secretary to the united brethren. He was author, also, of an Essay towards giving some just ideas of the character of Count Zinzendorf, the inventor and founder of the sect.

Mr. Hutton was a person of pleasing though eccentric manners. His notions were uncommon; his language was impressive, though quaint: his imagination, notwithstanding his age, was playful, nay, poetical. He considered all mankind as his brethren, and himself, therefore, as every one's equal; alike in his readiness to serve them, and in the frankness with which he demanded their services in return.

His desire to make acquaintance, and to converse with every body to whom any species of celebrity was attached, was insatiable, and was dauntless. He approached them without fear, and accosted them without introduction. But the genuine kindness of his smile made way for him wherever there was heart and observation; and with such his encounter, however uncouth, brought on, almost invariably, a friendly intercourse.

Yet where, on the contrary, he met not with those delicate developers and interpreters, heart and observation, to instil into those he addressed a persuasion of the benevolence of his intentions in seeking fair and free fraternity with all his fellow creatures, he suffered not his failures to dishearten him; for as he never meant, he never took offence. And even when turned away from with rudeness or alarm, as a man conceived to be intrusive, impertinent, or suspicious, he would neither be angry nor affronted; but, sorrowfully shaking his head, would hope that some happy accident would inspire them with softer feelings, ere some bitter misfortune should retaliate their unkindness.

The immediate, it might, perhaps, be said, the instinctive cause of any rebuff that he met with in public, namely, his extraordinary appearance, and apparel, never seemed to occur to him; for as he looked not at the finest garb of the wealthy or modish with the smallest respect, he surmised not that the shabbiness of his own could influence his reception. By him, the tailor and the mantua-maker were regarded merely as manufacturers of decency, not of embellishment; and he had full as much esteem for his own clumsy cobbler or second-hand patching tailor, as the finest beau or belle of Almack's could have for their Parisian attirers.

Nevertheless, so coarse was the large, brown, slouching surtout, which infolded his body; so rough and blowsy was the old mop-like wig that wrapt up his head; that, but for the perfectly serene mildness of his features, and the venerability of his hoary eye-brows, he might at all times have passed for some constable, watchman, or policeman, who had mistaken the day for the night, and was prowling into the mansions of gentlemen, instead of public-houses, to take a survey that all was in order.

That a man such as this, with every mark of a nature the most unstained, and of a character the most unsophisticated, could belong to a sect, which, by all popular report at least, was stampt, at that time, as dark and mystic; and as being wild and strange in some of its doctrines even to absurdity; must make every one who had witnessed the virtuous tenor of the life of Mr. Hutton, and shared in the inoffensive gaiety of his discourse, believe the sect to have been basely calumniated; for not a word was ever uttered by this singular being that breathed not good will to all mankind; and not an action is recorded, or known of him, that is irresponsive of such universal benevolence.

* * * * * * *

Dr. Burney, now, without a single black-ball, was elected a fellow of the Royal Society; of which honour his first notice was received through the amiable and zealous Miss Phipps,* who, knowing the day of election, had impatiently gathered the tidings of its success from her brother, Sir Constantine Phipps : † and before either the president, or the friend who had nominated the Doctor for a candidate, could forward the news, she sportively anticipated their intelligence, by sending to Queen-square a letter directed in large characters, " For Dr. Burney, F. R. S." ‡

---

* Daughter of Lord Mulgrave.

† More known by the title of the Hon. Polar Captain. Afterwards Lord Mulgrave.

‡ Mr. Seward, author of Biographiana, was wont to say, that those three initial letters stood for a Fellow Remarkably Stupid.

HISTORY OF MUSIC.

From this period, the profession of Dr. Burney, however highly he was raised in it, seemed but of secondary consideration for him in the world; where, now, the higher rank was assigned him of a man of letters, from the general admiration accorded to his Tours; of which the climax of honour was the award of Dr. Johnson, that Dr. Burney was one of the most agreeable writers of travels of the age. And Baretti, to whom Dr. Johnson uttered this praise, was commissioned to carry it to Dr. Burney; who heard it with the highest gratification: though, since his bereavement of his Esther, he had ceased to follow up the intercourse he had so enthusiastically begun. Participation there had been so animated, that the charm of the connexion seemed, for awhile, dissolved by its loss.

Letters now daily arrived from persons of celebrity, with praises of the Tours, encouragement for the History, or musical information for its advantage. Mr. Mason, Mr. Harris of Salisbury, Dr. Warton, Dr. Thomas Warton, Dr. Harrington, Mr. Pennant, Montagu North, Mr. Bewley, Mr. Crisp, and Mr. Garrick, all bestowed what Dr. Burney sportively called sweet-scented bouquets on his journals.

But amongst the many distinguished personages who volunteered their services in honour of the History of Music, the Doctor peculiarly valued the name of Wellesley, Earl of Mornington, father of the preserver, not alone of England, and of France, but of Europe, at the awful crisis of general—almost chaotic—danger.

This nobleman, the Earl of Mornington, with the most liberal love of the arts, and most generous admiration of their high professors, upon being addressed by his friend, Mr. Rigby, in favour of Dr. Burney's pursuit, came forth, with a zeal the most obliging, to aid the Doctor's researches concerning the antiquity of music in Ireland; and the origin of the right of the Irish for bearing the harp in their arms.

Some of his lordship's letters will be found in the correspondence, replete with information and agreeability.

The Doctor held, also, a continental correspondence, enlightening and flattering, with the Baron d'Holbach, Diderot, the Abbé Morellet, M. Suard, M. Monnet, and Jean Jacques Rousseau himself.

Of this last-named, and certainly most rare of his epistolary cotemporaries, Jean Jacques Rousseau, the following note is copied from the Doctor's memorandums.

"Five years after the representation of 'The Cunning Man,' when, in 1770, I had visited Rousseau at Paris, and entered into correspondence with him, I sent him, in a parcel with other books, a copy of 'The Cunning Man,' as it was performed and printed in England to my translation of his *Devin du Village*, and adjusted to his original music; and I received from him the following answer.

   "*A Monsieur*,
    "*Monsieur le Docteur Burney*,
     "*A Londres.*

"Je recois, Monsieur, avec bien de la reconnoissance, les deux pièces de musique gravée, que vous m'avez fait remettre par M. Guy. 'La Passione de Jomelli,' dont je vous suppose l'editeur, montre que vous savez connoître et priser le beau en ce genre. Cet ouvrage admirable me paroit plein d'harmonie et d'expression. Il merite en cela d'être mis à côté du Stabat Mater de Pergolese. Je le trouve seulment au dessous en ce qu'il a moins de simplicité.

"Je vous dois aussi des remercimens pour avoir daigné vous occuper du 'Devin du Village; quoiqu'il m'ait paru toujours impossible à traduire avec succés* dans une autre langue. Je ne vous parlerai pas des changemens que vous avez jugé àpropos

---

* There seems here to be some word, or words, omitted. — ED.

d'y faire. Vous avez consulté, sans doute, le gôut de votre nation ; et il n'y a rien à dire à cela.

"Les ouvrages, Monsieur, dont vous m'avez fait le cadeau, me rappelleront souvent le plaisir que j'ai eu de vous voir, et de vous entendre ; et nourriront le regret de n'en pas jouir quelque fois.

"Agreez, Monsieur, je vous supplie, mes bien humbles salutations.

"J. J. Rousseau."

JOEL COLLIER.

The quick-spreading favour with which the Tours were received; the celebrity which they threw around the name and existence of Dr. Burney; the associations of rank, talents, literature, learning, and fashionable coteries, to which they opened an entrance, could not fail, ere long, to make their author become an object of envy, since they raised him to be one of admiration.

The character, conduct, and life of Dr. Burney were now, therefore, no doubt, critically examined, and morally sifted, by the jealous herd of cotemporary rivals, who had worked far longer, and far more laboriously, through the mazes of science; yet, working without similar genius, had failed of rising to similar heights.

Nevertheless, the immediate path in which Dr.

Burney flourished was so new, so untrodden, that he displaced no competitor, he usurped no right of others; and the world, unsought and uncanvassed, was so instinctively on his side, that, for a considerable time, his palpable pre-eminence seemed as willingly accorded, as it was unequivocally acknowledged.

But the viper does not part with its venom from keeping its body in ambush; and, before the History came out, though long after the publication of the Tours, a ludicrous parody of the latter was sent forth into the world, under the name of Joel Collier.

The Doctor, delicately anxious not to deserve becoming an object for satire, was much hurt, on its first appearance, by this burlesque production. It attacked, indeed, little beyond the technical phraseology of the Tours; the tourist himself was evidently above the reach of such anonymous shafts.

It was generally supposed to be a *jeu d'esprit* of some enemy, to counteract his rapid progress in public favour; and to undermine the promising success of his great work.

But the Doctor himself did not give way to this opinion: he had done nothing to incur enemies;

he had done much to conciliate friends; and, believing in virtue because practising it, he knew not how to conceive personal malice without personal offence. He imagined it, therefore, the work of some stranger, excited solely by the desire of making money from his own risible ideas; without caring whom they might harass, or how they might irritate, provided, in the words of Rodrigo, he "put money in his purse."

The Doctor, however, as has been said, from the unimpeachable goodness of his heart and character, had the fair feelings of mankind in his favour. The parody, therefore, though executed with burlesque humour, whether urged or not by malevolence, was never reprinted; and obtained but the laugh of a moment, without making the shadow of an impression to the disadvantage of the tourist.

MR. TWINING.

But the happiest produce to Dr. Burney of this enterprise, and the dearest mede of his musical labours, was the cordial connexion to which it led with Mr. Twining, afterwards called Aristotle Twining; which opened with an impulsive reciprocation of liking, and ended in a friendship as permanent as it was exhilarating.

Mr. Twining, urged by an early and intuitive taste, equally deep and refined, for learning and for letters, had begun life by desiring to make over the very high emoluments of a lucrative business, with its affluence and its cares, to a deserving younger brother; while he himself should be quietly settled, for the indulgence of his literary propensities, in some retired and moderate living, at a distance from the metropolis.

His father listened without disapprobation; and at the vicarage of Colchester, Mr. Twining established his clerical residence.

His acquaintance with Dr. Burney commenced by a letter of singular merit, and of nearly incomparable modesty. After revealing, in terms that showed the most profound skill in musical science, that he had himself not only studied and projected, but, in various rough desultory sections, had actually written certain portions of a History of Music, he liberally acknowledged that he had found the plan of the Doctor so eminently superior to his own, and the means that had been taken for its execution so far beyond his power of imitation, that he had come to a resolution of utterly renouncing his design; of which not a vestige would now remain that could reflect any pleasure upon his lost time and pains, unless he might appease his abortive attempt by presenting its fruits, with the hope that they would not be found utterly useless, to Dr. Burney.

So generous an offering could not fail of being delightedly accepted; and the more eagerly, as the whole style of the letter decidedly spoke its writer to be a scholar, a wit, and a man of science.

Dr. Burney earnestly solicited to receive the manuscript from Mr. Twining's own hands: and Mr. Twining, though with a timidity as rare in accompanying so much merit as the merit itself, complied with the request.

The pleasure of this first interview was an immediate guarantee of the mental union to which it gave rise. Every word that issued from Mr. Twining confirmed the three high characters to which his letter had raised expectation,—of a man of science, a scholar, and a wit. Their taste in music, and their selection of composers and compositions, were of the same school; *i. e.* the modern and the Italian for melody, and the German for harmony.

Nor even here was bounded the chain by which they became linked: their classical, literary, and poetical pursuits, nay, even their fancies, glided so instinctively into the same channel, that not a dissonant idea ever rippled its current: and the animal spirits of both partook of this general coincidence, by running, playfully, whimsically, or ludicrously, with equal concord of pleasantry, into similar inlets of imagination.

The sense of this congeniality entertained by Dr. Burney, will be best shewn by the insertion of some biographical lines, taken from a chronological series of events which he committed to paper, about this time, for the amusement of Mrs. Burney.

* * * after toil and fatigue — —
To Twining I travel, in hopes of relief,
Whose wit and good-humour soon drive away grief.
And now, free from care, in night-gown and sandals,
Not a thought I bestow on the Goths and the Vandals.
Together we fiddled, we laugh'd, and we sung,
And tried to give sound both a soul and a tongue.
Ideas we sift, we compare, and commute,
And, though sometimes we differ, we never dispute;
Our minds to each other we turn inside out,
And examine each source of belief and of doubt;
For as musical discord in harmony ends,
So our's, when resolv'd, makes us still better friends.

The whole family participated in this delightful accession to the comfort and happiness of its chief; and, Mr. Crisp alone excepted, no one was received by the Burnean tribe with such eagerness of welcome as Mr. Twining.

A correspondence, literary, musical, and social, took place between this gentleman and the Doctor, when they separated, that made a principal pleasure, almost an occupation, of their future lives. And Dr. Burney thenceforward found in this willing and accomplished fellow-labourer, a charm for his work that made him hasten to it after his business and cares, as to his most grateful recreation. While Mr. Twining, exchanging a shyness that amounted nearly to bashfulness, for a friendly trust that gave free play to his sportive and original colloquial powers, felt highly gratified to converse at his ease with the man whose enterprise had filled him with an admiration to which he had been almost bursting to give some vent; but which he had so much wanted courage to proclaim, that, as he afterwards most humorously related, he had no sooner sent his first letter for Dr. Burney to the post-office, than he heartily hoped it might miscarry! and had hardly, though by appointment, softly knocked at the door of the Doctor, than he all but prayed that he should not find him at home!

MR. BEWLEY.

During a visit which, at this time, Dr. Burney made to his old friends and connexions in Norfolk, he spent a week or two with his truly-loved and warmly-admired favourite, Mr. Bewley, of Massingham; whose deep theoretical knowledge of the science, and passion for the art of music, made, now, a sojourn under his roof as useful to the work of the Doctor, as, at all periods, it had been delightful to his feelings.

Of this visit, which took place immediately after one that had been fatiguingly irksome from stately ceremony, he speaks, in his chronological rhymes, in the following manner.

> To Bewley retiring, in peace and in quiet,
> Where our* welcome was hearty, and simple our diet;
> Where reason and science all jargon disdain'd,
> And humour and wit with philosophy reign'd—

---

* Mrs. Doctor Burney accompanied the Doctor in this visit to Mr. and Mrs. Bewley.

Not a muse but was ready to answer his call;
By the virtues all cherish'd, the great and the small.
There Clio I court, to reveal every mystery
Of musical lore, with its practice and history.

Mr. Bewley, now, was the principal writer for scientific articles in the Monthly Review, under the editorship of Mr. Griffith. He was, also, in close literary connexion with Dr. Priestley, Mr. Reid, and Padre Beccaria; with whom to correspond he had latterly dedicated some weeks exclusively to the study of Italian, that he might answer the letters of that celebrated man in his own language.

In company with this learned and dear friend, Dr. Burney afterwards passed a week at Haughton Hall, with the Earl of Orford, who invariably received him with cordial pleasure; and who had the manly understanding, combined with the classical taste, always to welcome with marked distinction the erudite philosopher of Massingham; though that obscure philosopher was simply, in his profession, a poor and hard-working country surgeon; and though, in his habits, partly from frugal necessity, and partly from negligent indifference, he was the man the most miserably and meanly accoutred, and withal the most slovenly, of any who had ever found his way into high society.

Lord Orford, with almost unexampled liberality, was decidedly blind to all these exterior imperfections; and only clear-sighted, for this gifted man of mind, to the genius that, at times, in the arch meaning of his smile, sparkled knowledge from his eye, with an intelligent expression that brightened into agreeability his whole queer face. And to call into play those rugged features, beneath which lurked the deepest information, and the most enlightened powers of entertainment, was the pleasure of the noble host; a distinction which saved this unknown and humble country practitioner from the stares, or the ridicule, of all new-arrived guests; though secretly, no doubt, they marvelled enough who he could be; and still more how he came there.

DR. HAWKESWORTH.

At Haughton Hall these two friends found now a large assembled party, of which the Earl of Sandwich, then first lord of the Admiralty, was at the head. The whole conversation at the table turned upon what then was the whole interest of the day, the first voyage round the world of Captain Cooke, which that great circumnavigator had just accomplished. The Earl of Sandwich mentioned that he had all the papers relating to the voyage in his hands; with the circumnavigations preceding it of Wallace and Byron; but that they were mere rough draughts, quite unarranged for the public eye; and that he was looking out for a proper person to put them into order, and to re-write the voyages.

Dr. Burney, ever eager upon any question of literature, and ever foremost to serve a friend, ventured to recommend Dr. Hawkesworth; who though, from his wise and mild character, contented with his lot, Dr. Burney knew to be neither rich enough for retirement, nor employed enough to refuse any new and honourable occupation. The *Adventurer* was in every body's library; but the author was less generally known: yet the account now given of him was so satisfactory to Lord Sandwich, that he entrusted Dr. Burney with the commission of sending Dr. Hawkesworth to the Admiralty.

Most gladly this commission was executed. The following is the first paragraph of Dr. Hawkesworth's answer to its communication :

"Many, many thanks for your obliging favour, and the subject of it. There is nothing about which I would so willingly be employed as the work you mention. I would do my best to make it another Anson's Voyage.

Lord Sandwich, upon their meeting, was extremely pleased with Dr. Hawkesworth, to whom the manuscripts were immediately made over; and who thus expressed his satisfaction in his next letter to Dr. Burney.

" I am now happy in telling you, that your labour of love is not lost; that I have all the journals of the Dolphin, the Swallow, and the Endeavour in my possession; that the government will give me the cuts, and the property of the work will be my own.

" Is it impossible I should give you my hand, and the thanks of my heart, here ? *i. e.* at Bromley."

CAPTAIN COOKE.

Some time afterwards, Dr. Burney was invited to Hinchinbroke, the seat of the Earl of Sandwich, to meet Sir Joseph Banks, Dr. Solander, Dr. Hawkesworth, and the celebrated circumnavigator, Captain Cooke himself.

It was the earnest request of James, the eldest son of Dr. Burney, to be included in the approaching second expedition of this great seaman ; a request which Lord Sandwich easily, and with pleasure, accorded to Dr. Burney ; and the young naval officer was invited to Hinchinbroke, and presented to his new commander, with a recommendation that he should stand foremost on the list of promotion, should any occasion of change occur during the voyage.

The following note upon Captain Cooke, is copied from a memorandum-book of Dr. Burney's.

" In February, I had the honour of receiving the illustrious Captain Cooke to dine with me in Queen-square, previously to his second voyage round the world.

" Observing upon a table Bougainville's *Voyage autour du Monde*, he turned it over, and made some curious remarks on the illiberal conduct of that circumnavigator towards himself, when they met and crossed each other ; which made me desirous to know, in examining the chart of M. de Bougainville, the several tracks of the two navigators ; and exactly where they had crossed or approached each other.

" Captain Cooke instantly took a pencil from his pocket-book, and said he would trace the route ; which he did in so clear and scientific a manner, that I would not take fifty pounds for the book. The pencil marks having been fixed by skim milk, will always be visible."

This truly great man appeared to be full of sense and thought; well-mannered, and perfectly unpretending; but studiously wrapped up in his own purposes and pursuits; and apparently under a pressure of mental fatigue when called upon to speak, or stimulated to deliberate, upon any other.

The opportunity which thus powerfully had been prepared of promotion for the Doctor's son, occurred early in the voyage. Mr. Shanks, the second lieutenant of the Discovery, was taken ill at the Cape of Good Hope, and obliged to leave the ship. "In his place," Captain Cooke wrote to Lord Sandwich, "I have appointed Mr. Burney, whom I have found very deserving."

DOCTOR GOLDSMITH.

Dr. Goldsmith, now in the meridian of his late-earned, but most deserved prosperity, was projecting an English Dictionary of Arts and Sciences, upon the model of the French Encyclopædia. Sir Joshua Reynolds was to take the department of painting; Mr. Garrick, that of acting; Dr. Johnson, that of ethics: and no other class was yet nominated, when Dr. Burney was applied to for that of music, through the medium of Mr. Garrick.

Justly gratified by a call to make one in so select a band, Dr. Burney willingly assented; and immediately drew up the article "Musician;" which he read to Mr. Garrick; from whom it received warm plaudits.

The satisfaction of Dr. Goldsmith in this acquisition to his forces, will be seen by the ensuing letter to Mr. Garrick; by whom it was enclosed, with the following words, to Dr. Burney.

"*June* 11, 1773.

"My dear Doctor,

"I have sent you a letter from Dr. Goldsmith. He is proud to have your name among the elect.

"Love to all your fair ones.

"Ever yours,

"D. GARRICK."

To DAVID GARRICK, ESQ.

"*Temple, Jan.* 10, 1773.

"Dear Sir,

"To be thought of by you, obliges me; to be served by you, still more. It makes me very happy to find that Dr. Burney thinks my scheme of a Dictionary useful; still more that he will be so kind as to adorn it with any thing of his own. I beg you, also, will accept my gratitude for procuring me so valuable an acquisition.

"I am,
"Dear Sir,
"Your most affectionate servant,
"Oliver Goldsmith."

The work, however, was never accomplished, and its project sunk away to nothing; sincerely to the regret of those who knew what might be expected from that highly qualified writer, on a plan that would eminently have brought forth all his various talents; and which was conceived upon so grand a scale, and was to be supported by such able coadjutors. And deeply was public regret heightened that it was by the hand of Death that this noble enterprise was cut short; Death, which seemed to have awaited the moment of the reversal of poverty and hardship into prosperity and fame, for striking that blow which, at an earlier period, might frequently, for Dr. Goldsmith, have taken away a burthen rather than a blessing. But such is the mysterious construction of Life—that mere harbinger of Death! —always obedient to the fatal knell he tolls, though always longing to implore that he would toll it a little—little later!

DOCTOR HAWKESWORTH.

The sincere satisfaction that Dr. Burney had experienced in having influenced the nomination of Dr. Hawkesworth to be editor of the first voyage of Captain Cooke round the world, together with the revisal and arrangement of the voyages of Captain Wallace and Admiral Byron, was soon overcast by sorrow, through circumstances as impossible to have foreseen as not to lament.

Dr. Hawkesworth, though already in a delicate state of health, was so highly animated by his election to this office, and with the vast emolument which, with scarcely any labour, promised to give the dignity of ease and comfort to the rest of his life; that he performed his task, and finished the narratory compilation, with a rapidity of pleasure, resulting from a promise of future independence, that filled him with kind gratitude to Dr. Burney; and seemed to open his heart, temper, and manners, to the most cordial feelings of happiness.

But the greatness of his recompense for the smallness of his trouble, immediately disposed all his colleagues in the road of renown to censure; and all his competitors in that of profit, to jealousy and ill-will. Unfortunately, in his Introduction to the Voyages, he touched upon some controversial points of religious persuasion, which proved a fatal opening to malignity for the enemies of his success; and other enemies, so upright was the man, it is probable he had none. His reasoning here, unhappily, was seized upon with avidity by his infuriated enviers; and the six thousand pounds which flowed into his coffers, brought six millions of pungent stings to his peace, by arraigning his principles.

A war so ungenial to his placid nature, and hitherto honoured life, breaking forth, with the offensive enmity of assumed superior piety, in calumnious assertions, that strove to blacken the purity of his faith and doctrine; occurring at the moment when he had thought all his worldly cares blown away, to be succeeded by soft serenity and easy affluence; made the attack so unexpected, that its shock was enervating; and his wealth lost its charms, from a trembling susceptibility that detached him from every pleasure it could procure —save that of a now baneful leisure for framing answers to his traducers.

In his last visit, as it proved, to Queen-square, where he dined and spent the evening, Dr. Burney was forcibly struck with concern at sight of the evident, though uncomplaining invalid; so changed, thin, and livid was his appearance.

He conversed freely upon the subject of his book, and the abuse which it had heaped upon him, with the Doctor; who strongly exhorted him to repel such assaulters with the contempt that they deserved: adding, " They are palpably the offsprings of envy at your success. Were you to become a bankrupt, they would all turn to panegyrists; but now, there is hardly a needy man in the kingdom, who has ever held a pen in his hand for a moment, who, in pondering upon the six thousand pounds, does not think he could have done the work better."

Dr. Hawkesworth said that he had not yet made any answer to the torrent of invective poured upon him, except to Dalrymple, who had attacked him by name; for a law-suit was then impending upon Parkinson's publication, and he would write nothing that might seem meant to influence justice: but when that law-suit, by whatever result, should be decided, he would bring out a full and general reply to all the invidious aspersions that so cruelly and wantonly had been cast upon him, since the publication of the Voyages.

He then further, and confidentially, opened to Dr. Burney upon his past life and situation: " Every thing that I possess," he cried, " I have earned by the most elaborate industry, except this last six thousand pounds! I had no education, and no advantage but such as I sedulously worked to obtain for myself; but I preserved my reputation and my character as unblemished as my principles—till this last year! "

Rallying a little then, from a depression which he saw was becoming contagious, he generously changed the subject to the History of Music; and begged to be acquainted with its progress; and to learn something of its method, manner, and meaning; frankly avowing an utter ignorance of the capabilities, or materials, that such a work demanded.

Dr. Burney read to him the dissertation,—then but roughly sketched,—on the Music of the Ancients, by which the History opens: and Dr. Hawkesworth, confessing its subject to be wholly new to him, warmly declared that he found its treatment extremely entertaining, as well as instructive.

After a visit, long, and deeply interesting, he left his friend very anxious about his health, and very impatient for his promised pamphlet: but, while still waiting, with strong solicitude, the appearance of a vindication that might tranquillize the author's offended sensibility, the melancholy tidings arrived, that a slow fever had robbed the invalid of sleep and of appetite; and had so fastened upon his shattered nerves, that, after lingering a week or two, he fell a prey to incurable atrophy; and sunk to his last earthly rest exactly a month after the visit to Dr. Burney, the account of which has been related.

Had the health of Dr. Hawkesworth been more sound, he might have turned with cold disdain from the outrages of mortified slanderers; or have scoffed the impotent rage of combatants whom he had had the ability to distance:—but, who shall venture to say where begins, and where ends, the complicate reciprocity of influence which involves the corporeal with the intellectual part of our being? Dr. Hawkesworth foresaw not the danger, to a constitution already, and perhaps natively, fragile, of yielding to the agitating effects of resentful vexation. He brooded, therefore, unresistingly, over the injustice of which he was the victim; instead of struggling to master it by the only means through which it is conquerable, namely, a calm and determined silence, that would have committed his justification to personal character;—a still, but intrepid champion, against which falsehood never ultimately prevails.

KIT SMART.

If thus untimely fell he who, of all the literary associates of Dr. Burney, had attained the most prosperous lot, who shall marvel that untimely should be the fate of the most unfortunate of his Parnassian friends, Christopher Smart? who, high in literary genius, though in that alone, had a short time previously, through turns of fortune, and concurrences of events, wholly different in their course from those which had undermined the vital powers of Dr. Hawkesworth, paid as prematurely the solemn debt relentlessly claimed by that dread accomptant-general, Death!—of all alike the awful creditor!— and paid it as helplessly the victim of substantial, as Dr. Hawkesworth was that of shadowy, disappointment.

With failure at the root of every undertaking, and abortion for the fruit of every hope, Kit Smart finished his suffering existence in the King's Bench prison; where he owed to a small subscription, of which Dr. Burney was at the head, a miserable little pittance beyond the prison allowance; and where he consumed away the blighted remnant of his days, under the alternate pressure of partial aberration of intellect, and bacchanalian forgetfulness of misfortune.

His learning and talents, which frequently, in his youth, had been crowned with classical laurels at the University of Cambridge, had seemed to prognosticate a far different result : but, through whatever errors or irregularities such fair promises may have been set aside, he, surely, must always call for commiseration rather than censure, who has been exposed, though but at intervals, to the unknown disorders of wavering senses.

Nevertheless, whenever he was master of his faculties, his piety, though rather fanatical than rational, was truly sincere; and survived all his calamities, whether mental or mundane.

He left behind him none to whom he was more attached than Dr. Burney, who had been one of his first favourite companions, and who remained his last and most generous friend.

Alike through his malady and his distresses,

the goodness of his heart, and his feeling for others, were constantly predominant. In his latest letter to Dr. Burney, which was written from the King's Bench prison, he passionately pleaded for a fellow-sufferer, "whom I myself," he impressively says, "have already assisted according to my willing poverty."

Kit Smart is occasionally mentioned in Boswell's Life of Dr. Johnson, and with anecdotes given to Mr. Boswell by Dr. Burney.

Mrs. Le Noir, the ingenious daughter of Mr. Smart, is authoress of a pleasing production entitled *Village Manners*, which she dedicated to Dr. Burney.

QUEEN SQUARE.

Dr. Burney now, in the intervals of his varied, but never-ceasing occupations, gently, yet gaily, enjoyed their fruits. All classes of authors offered to him their services, or opened to him their stores. The first musical performers then in vogue, Millico, Giardini, Fischer, Cervetto, Crosdill, Barthelemon, Dupont, Celestini, Parke, Corri, the blind Mr. Stanley, La Baccelli, and that composer for the heart in all its feelings, Sacchini; with various others, were always eager to accept his invitations, whether for concerts, which occasionally he gave to his friends and acquaintance; or to private meetings for the regale of himself and family.

OMIAH.

But his most serious gratification of this period, was that of receiving in safety and honour, James, his eldest son, the lieutenant of Captain Cooke, on the return from his second voyage round the world, of that super-eminent navigator.

The Admiralty immediately confirmed the nomination of Captain Cooke; and further, in consideration of the character and services of the young naval officer, promoted him to the rank of master and commander.

The voyagers were accompanied back by Omiah, a native of Ulitea, one of the Otaheitean islands. Captain Burney, who had studied the language of this stranger during the voyage home, and had become his particular favourite, was anxious to introduce the young South-Sea islander to his father and family; who were at least equally eager to behold a native of a country so remote, and of such recent discovery.

A time was quickly fixed for his dining and spending the day in Queen-square; whither he was brought by Mr., afterwards Sir Joseph, Bankes, and Dr. Solander; who presented him to Dr. Burney.

The behaviour of this young Otaheitean, whom it would be an abuse of all the meaning annexed to the word, to call a savage, was gentle, courteous, easy, and natural; and shewed so much desire to please, and so much willingness to be pleased himself, that he astonished the whole party assembled to receive him; particularly Sir Robert Strange and Mr. Hayes; for he rather appeared capable to bestow, than requiring to want, lessons of conduct and etiquette in civilized life.

He had a good figure, was tall and well-made; and though his complexion was swarthy and dingy, it was by no means black; and though his features partook far more of the African than of the European cast, his eyes were lively and agreeable, and the general expression of his face was good-humoured and pleasing.

He was full dressed on this day, in the English costume, having just come from the House of Lords, whither he had been taken by Sir Joseph Bankes, to see, rather than to hear, for he could not understand it, the King deliver his speech from the throne. He had also been admitted to a private audience of his Majesty, whom he had much entertained.

A bright Manchester velvet suit of clothes, lined with white satin, in which he was attired, sat upon him with as much negligence of his finery, as if it had been his customary dress from adolescence.

But the perfect ease with which he wore and managed a sword, which he had had the honour to receive from the king, and which he had that day put on for the first time, in order to go to the House of Lords, had very much struck, Sir Joseph said, every man by whom it had been observed; since, by almost every one, the first essay of that accoutrement had been accompanied with an awkwardness and inconvenience ludicrously risible; which this adroit Otaheitean had marvellously escaped.

Captain Burney had acquired enough of the Otaheitean language to be the ready interpreter of Omiah with others, and to keep him alive and in spirits himself, by conversing with him in his own dialect. Omiah understood a little English, when addressed in it slowly and distinctly; but could speak it as yet very ill; and with the peculiarity, whether adopted from the idiom of his own tongue, or from the apprehension of not being clearly comprehended, of uttering first affirmatively, and next negatively, all the little sentences that he attempted to pronounce.

Thus, when asked how he did, he answered " Ver well; not ver ill." Or how he liked any thing, " Ver nice; not ver nasty." Or what he thought of such a one, " Ver dood; not ver bad."

On being presented by Captain Burney to the several branches of the family, when he came to this memorialist, who, from a bad cold, was enveloped in muslin wrappings, he inquired into the cause of her peculiar attire; and, upon hearing that she was indisposed, he looked at her for a moment with concern, and then, recovering to a cheering nod, said, " Ver well to-morrow morrow?"

There had been much variation, though no serious dissension, among the circumnavigators during the voyage, upon the manner of naming this stranger. Captain Burney joined those officers who called him Omai; but Omiah was more general; and Omy was more common still. The sailors, however, who brought him over, disdaining to scan the nicety of these three modes of pronunciation, all, to a man, left each of them unattempted and undiscussed, and, by universal, though ridiculous agreement, gave him no other appellation than that of Jack.

His after visits to the house of Dr. Burney were frequent, and evidently very agreeable to him. He was sure of a kind reception from all the family, and he was sincerely attached to Captain Burney; who was glad to continue with him the study of the Otaheitean language, preparatory to accompanying Captain Cooke in his third circumnavigation, when Omiah was to be restored to his own island and friends.

In the currency of this intercourse, remarks were incessantly excited, upon the powers of nature unassisted by art, compared with those of art unassisted by nature; and of the equal necessity of some species of innate aptness, in civilized as well as in savage life, for obtaining success in personal acquirements.

The disserters on the instruction of youth were just then peculiarly occupied by the letters of Lord Chesterfield; and Mr. Stanhope, their object, was placed continually in a parallel line with Omiah: the first, beginning his education at a great public school; taught from an infant all attainable improvements; introduced, while yet a youth, at foreign courts; and brought forward into high life with all the favour that care, expense, information, and refinement could furnish; proved, with all these benefits, a heavy, ungainly, unpleasing character: while the second, with neither rank nor wealth, even in his own remote island; and with no tutor but nature; changing, in full manhood, his way of life, his dress, his country, and his friends; appeared, through a natural facility of observation, not alone unlike a savage, but with the air of a person who had devoted his youth to the practice of those graces, which the most elaborately accomplished of noblemen had vainly endeavoured to make the ornament of his son.

MR. CRISP.

Another severe illness broke into the ease, the prosperity, and the muse of Dr. Burney, and drove him, perforce, to sojourn for some weeks at Chesington, with his friend, Mr. Crisp; whose character, in the biographical and chronological series of events, is thus forcibly, though briefly, sketched.

" To Crisp I repair'd—that best guide of my youth,
Whose decisions all flow from the fountain of truth;

> Whose oracular counsels seem always excited
> By genius, experience, and wisdom united.
> Then his taste in the arts —happy he who can follow!
> 'Tis the breath of the muses when led by Apollo.
> His knowledge instructs, and his converse beguiles."

To this inestimable Mentor, and to Chesington, that sanctuary of literature and of friendship, Dr. Burney, even in his highest health, would uncompelled have resorted, had Fortune, as kind to him in her free gifts as Nature, left his residence to his choice.

But choice has little to do with deciding the abode of the man who has no patrimony, yet who wishes to save his progeny from the same hereditary dearth: the Doctor, therefore, though it was to the spot of his preference that he was chased, could not, now, make it that of his enjoyment: he could only, and hardly, work at the recovery of his strength; and, that regained, tear himself away from this invaluable friend, and loved retreat, to the stationary post of his toils, the metropolis.

ST. MARTIN'S STREET.

His house in Queen-square had been relinquished from difficulties respecting its title; and Mrs.

Burney, assiduously and skilfully, purchased and prepared another, during his confinement, that was situated in St. Martin's-street, Leicester-fields.

If the house in Queen-square had owed a fanciful part of its value to the belief that, formerly, in his visits to Alderman Barber, it had been inhabited occasionally by Dean Swift, how much higher a local claim, was vested in imagination, for a mansion that had decidedly been the dwelling of the immortal Sir Isaac Newton!

Dr. Burney entered it with reverence, as may be gathered from the following lines in his doggrel chronology.

> " This house, where great Newton once deign'd to reside,
> Who of England, and all Human Nature the pride,
> Sparks of light, like Prometheus, from Heaven purloin'd,
> Which in bright emanations flash'd full on mankind."

This change of position from Queen-square to St. Martin's-street, required all that it could bestow of convenience to business, of facilitating fashionable and literary intercourse, of approximation to travelling foreigners of distinction, and of vicinity to the Opera House; to somewhat counter-balance its unpleasant site, its confined air, and its shabby immediate neighbourhood; after the beautiful prospect which the Doctor had quitted of the hills, ever verdant and smiling, of Hampstead and Highgate; which, at that period, in unobstructed view, had faced his dwelling in Queen-square.

St. Martin's-street, though not narrow, except at its entrance from Leicester-square, was dirty, ill built, and vulgarly peopled.

The house itself was well-constructed, sufficiently large for the family, and, which now began to demand nearly equal accommodation, for the books of the Doctor. The observatory of Sir Isaac Newton, which surmounted its roof, over-looked all London and its environs. It still remained in the same simple state in which it had been left by Sir Isaac; namely, encompassed completely by windows of small old-fashioned panes of glass, so crowded as to leave no exclusion of the glazier, save what was seized for a small chimney and fire-place, and a cupboard, probably for instruments. Another cupboard was borrowed from the little landing-place for coals.

The first act of Dr. Burney, after taking possession of this house, was to repair, at a considerable expense, the observatory of the astronomical chief of nations: and he had the enthusiasm, soon afterwards, of nearly re-constructing it a second time, in consequence of the fearful hurricane of 1778, by which its glass sides were utterly demolished; and its leaden roof, in a whirl of fighting winds, was swept wholly away.

Dr. Burney, who was as elevated in spirit as he was limited in means, for being to all the arts, and all the artists, a patron, preferred any self-denial to suffering such a demolition. He would have thought himself a ruthless Goth, had he permitted the *sanctum sanctorum* of the developer of the skies in their embodied movements, to have been scattered to nonentity through his neglect or parsimony; and sought for, thenceforward, in vain, by posterity.

* * * * *

Amongst the earliest hailers of this removal, stood forth the worthy and original Mr. Hutton, who was charmed to visit his enthusiastically esteemed new friend in the house of the great Newton; in which he flattered himself with retaining a faint remembrance that he had been noticed, when a boy, by the niece of that most stupendous of human geniuses.

In shaking hands around with the family upon this occasion, Mr. Hutton related that he had just come from the apartment of M. de Solgas, sub-preceptor to his Royal Highness the Prince of Wales;* in which he had had the high honour of being permitted to discourse with his Majesty; whom he had found the best of men, as well as the best of Kings; for, in talking over the letters of Lord Chesterfield, and his Lordship's doctrines, and subtle definitions of simulation and dissimulation, his Majesty said, "It is very deep, and may be it is very clever; but for me, I like more straight-forward work."

This tribute to the honour of simple truth excited a general plaudit. Mr. Hutton then, with a smile of benevolent pleasure, said that the subject had been changed, by Mr. Smelt, from Lord Chesterfield's letters to Dr. Burney's Tours, which had been highly commended: "And then I," added the good old man, "could speak my notions, and my knowledge, too, of my excellent friend the tourist, as well as of his writings; and so, openly and plainly, as one honest man should talk to another, I said it outright to my sovereign lord the King—who is as honest a man himself as any in his own three kingdoms. God bless him!"

---

* Afterwards George IV.

All the party, greatly pleased, smiled concurrence; and Mrs. Burney said that the Doctor was very happy to have had a friend to speak of him so favourably before the King.

"Madam," cried the good man, with warmth, "I will speak of him before my God! And that is doing much more."

The Stranges, who lived in the immediate neighbourhood of St. Martin's-street, were speedy welcomers to the new dwelling; where heartily they were welcomed.

The Doctor's worthy and attached old friend, Mr. Hayes, rejoiced in this near approach to his habitation, which was in James-street, Westminster; though the fast advancing ravages and debilities of time and infirmities, soon bereaved him of all other advantage from the approximation, than that which he could court to his own house.

Mr. Twining, when in town, which was only for a week or two every year, loved not to pass even a day without bestowing a few minutes of it upon a house at which he was always hailed with delight.

But Mr. Crisp, though unalterably he maintained that first place in the heart of Dr. Burney, to which priority of every species entitled him, had become subject to such frequent fits of the gout, that to London he was almost lost: he dreaded sleeping even a night from Chesington, which now was his nearly unbroken residence.

The learned and venerable Mr. Latrobe, and his two sons, each of them men of genius, though of different characters, were frequent in their visits, and amongst the Doctor's warmest admirers; and, in the study of the German language and literature, amongst his most useful friends.

The elegant translator of Tasso, Mr. Hoole, and his erudite and poetical son, the Rev. Samuel Hoole, * to form whose characters worth and modesty went hand in hand, were often of the social circle.

The Doctor's two literary Italian friends, Martinelli and Baretti, were occasional visitors; and by the rapidity of their elocution, the exuberance of their gestures, and the distortion of their features, upon even the most trivial contradiction, always gave to the Doctor a divertingly national reminiscence of the Italian, or Volcanic, portion of his tours.

---

* Now rector of Abinger, mentioned several times in Boswell's Life of Dr. Johnson.

Mr. Nollekens, the eminent sculptor, was one of the travelled acquaintances of Dr. Burney, with whom he had frequently assorted while in Italy; and with whom now, and through life, he kept up the connexion then formed.

Nollekens was one of those who shewed, in the most distinct point of view, the possible division of partial from general talent. He was uncultivated and under-bred; his conversation was without mark; his sentiments were common; and his language was even laughably vulgar; yet his works belong to an art of transcendant sublimity, and are beautiful with elegance and taste.

MR. BRUCE.

But more peculiarly this new residence was opened by the distinction of a new acquaintance, who was then as much the immediate lion of the day, as had been the last new acquaintance, Omiah, who had closed the annals of the residence in Queen-square.

This personage was no other than the famous Mr. Bruce, who was just returned to England, after having been wandering, and thought to be lost, during four years, in the deserts and sands of the hitherto European-untrodden territory of Africa, in search of the source, or sources, of the Nile.

The narrations, and even the sight of Mr. Bruce, were at this time vehemently sought, not only by all London, but, as far as written intercourse could be stretched, by all Europe.

The tales spread far and wide, first of his extraordinary disappearance from the world, and next of his unexpected re-appearance in the heart of Africa, were so full of variety, as well as of wonder, that they raised equal curiosity in the most refined and the most uncultivated of his cotemporaries.

Amongst these multifarious rumours, there was one that aroused in Dr. Burney a more eager desire to see and converse with this eminent traveller, than was felt even by the most ardent of the inquirers who were pressing upon him, in successive throngs, for intelligence.

The report here alluded to, asserted, that Mr. Bruce had discovered, and personally visited, the long-famed city of Thebes; and had found it such as Herodotus had described: and that he had entered and examined its celebrated temple; and had made, and brought home, a drawing of the Theban harp, as beautiful in its execution as in its form, though copied from a model of at least three thousand years old.

Mr. Bruce had brought, also, from Egypt, a drawing of an Abyssinian lyre in present use.

The assiduity of Dr. Burney in devising means of introduction to whosoever could increase, or ameliorate, the materials of his history, was not here put to any proof. Mr. Bruce had been an early friend of Mrs. Strange, and of her brother, Mr. Lumisden; and that zealous lady immediately arranged a meeting between the parties at her own house.

As this celebrated narrator made the opening of his career as an author, in the History of Music of Dr. Burney; to the eclat of which, on its first appearance, he not slightly contributed, by bestowing upon it the two admirable original drawings abovementioned, with a letter historically descriptive of their authenticity; some account of him seems naturally to belong to this place: and the Editor is persuaded, that two or three genuine, though juvenile letters which she wrote, at the time, to Mr. Crisp, may be more amusing to the reader, from their natural flow of youthful spirits, in describing the manners and conversation of this extraordinary wanderer, than any more steady recollections that could at present be offered from the same pen. And, led by this persuasion, she here copies a part of her early and confidential correspondence with her father's, her family's, and her own first friend.*

"To Samuel Crisp, Esq.
"Chesington, near Kingston, Surrey.

"St. Martin's Street, 1775.

"Well, now then, my dear Daddy,† I have got courage to obey your call for more! more! more! without fear of fatiguing you, for I have seen the great man-mountain, Mr. Bruce; and have been in

---

* These little narrations, selected and transcribed from a large packet of letters, written by the Editor, at a very early period of life, to Mr. Crisp, were by him bequeathed to his sister, Mrs. Gast; at whose death they became the property of Mrs. Frodsham, their nearest of kin; who, unsolicited, most generously and delicately restored the whole collection to its writer. She is gone hence before this little tribute of gratitude could be offered to her; but she has left two amiable daughters, who will not read it with indifference.

† This familiar, but affectionate, appellation, had been given by Dr. Burney, during his own youth, to Mr. Crisp; and was now, by prescription, adopted by the whole of the Doctor's family.

his high and mighty presence three times; as I shall proceed to tell you in due form and order, and with all the detail you demand.

"MEETING THE FIRST

took place at the tea-table, at Mrs. Strange, to which my mother, by appointment, had introduced her Lynn friends, Mr. and Mrs. Turner, who were extremely curious to see Mr. Bruce. My dear father was to have escorted us; but that provoking marplot, commonly called Business, came, as usual, in the way, and he could only join us afterwards.

" The man-mountain, and Mr. and Mrs. Turner, were already arrived; and no one else was invited, or, at least, permitted to enter.

" Mr. Bruce, as we found, when he arose—which he was too stately to do at once—was placed on the largest easy chair; but which his vast person covered so completely, back and arms, as well as seat, that he seemed to have been merely placed on a stool; and one was tempted to wonder who had ventured to accommodate him so slightly. He is the tallest man you ever saw in your life — at least, *gratis*. However, he has a very good figure, and is rather handsome; so that there is nothing alarming, or uncomely, or, I was going to say, ungenial—but I don't think that is the word I mean——in his immense and authoritative form.

"My mother was introduced to him, and placed by his side; but, having made her a cold, though civilish bow, he took no further notice even of her being in the room. I, as usual, glided out of the way, and got next to Miss Strange, who is agreeable and sensible: and who, seeing me, I suppose, very curious upon the subject, gave me a good deal of information about Man-Mountain.

"As he is warmly attached to Mrs. Strange and her family, he spends all his disengaged evenings at their house, where, when they are alone, he is not only chatty and easy, but full of comic and dry humour; though, if any company enters, he sternly, or gloutingly, Miss Strange says, shuts up his mouth, and utters not a word—except, perhaps, to her parrot; which, I believe, is a present from himself. Certainly he does not appear more elevated above the common race in his size, than in his ideas of his own consequence. Indeed, I strongly surmise, that he is not always without some idea how easy it would be to him—and perhaps how pleasant—in case any one should dare to offend him, to toss a whole company of such pigmies as the rest of mankind must seem to him, pell-mell down stairs,—if not out of the window.

"There is some excuse, nevertheless, for this proud shyness, because he is persuaded that nobody comes near him but either to stare at him as a curiosity, or to pick his brains for their own purposes: for, when he has deigned to behave to people as if he considered himself as their fellow-creature, every word that has been drawn from him has been printed in some newspaper or magazine; which, as he intends to publish his travels himself, is abominably provoking; and seems to have made him suspicious of some dark design, or some invidious trick, when any body says to him 'How do you do, Sir?' or, 'Pray, Sir, what's o'clock?'

"And, after all, if his nature in itself is as imperious as his person and air are domineering, it is hardly fair to expect that having lived so long among savages should have softened his manners.

"Well, when all the placements, and so forth, were over, we went to tea. There's an event for you, my dear Sir!

"There was, however, no conversation. Mr. Bruce's grand air, gigantic height, and forbidding brow, awed every body into silence, except Mrs. Strange; who, with all her wit and powers, found it heavy work to talk without reply.

" But Mr. Turner suffered the most. He is, you know, a very jocular man, and cannot bear to lose his laugh and his *bon mot*. Yet he durst not venture at either; though he is so accustomed to indulge in both, and very successfully, in the country, that he seemed in blank dismay at finding himself kept in such complete subordination by the fearful magnitude of Mr. Bruce, joined to the terror of his looks.

" Mrs. Turner, still less at her ease, because still less used to the company of strangers, attempted not to obtain any sort of notice. Yet, being gay in her nature, she, too, did not much like being placed so totally in the back ground. But she was so much impressed by the stateliness of this renowned traveller, that I really believe she sat saying her prayers half the evening, that she might get away from the apartment without some affront.

" Pray have you happened to read a paragraph in the newspapers, importing that Mr. Bruce was dying, or dead? My father, who had seen him alive and well the day before it appeared, cut it out, and wafered it upon a sheet of paper, and sent it to him without comment.

"My mother now inquired of Mr. Bruce whether he had seen it?

"'Yes,' answered he, coolly; 'but they are welcome to say what they please of me. I read my death with great composure.' Then, condescending to turn to me,—though only, I doubt not, to turn away from my elders,—he added: 'Were you not sorry, Miss Burney, to hear that I was dead?'

"Finding him thus address himself, and rather courteously, for he really smiled, to so small a personage as your very obedient servant, Mr. Turner, reviving, gathered courage to open his mouth, and, with a put-on air of easy jocularity, ventured to exclaim, with a laugh, 'Well, sir, as times go, I think, when they killed you, it is very well they said no harm of you.'

"'I know of no reason they had!' replied Mr. Bruce, in so loud a tone, and with an air of such infinite haughtiness, that poor Mr. Turner, thus repulsed in his first attempt, never dared to again open his lips.

"Soon afterwards, a servant came into the room, with General Melville's compliments, and he begged to know of Mrs. Strange whether it was true that Mr. Bruce was so dangerously ill.

" 'Yes!' cried he, bluffly; 'tell the General I am dead.'

" 'Ay, poor soul! poor mon!' cried Mrs. Strange, 'I dare say he has been vexed enough to hear such a thing! Poor honest mon! I dare be sworn he never wronged or deceived a human being in all his life.'

" 'Will you, faith?' cried Mr. Bruce: 'Will you be sworn to that? It's more than I would dare to be for any man alive! Do you really think he has risen to the rank of General, with so little trouble?'

" 'Troth, yes,' she answered; you men, you know, never deceive men! you have too much honour for that. And as to us women,—ah, troth! the best among you canno' deceive me! for whenever you say pretty things to me, I make it a rule to believe them all to be true: so the prettier the better!'

"Miss Bell Strange, the youngest daughter, a very sensible little girl, about ten years old, now brought him his tea. He took it, in chucking her under the chin; which was evidently very annoying to her, as a little womanly consciousness is just stealing upon her childhood: but, not heeding that, he again turned to me, and said, 'Do you know, Miss Burney, that I intend to run away with Bell? We are going to Scotland together. She won't let me rest till I take her to Gretna Green.'

"'La! how can you say so, sir,?' cried Bell, colouring, and much fidgetted. 'Pray, Ma'am, don't believe it!'

"'Why, how now, Bell? — What! won't you go?'

"'No, sir, I won't!' answered Bell, very demurely.

"'Well,' cried he, with a scoffing smile, and rising, 'this is the first lady that ever refused me.'

"He then inquired of Mrs. Strange whether she had heard any thing lately of Lord R., of whom they joined in drawing a most odious character; especially for his avarice. And when they had finished the portrait, Mr. Bruce, advancing his great figure towards me, exclaimed, 'And yet this man is my rival!'

"'Really?' cried I, hardly knowing what he expected I should say, but afraid to affront him by a second total silence.

"'O, it's true!' returned he, in a tone that implied

though not credible ; ' Is it not true, Mrs. Strange, that he is my rival?'

" ' Troth, they say so,' answered she, calmly.

" ' I wonder he should dare !' cried my mother. ' I wonder he should not apprehend that the long residence in Egypt of Mr. Bruce, had made him so well acquainted with magic, that '—

" ' O,' interrupted Mr. Bruce, coolly, ' I shall not poison him. But I may bribe his servant to tie a rope across his staircase, on some dark night, and then, as I dare say the miserly wretch never allows himself a candle to go up and down stairs, he may get a tumble, and break his neck.'

" This idea set him into a fit of laughter quite merry to behold ; and as I caught, from surprise, a little of its infection, he was again pleased to address himself to me, and to make inquiry whether I was musical; expressing his hopes that he should hear me play, when Mrs. Strange fulfilled her engagement of bringing him to our house; adding, that he had a passionate love of music.

" ' I was once,' said Mrs. Strange, ' with a young lady, a friend of mine, when she was at a concert for the first time she ever heard any music, except nursery lullabys, or street holla-balloos, or perhaps a tune on a fiddle by some poor blind urchin. And the music was very pretty, and quite tender; and she liked it so weel, it almost made her swoon; and she could no' draw her breath; and she thrilled all over; and sat sighing and groaning, and groaning and sighing, with over-much delight, till, at last, she burst into a fit of tears, and sobbed out, 'I can't help it!'

"' There's a woman,' said Mr. Bruce, with some emotion, 'who could never make a man unhappy! Her soul must be all harmony.'

"My dear father now arrived; and he and Mr. Bruce talked apart for the rest of the evening, upon the harp and the letter.

"But when the carriage was announced, imagine my surprise to see this majestic personage take it into his fancy to address something to me almost in a whisper! bending down, with no small difficulty, his head to a level with mine. What it was I could not hear. Though perhaps 'twas some Abyssinian compliment that I could not understand! It's flattery, however, could not have done me much mischief, after Miss Strange's information, that, when he is not disposed to be social with the company at large, he always singles out for notice the youngest female present—except, indeed, a dog, a bird, a cat, or a squirrel, be happily at hand.

"As I had no 'retort courteous' ready, he grandly re-erected himself to the fullest extent of his commanding height; setting me down, I doubt not, in his black book, for a tasteless imbecile. Every body, however, as all his motions engage all attention, looked so curious, that my only gratitude for his condescension, was heartily wishing him at one of the mouths of his own famous Nile.

"Will you not wish me there too, my dearest Mr. Crisp, for this long detail, without one word of said Nile, and its endless sources? or of Thebes and its hundred gates? or of the two harps of harps that are to decorate the History of Music? But nothing of all this occurred; except it might be in his private confab. with my father.

"You demanded, however, an account of his manner, his air, and his discourse; and what sort of mode, or fashion, he had brought over from Ethiopia.

"And here, so please you, all that is at your feet.

"I have only to add, that his smile, though rare, is really graceful and engaging. But his laugh, when his dignity is off its guard, and some sportive or active mischief comes across his ideas— such as the image of his miserly rival, Lord R., dangling from a treacherous rope on his own staircase; or tumbling headlong down,—is a chuckle of delight that shines his face of a bright scarlet, and shakes his whole vast frame with a boyish ecstacy.

"But I forgot to mention, that while Mr. Bruce was philandering with little Miss Bell Strange, who, with comic childish dignity, resented his assumed success, he said he believed he had discovered the reason of her shyness; 'Somebody has told you, I suppose, Bell, that when I am taken with a hungry fit in my rambles, I make nothing of seizing on a young bullock, and tying him by the horns to a tree, while I cut myself off a raw beef-steak, and regale myself upon it with its own cold gravy? according to my custom in Abyssinia? Perhaps, Bell, you may think a young heifer might do as well? and are afraid you might serve my turn, when my appetite is rather keen, yourself? Eh, Bell?'

* * * *

"You have accepted Meeting the First with so

much indulgence, my dear Mr. Crisp, that I am all alertness for presenting you with

MEETING THE SECOND,

which took place not long after the First, already recorded in these my elaborate annals.

"My father invited Mr. Twining, the great Grecian, to said meeting. What a contrast did he form with Mr. Bruce, the great Ethiopian! I have already described Mr. Twining to you, though very inadequately; for he is so full of merits, it is not easy to find proper phrases for him. There is only our dear Mr. Crisp whom we like and love half as well.

"Mr. Twining, with all his excellencies,—and he is reckoned one of the first scholars living; and is now engaged in translating Aristotle,—is as modest and unassuming as Mr. Bruce is high and pompous. He came very early, frankly owning, with a sort of piteous shrug, that he really had not bronze to present himself when the party should be assembled, before so eminent, but tremendous a man, as report painted Mr. Bruce; though he was extremely gratified to nestle himself into a corner, as a private spectator.

"Mrs. Strange, with her daughter, arrived next; and told us that his Abyssinian Majesty, as she calls Mr. Bruce, had dined at General Melville's, but would get away as quickly as possible.

"We waited tea, in our old-fashioned manner, a full hour; but no Mr. Bruce. So then we—or rather I—made it. And we all united to drink it. There, Sir; there's another event for you!

"Mr. Twining entreated that we might no longer postpone the concert, and was leading the way to the library, where it was to be held; but just then, a thundering rap at the door raised our expectations, and stopt our steps;—and Mr. Bruce was announced.

"He entered the room with the state and dignity of a tragedy giant.

"We soon found that something had displeased him, and that he was very much out of humour: and when Mrs. Strange inquired after General Melville, he answered her, with a face all made up of formidable frowns, that the General had invited a most stupid set of people to meet him. He had evidently left the party with disgust. Perhaps they had asked him whether there were any real men and women in Abyssinia, or only bullocks and heifers.

" He took his tea in stern silence, without deigning to again open his lips, till it was to demand a private conference with my father. They then went together to the study,—erst Sir Isaac Newton's—which is within the library.

" In passing through the latter, they encountered Mr. Twining, who would hastily have shrunk back; but my father immediately, and with distinction to Mr. Twining, performed the ceremony of introduction. Mr. Bruce gravely bowed, and went on; and he was then shut up with my father at least an hour, in full discussion upon the Theban harp, and the letter for the history.

" Mr. Twining returned, softly and on tiptoe, to the drawing room; and advancing to Mrs. Strange and my mother, with uplifted hands and eyes, exclaimed, ' This is the most awful man I ever saw!—I never felt so little in all my life!'

" ' Well, troth,' said Mrs. Strange, ' never mind! If you were six feet high he would overlook you; and he can do no more now.'

" Mr. Twining then, to recover breath he said, sat down, but declared he was in fear of his life; ' for if Mr. Bruce,' he cried, ' should come in hastily, and, not perceiving such a pitiful Lilliputian, should take the chair to be empty—it will soon be over with me! I shall be jammed in a moment—while he will think he is only dropping down upon a cushion!'

"As the study confab. seemed to menace duration, Mr. Twining petitioned Mr. Burney to go to the piano-forte; where he fired away in a voluntary with all the astonishing powers of his execution, and all the vigour of his genius.

"He might well be animated by such an auditor as Mr. Twining, who cannot be a deeper Grecian than he is a refined musician. How happy is my dear father that the three best, and dearest, and wisest, of his friends, should be three of the most scientific judges of his own art,—Mr. Twining, Mr. Bewley, and Mr. Crisp.

"Dear me! how came that last name into my head? I beg your pardon a thousand times. It was quite by accident. A mere slip of the pen.

"Mr. Twining, astonished, delighted, uttered the warmest praises, with all his heart; but that fervent effusion over, dropped his voice into its lowest key, to add, with a look full of arch pleasantry, 'Now, is not this better than being tall?'

"My poor sister, Burney, was not quite well,

and had a hurt on one of her fingers. But though she could not exert herself to play a solo, she consented to take her part in the noble duet for the piano-forte of Müthel; and she was no sooner seated, than Mr. Bruce re-appeared in our horizon.

" You well know that enchanting composition, which never has been more perfectly executed.

" Mr. Twining was enraptured; Mrs. Strange listened in silent wonder and pleasure; and Mr. Bruce himself was drawn into a charmed attention. His air lost its fierceness; his features relaxed into smiles; and good humour and complacency turned pride, sternness, and displeasure, out of his phiz.

" I begin now to think I have perhaps been too criticising upon poor man-mountain; and that, when he is not in the way of provocation to his vanity, he may be an amiable, as well as an agreeable man. But I suppose his giant-form, which makes every thing around him seem diminutive, has given him a notion that he was born to lord it over the rest of mankind; which, peradventure, seems to him a mere huddle of Lilliputians, as unfit to cope with him, mentally, in discourse, as corporeally in a wrestling match.

" Mr. Twining had been invited to supper; and

as it now grew very late, my mother made the invitation general; which, to our great surprise, Mr. Bruce was the first to accept. Who, then, could start any objection?

"So softened had he been by the music, that he was become all courtesy. Nobody else was listened to, or looked at; and as he scarcely ever deigns to look at any body himself, he is a primary object for peering at.

"The conversation turned upon disorders of the senses; for Mrs. Strange has a female friend who is seized with them, from time to time, as other people might be seized with an ague. She had been on a visit at the house of Mrs. Strange, the day before, where she had met Mr. Bruce. When it was perceived that a fit of the disorder was coming on, Miss Strange took her home; for which extraordinary courage Mr. Bruce greatly blamed her.

"'How,' said he, 'could you be sure of your life for a single moment? Suppose she had thought proper to run a pair of scissors into your eyes? Or had taken a fancy to cutting off one of your ears?'

"Miss Strange replied, that she never feared, for she always knew how to manage her.

"Mr. Bruce then inquired what had been the

first symptom she had shewn of the return of her malady?

"Mrs. Strange answered, that the beginning of her wandering that evening, had been by abruptly coming up to her, and asking her whether she could make faces?

"'I wish,' said Mr. Bruce, 'she had asked me! I believe I could have satisfied her pretty well that way!'

"'O, she had a great desire to speak to you, sir,' said Miss Strange, 'she told me she had a great deal to say to you.'

"'If,' said Mr. Bruce, 'she had come up to me, without any preface, and made faces at me,—I confess I should have been rather surprised!'

"'Troth,' said Mrs. Strange, 'if we are not upon our guard, we are all of us mad when we are contradicted! for we are all of us so witty, in our own ideas, that we think every mon out of his head that does not see with our eyes. But when I tried to hold her, poor little soul, from running into the street, while we were waiting for the coach, she gave me such a violent scratch on the arm, that I piteously called out for help. See! here's the mark.'

"'Did she fetch blood,' cried Mr. Bruce, in a tone of alarm; 'if she did, you will surely go out of your own senses before a fortnight will be over! You may depend upon that! If you are bit by a wild cat, you will undoubtedly become crazy; and how much more if you are scratched by a crack-brained woman? I would advise you to go forthwith to the sea, and be well dipped. I assure you fairly I would not be in your situation.'

"I thought this so shocking, that I felt a serious impulse to expostulate with his giantship upon it myself, and *almost* the courage; but, whether perceiving my horror, or only imagining it, I cannot tell; he deigned to turn his magnificent countenance full upon me, to display that he was laughing. And he afterwards added, that he knew there was nothing in this case that was any way dangerous; though how he obtained the knowledge he kept to himself.

"My mother then expressed her hopes that the poor lady might not, meanwhile, be removed to a private asylum; as in these repositories, the patients were said to be goaded on to become worse, every time a friend or a physician was expected to visit them; purposely to lengthen the poor sufferer's detention.

"'Indeed!' cried Mr. Bruce, knitting his brows, 'why this is very bad encouragement to going out of one's senses!'

"The rest of the conversation was wholly upon this subject; and so, as I know you hate the horrors, I must bid good night to Meeting the Second with his Abyssinian Majesty.

"The *tête à tête* in the study had been entirely upon the two drawings; and in settling the points upon which Mr. Bruce had best expatiate in his descriptive and historical epistle.

"My father has great satisfaction in being the first to bring forth the drawings and the writings of this far-famed traveller before the public. The only bad thing was, that it kept him away from us all supper-time, to put down the communications he had received, and the hints he wished to give for more.

"Mr. Twining, too, wrapt himself up in his own observations, and would not speak—except by his eyes, which had a comic look, extremely diverting, of pretended fearful insignificance.

* * * * *

"Well, now, my dear Sir, to

MEETING THE THIRD.

"It was produced by a visit from Mrs. Strange, with a petition from his Majesty of Abyssinia for another musical evening; as he had spoken with so much rapture of the last to Mr. Nesbit, a great *amateur*, 'that the poor honest lad,' Mrs. Strange said, 'could no' sleep o' nights from impatience to be inoculated with the same harmony, to prevent the infection Mr. Bruce carried about with him from doing him a mischief.'

"Well, the time was fixed, and the evening proved so agreeable, that we heartily and continually wished our dear Mr. Crisp amongst us. Mr. Twining, too, was gone. All one likes best go quickest.

"The first who arrived was Mr. Solly. He, also, is a great traveller, though not a renowned one; for nothing less than the Nile, and no place short of Abyssinia, will do, at present, for the taste of the public. My father had met with Mr. Solly at four several cities in Italy, and all accidentally; namely, Bologna, Florence, Rome, and Naples. Since that time, Mr. Solly has been wandering to many more remote places; and at Alexandria, and at Grand Cairo, he had met with Mr. Bruce. He is a chatty, lively man;

and not at all wanting in marks of his foreign excursions, *i. e.* shrugs, jerks, and gestures. John Bull, you know, my dear Mr. Crisp, when left to himself, is so torpid a sort of figure, with his arms slung so lank to his sides, that, at a little distance, one might fancy him without any such limb. While the Italians and French make such a flourishing display of its powers, that I verily believe it quickens circulation, and helps to render them so much more vivacious than philosopher Johnny.

" Yet I love Johnny best, for all that; as well as honour him the most; only I often wish he was a little more entertaining.

" Mr. Solly and my father 'fought all their battles o'er again' through Italy; and kept fighting them on till the arrival of Dr. Russel, a learned, and likewise a travelled physician, who seems droll and clever; but who is so very short-sighted, that even my father and I see further a-field. He loses nothing, however, through this infirmity, that trouble can supply; for he peers in every body's face at least a minute, to discover whether or not he knows them; and, after that, he peers a minute or two more, to discover, I suppose, whether or not he likes them. Yet, without boldness. 'Tis merely a look of earnest investigation, which he bestowed, in turn, upon every one present, as they came in his way; never fastening his eyes, even for an instant, upon the ground, the fire, the wainscot, or any thing inanimate, but always upon the 'human face divine.'

" He, also, is another travelled friend of Mr. Bruce, whom he knew at Aleppo, where Dr. Russel resided some years.*

" Then came Mrs. and Miss Strange, and his Abyssinian majesty, with his companion, Mr. Nesbit, who is a young Scotchman of distinction, infinitely *fade*, conceited, and coxcombical. He spoke very little, except to Mr. Bruce, and that, very politely, in a whisper. I cannot at all imagine what could provoke this African monarch to introduce such a fop here. We heartily wished him back in his own quarters; or at least at 'the Orkneys,' or at 'the Lord knows where.'

" Mr. Bruce himself was in the most perfect good humour; all civility and pleasantry; and his smiles seemed to give liberty for general ease.

---

* Dr. Russel, after this meeting, procured for Dr. Burney some curious information from Aleppo, of the modern state of music in Arabia.

"Having paid his compliments to my mother, he addressed himself to my sister Burney, inquiring courteously after her finger, which Miss Strange had told him she had hurt.

"' Mrs. Burney's fingers,' cried Dr. Russel, snatching at the opportunity for a good gaze, not upon her finger, but her phiz, ' ought to be exempt from all evil.'

"Your Hettina smiled, and assured them it was almost well.

"' O, I prayed to Apollo,' cried Mr. Bruce, ' for its recovery, and he has heard my prayer.'

"' I have no doubt, sir,' said Hetty, ' of your influence with Apollo.'

"' I ought to have some, Madam,' answered he grandly, ' for I have been a slave to him all my life!'"

"He then came to hope that I should open the concert; speaking to me with just such an encouraging sort of smile as if I had been about eleven years old; and strongly admonishing me not to delay coming forward at once, as he was prepared for no common pleasure in listening to me.

"Next he advanced to Susanna, begging her to exhibit her talent; and telling her he had had a dream, that if she refused to play, some great misfortune would befal him.

"When he had gone through this little circle of gallantry, to his own apparent satisfaction, he suffered Mr. Nesbit to seize upon him for another whispering dialogue; in which, as Mrs. Strange has since told my mother, that pretty swain lamented that he must soon run away, a certain lady of quality having taken such an unaccountable fancy to him at the opera of the preceding night, that she had appointed him to be with her this evening *tête à tête!*

"Mr. Bruce gave so little credit to this *bonne fortune*, that he laughed aloud in relating it to Mrs. Strange.

"Mr. Bruce then called upon Dr. Russel to take a violin, saying he was a very fine performer; but adding, 'We used to disgrace his talents, I own, at Aleppo; for, having no blind fiddler at hand, we kept him playing country dances by the hour.

"Dr. Russel mentioned some town *in those parts*, Asia or Africa, where a concert, upon occasion of a marriage, lasted three days.

". 'Three days?' repeated Mr. Bruce; 'why marriage is a more formidable thing there than even here!'

"Then came music, and the incomparable duet; which, as they could not forbear encoring, filled up all the rest of the evening, till the company at large departed; for there were several persons present whom I have not mentioned, being of no zest for your notice.

"Mr. Bruce, however, with the Stranges, again consented to stay supper; which, you know, with us, is nothing but a permission to sit over a table for chat, and roast potatoes, or apples.

"But now, to perfect your acquaintance with this towering Ethiopian, where do you think he will take you during supper?

"To the source, or sources, you cry, of the Nile? to Thebes? to its temple? to an arietta on the Theban Harp? or, perhaps, to banquetting on hot raw beef in Abyssinia?

"No such thing, my dear Mr. Crisp, no such thing. Travellers who mean to write their travels, are fit for nothing but to represent the gap at your whist table at Chesington, when you have only three players; for they are mere dummies.

"Mr. Bruce left all his exploits, his wanderings, his vanishings, his re-appearances, his harps so celestial, and his bullocks so terrestrial, to plant all our entertainment within a hundred yards of our own coterie; namely, at the masquerades at the Haymarket.

"Thus it was. He inquired of Mrs. Strange where he could find Mrs. Twoldham, a lady of his acquaintance; a very fine woman, but remarkably dissipated, whom he wished to see.

"'Troth,' Mrs. Strange answered, 'she did not know; but if he would take a turn to a masquerade or two, he would be sure to light upon her, as she never missed one.'

"'What,' cried he, laughing, 'has she not had enough yet of masquerades? Brava, Mrs. Twoldham! I honour your spirit.'

"He then laughed so cordially, that we were tempted, by such extraordinary good-humour, to beg him, almost in a body, to permit us to partake of his mirth.

"He complied very gaily. 'A friend of mine,' he cried, 'before I went abroad, had so often been teazed to esquire her to some of these medleys, that he thought to give the poor woman a surfeit of them to free himself from her future importunity. Yet she was a very handsome woman, very handsome indeed. But just as they were going into the great room, he had got one of her visiting cards ready, and contrived, as they passed through a crowded passage, to pin to the back of her robe, Mrs. Twoldham, Wimpole Street. And not three steps had she tript forward, before some one called out: "Hah! Mrs. Twoldham! how do you do, Mrs. Twoldham?"—"Oho, Mrs. Twoldham, are you here?" cried another; "Well, Ma'am, and how do all friends in Wimpole Street do?" till the poor woman was half out of her wits, to know how so many people had discovered her. So she thought that perhaps her forehead was in sight, and she perked up her mask; but she did not less hear, "Ah! it's you, Mrs. Twoldham, is it?" Then she supposed she had left a peep at her chin, and down again was tugged the poor mask; but still, "Mrs. Twoldham!" and, "how do you do, my dear Mrs. Twoldham?" was rung in her ears at every step; till at last, she took it into her head that some one, who, by chance, had detected her, had sent her name round the room; so she hurried off like lightning to the upper suite of apartments. But 'twas all the same. "Well, I declare, if here is not Mrs. Twoldham!" cries the first person that passed her. "So she is, I protest," cried another; "I am very glad to see you, my dear

Ma'am! what say you to giving me a little breakfast to morrow morning? you know where, Mrs. Twoldham; at our old haunt in Wimpole Street." But, at last, the corner of an unlucky table rubbed off the visiting card; and a waiter, who picked it up, grinned from ear to ear, and asked whether it was hers. And the poor woman fell into such a trance of passion, that my friend was afraid for his eyes; and all the more, because, do what he would, he could not refrain from laughing in her face.'

"You can scarcely conceive how heartily he laughed himself; he quite chuckled, with all the enjoyment in mischief of a holiday school boy.

"And he harped upon the subject with such facetious pleasure, that no other could be started.

"'I once knew,' he cried, 'a man, his name was Robert Chambers, and a good-natured little fellow he was, who was served this very trick the first masquerade he went to in London, upon fresh coming from Scotland. A gentleman who went to it with him, wrote upon his black domino, with chalk, " this is little Bob Chambers, fresh come from Edinburgh;" and immediately some one called out, in passing him, "What Bob? little Bob Chambers? how do do, my boy?" "Faith," says Bob, to his friend, "the people of this fine London are pretty impudent! I don't know that I know a soul in the whole town, and the first person I meet makes free to call me plain Bob?" But when he went on, and found that every creature in every room did the same, he grew quite outrageous at being treated with so little ceremony; and he stamped with his foot at one, and clenched his fist at another, and asked how they dared call him Bob? "What! a'n't you Bob, then?" replies one; "O yes, you are! you're Bob, my Bob, as sure as a gun! Bob Chambers! little Bob Chambers. And I hope you have left all well at Edinburgh, my Bob?" In vain he rubbed by them, and tried to get on, for they called to him quite from a distance; "Bob!—Bob! come hither, I say!—come hither, my Bobby! my Bob of all Bobs! you're welcome from Edinburgh, my Bob!" Well, then, he said, 'twas clear the devil owed him a spite, and had told his name from top to bottom of every room. Poor Bob! he made a wry face at the very sound of a masquerade to the end of his days.'

"To have looked at Mr. Bruce in his glee at this buffoonery, you must really have been amused; though methinks I see, supposing you had been with us, the picturesque rising of your brow, and all the dignity of your Roman nose, while you would have stared at such familiar delight in an active joke, as to transport into so merry an *espiegle*, the seven-footed loftiness of the haughty and imperious tourist from the sands of Ethiopia, and the waters of Abyssinia; whom, nevertheless, I have now the honour to portray in his *robe de chambre*, i. e. in private society, to my dear Chesington Daddy.

" What says he to the portrait?"

With fresh pleasure and alacrity, Dr. Burney now went on with his work. So unlooked for a re-inforcement of his means could not have arrived more seasonably. Every discovery, or development, relative to early times, was not only of essential service to the Dissertation on the Music of the Ancients, upon which, now, he was elaborately engaged, but excited general curiosity in all lovers of antiquity.

SIR JOSHUA REYNOLDS.

Amongst other new friends that this new neighbourhood procured, or confirmed, to Dr. Burney, there was one of so congenial, so Samaritan, a sort, that neighbour he must have been to the Doctor from the time of their first acquaintance, had his residence been in Dorset-square, or at Botolph's Wharf; instead of Leicester-square, and scarcely twenty yards from the Doctor's own short street.

Sir Joshua Reynolds, this good Samaritan, was, like Dr. Burney, though well-read and deeply studious, as easy and natural in discourse as if he had been merely a man of the world; and though his own art was his passion, he was open to the warmest admiration of every other: and again, like the Doctor, he was gay though contemplative, and flew from indolence, though he courted enjoyment. There was a striking resemblance in the general amenity of their intercourse, that not only made them, at all times, and with all persons, free from any approach to envy, peevishness, or sarcasm themselves, but seemed to spread around them a suavity that dissolved those angry passions in others.

In his chronological doggrels, Dr. Burney records that he now began his intimacy with the great English Raphael; of whom he adds,

> " 'Twere vain throughout Europe to look for his peer
> Who by converse and pencil alike can endear."

MRS. REYNOLDS.

Sir Joshua had a maiden sister, Mrs. Frances Reynolds; a woman of worth and understanding, but of a singular character; who, unfortunately for herself, made, throughout life, the great mistake of nourishing that singularity which was her bane, as if it had been her blessing.

She lived with Sir Joshua at this time, and stood

high in the regard of his firm and most honoured friend, Dr. Johnson; who saw and pitied her foible, but tried to cure it in vain. It was that of living in an habitual perplexity of mind, and irresolution of conduct, which to herself was restlessly tormenting, and to all around her was teazingly wearisome.

Whatever she suggested, or planned, one day, was reversed the next; though resorted to on the third, as if merely to be again rejected on the fourth; and so on, almost endlessly; for she rang not the changes in her opinions and designs in order to bring them into harmony and practice; but waveringly to stir up new combinations and difficulties; till she found herself in the midst of such chaotic obstructions as could chime in with no given purpose; but must needs be left to ring their own peal, and to begin again just where they began at first.

This lady was a no unfrequent visitor in St. Martin's street; where, for her many excellent qualities, she was much esteemed.

The Miss Palmers,* also, two nieces of Sir Joshua,

---

* The eldest was afterwards Marchioness of Thomond; the second is now Mrs. Gwatken.

lived with him then occasionally; and one of them, afterwards, habitually; and added to the grace of his table, and of his evening circles, by the pleasingness of their manners, and the beauty of their persons.

Mrs. Frances Reynolds desired to paint Dr. Burney's portrait, that she might place it among certain other worthies of her choice, already ornamenting her dressing-room. The Doctor had little time to spare; but had too natively the spirit of the old school, to suffer No! and a lady, to pair off together.

During his sittings, one trait of her tenacious humour occurred, that he was always amused in relating. While she was painting his hair, which was remarkably thick, she asked him, very gravely, whether he could let her have his wig some day to work at, without troubling him to sit.

" My wig?" repeated he, much surprised.

" Yes;" she answered; " have not you more than one? can't you spare it?"

" Spare it?—Why what makes you think it a wig? It's my own hair."

" O then, I suppose," said she, with a smile, " I must not call it a wig?"

"Not call it a wig?—why what for, my dear Madam, should you call it a wig?"

"Nay, Sir," replied she, composedly, "if you do not like it, I am sure I won't."

And he protested, that though he offered her every proof of twisting, twitching, and twirling that she pleased, she calmly continued painting, without heeding his appeal for the hairy honours of his head; and only coolly repeating, "I suppose, then, I must not call it a wig?"

MRS. BROOKES.

Mrs. Brookes, authoress of "Lady Julia Mandeville," &c., having become a joint proprietor of the Opera House with Mr. and Mrs. Yates, earnestly coveted the acquaintance of Dr. Burney; in which, of course, was included the benefit of his musical opinions, his skill, and his counsel.

Mrs. Brookes had much to combat in order to receive the justice due to her from the world; for nature had not been more kind in her mental, than hard in her corporeal gifts. She was short, broad, crooked, ill-featured, and ill-favoured; and she had a cast of the eye that made it seem looking every way rather than that which she meant for its direction. Nevertheless, she always ultimately obtained the consideration that she merited. She was free from pretension, and extremely good-natured. All of assumption, by which she might have claimed literary rank, from the higher and graver part of her works, was wholly set aside in conversation; where, however different in grace and appearance, she was as flowing, as cheerful, and as natural in dialogue, as her own popular and pleasing "Rosina."*

MISS REID.

Miss Reid, the Rosalba of Britain, who, in crayons, had a grace and a softness of colouring rarely surpassed, was a visitor likewise at the house, whose works and whose person were almost divertingly, as was remarked by Mr. Twining, at variance with one another; for while the works were all loveliness, their author was saturnine, cold, taciturn; absent to an extreme; awkward and full of mischances in every motion; ill-accoutred, even beyond negligence, in her dress; and plain enough to

---

* An afterpiece of Mrs. Brookes's composition.

produce, grotesquely, an effect that was almost picturesque.

Yet, with all this outward lack of allurement, her heart was kind, her temper was humane, and her friendships were zealous. But she had met with some misfortunes in early life that had embittered her existence, and kept it always wavering, in a miserable balance, between heartless apathy, and pining discontent.

MRS. ORD.

An acquaintance was now, also, begun, with one of the most valued, valuable, and lasting friends of Dr. Burney and his family, Mrs. Ord; a lady of great mental merit, strict principles, and dignified manners.

Without belonging to what was called the Blues, or *Bas Bleu* Society, except as a receiver or a visitor, she selected parties from that set to mix with those of other, or of no denomination, that were sometimes peculiarly well assorted, and were always generally agreeable.

Mrs. Ord's was the first coterie into which the Doctor, after his abode in St. Martin's Street, initiated his family; Mrs. Burney as a participator, his daughters as appendages, of what might justly be called a *conversatione*.

The good sense, serene demeanour, and cheerful politeness of the lady of the house, made the first meeting so pleasingly animating to every one present, that another and another followed, from time to time, for a long series of years. What Dr. Burney observed upon taking leave of this first little assemblage, may be quoted as applicable to every other.

" I rejoice, Madam," he said, " to find that there are still two or three houses, even in these dissipated times, where, through judgment and taste in their selection, people may be called together, not with the aid of cards, to kill time, but with that of conversation, to give it life."

" And I rejoice the more in the success of Mrs. Ord," cried Mr. Pepys,* " because I have known many meetings utterly fail, where equal pleasure has been proposed and expected; but where, though the ingredients, also, have been equally good—the pudding has proved very bad in the eating!"

" The best ingredients," said Dr. Burney, " how-

---

* Afterwards Sir William Weller Pepys.

ever excellent they may be separately, always prove inefficient if they are not well blended; for if any one of them is a little too sour, or a little too bitter—nay, or a little too sweet, they counteract each other. But Mrs. Ord is an excellent cook, and employs all the refinements of her art in taking care not to put clashing materials into the same mess."

HON. MR. BRUDENEL.

His Honour, Brudenel,* loved and sought Dr. Burney with the most faithful admiration from a very early period; and, to the latest in his power, he manifested the same partiality. Though by no means a man of talents, he made his way to the grateful and lasting regard of Dr. Burney, by constancy of personal attachment, and a fervour of devotion to the art through which the distinction of the Doctor had had its origin.

Dr. Ogle, Dean of Winchester,† a man of facetious pleasantry, yet of real sagacity; though mingled with eccentricities, perversities, and decidedly repub-

---

* Afterwards Earl of Cardigan.
† Father of the second Mrs. Sheridan.

lican principles, became a warm admirer of the character and conversation of the Doctor; while the exemplary Mrs. Ogle and her sprightly daughters united to enliven his reception, in Berkeley-square, as an honoured instructor, and a cordial friend.

But with far more political congeniality the President of the Royal Society, Sir Joseph Banks, was included in this new amical committee.

In a loose manuscript of recurrence to the year 1776, stand these words upon the first Dr. Warren.

" In January of this year, an acquaintance which I had already begun with that most agreeable of men, Dr. Warren, grew into intimacy. His conversation was the most pleasant, and, nearly, the most enlightened, without pedantry or dogmatism, that I had ever known."

Amongst the distinguished persons appertaining to this numerous list of connexions upon the opening of the St. Martin's-street residence during the last century, one, at least, still remains to ornament, both by his writings and his conversation, the present, Dr. Gillies; whose urbanity of mind and manners, joined to his literary merits, made him, at his own pleasure, one of the most estimable and honourable contributors to the Doctor's social circle.

MR. CUTLER.

But the most prominent in eagerness to claim the Doctor's regard, and to fasten upon his time, with wit, humour, learning, and eccentric genius, that often made him pleasant, and always saved him from becoming insignificant; though with an officious zeal, and an obtrusive kindness that frequently caused him to be irksome, must be ranked Mr. Cutler, a gentleman of no common parts, and certainly of no common conduct; who loved Dr. Burney with an ardour the most sincere, but which he had not attraction to make reciprocal; who wrote him letters of a length interminable, yet with a frequency of repetition that would have rendered even little billets wearisome; and who, satisfied of the truth of his feelings, investigated not their worth, and never doubted their welcome.

The Doctor had a heart too grateful and too gentle to roughly awaken such friendship from its error; he endured, therefore, its annoyance, till the intrusion upon his limited leisure became a serious persecution. He then, almost perforce, sought to render him more considerate by neglect, in wholly omitting to answer his letters.

But Mr. Cutler, though hurt and chagrined, was not quieted. Letter still followed letter, detailing at full length his own ideas upon every subject he could start; with kind assurances of his determined patient expectance of future replies.

The Doctor then was reduced to frankly offer a remonstrance upon the difference of their position with respect to time,—and its claims.

This, though done with softness and delicacy, opened all at once the eyes of this pertinacious friend to his unreflecting insufficiency; but, of course, rather with a feeling of injury, than to a sense of justice; and he withdrew abruptly from all correspondence; powerfully piqued, yet in silent, uncomplaining dismay.

To give an idea of his singular style, some few extracts, of the most uncommon sort, will be selected for the correspondence, from the vast volume of letters that will be consigned to the flames.*

MR. BARRY.

The most striking, however, though by no means the most reasonable converser amongst those who

---

* See Correspondence.

generally volunteered their colloquial services in St. Martin's-street, was that eminent painter, and entertaining character, Mr. Barry; who, with a really innocent belief that he was the most modest and moderate of men, nourished the most insatiable avidity of applause; who, with a loudly laughing defiance of the ills of life, was internally and substantially sinking under their annoyance; and who, with a professed and sardonic contempt of rival prosperity or superiority, disguised, even to himself, the bitterness with which he pined at the success which he could not share, but to which he flattered himself that he was indifferent, or above; because so to be, behoved the character of his believed adoption, that of a genuine votary to philanthropy and philosophy.

His ideas and his views of his art he held, and justly, to be sublime; but his glaring execution of the most chaste designs left his practice in the lurch, even where his theory was most perfect.

He disdained to catch any hints from the works, much less from the counsel, of Sir Joshua Reynolds; from whose personal kindness and commanding abilities he had unfortunately been cut off by early disagreement; for nearly as they approached each other in their ideas, and their knowledge of their art, their process, in cultivating their several talents, had as little accord, as their method of organizing their intellectual attributes and characters. And, indeed, the inveterate dissension of Barry with Sir Joshua Reynolds, must always be in his own disfavour, though his harder fate must mingle pity with censure—little thankfully as his high spirit would have accepted such a species of mitigation. It is not, however, probable, that the fiery Mr. Barry should have received from the serene and candid Sir Joshua, the opening provocation; Sir Joshua, besides his unrivalled professional merits,* had a negative title to general approbation, that included many an affirmative one; " Sir Joshua Reynolds," said Dr. Johnson,† "possesses the largest share of inoffensiveness of any man that I know.

Yet Mr. Barry had many admirable as well as uncommon qualities. His moral sentiments were liberal, nay, noble; he was full fraught, almost bursting with vigorous genius; and his eccentrici-

---

* His brilliant successor in deserved renown, Sir Thomas Lawrence, was then scarcely in being.
† To this Editor.

ties, both in manner and notions, made his company generally enlightening, and always original and entertaining.

GARRICK.

The regret that stood next, or, rather, that stood alone with Dr. Burney, to that of losing the pure air and bright view of Hampstead and Highgate, by this change to St. Martin's-street, was missing the frequency of the visits of Mr. Garrick; to whom the Queen-square of that day was so nearly out of town, that to arrive at it on foot had almost the refreshment of a country walk.

St. Martin's-street, on the contrary, was situated in the populous closeness of the midst of things; and not a step could Garrick take in its vicinity, without being recognised and stared at, if not pursued and hailed, by all the common herd of his gallery admirers; those gods to whom so often he made his fond appeal; and who formed, in fact, a principal portion of his fame, and, consequently, of his happiness, by the honest tribute of their vociferous plaudits.

Nevertheless, these jovial gods, though vivifying

to him from their high abode, and in a mass, at the theatre, must, in partial groups, from the exertions he could never refrain from making to keep alive with almost whatever was living, his gay popularity, be seriously fatiguing, by crowding about him in narrow streets, dirty crossings, and awkward nooks and corners, such as then abounded in that part of the town; though still his buoyant spirits, glowing and unequalled, retained their elastic pleasure in universal admiration.

An instance of this preponderating propensity greatly diverted Dr. Burney, upon the first visit of Mr. Garrick to St. Martin's-street.

This visit was very matinal; and a new housemaid, who was washing the steps of the door, and did not know him, offered some resistance to letting him enter the house unannounced: but, grotesquely breaking through her attempted obstructions, he forcibly ascended the stairs, and rushed into the Doctor's study; where his voice, in some mock heroics to the damsel, alone preceded him.

Here he found the Doctor immersed in papers, manuscripts, and books, though under the hands of his hair-dresser; while one of his daughters was reading a newspaper to him;* another was making his tea,† and another was arranging his books.‡

The Doctor, beginning a laughing apology for the literary and littered state of his apartment, endeavoured to put things a little to rights, that he might present his ever welcome guest with a vacated chair. But Mr. Garrick, throwing himself plumply into one that was well-cushioned with pamphlets and memorials, called out: "Ay, do now, Doctor, be in a little confusion! whisk your matters all out of their places; and don't know where to find a thing that you want for the rest of the day;—and that will make us all comfortable!"

The Doctor now, laughingly leaving his disorder to take care of itself, resumed his place on the stool; that the furniture of his head might go through its proper repairs.

Mr. Garrick then, assuming a solemn gravity, with a profound air of attention, fastened his eyes upon the hair-dresser; as if wonder-struck at his amazing skill in decorating the Doctor's *tête*.

The man, highly gratified by such notice from

---

* Susanna. † Charlotte. ‡ Frances.

the celebrated Garrick, briskly worked on, frizzing, curling, powdering, and pasting, according to the mode of the day, with assiduous, though flurried importance, and with marked self-complacency.

Mr. Garrick himself had on what he called his scratch wig; which was so uncommonly ill-arranged and frightful, that the whole family agreed no one else could have appeared in such a plight in the public streets, without a risk of being hooted at by the mob.

He dropt now all parley whatsoever with the Doctor, not even answering what he said; and seemed wholly absorbed in admiring watchfulness of the progress of the hair-dresser; putting on, by degrees, with a power like transformation, a little mean face of envy and sadness, such as he wore in representing Abel Drugger; which so indescribably altered his countenance, as to make his young admirers almost mingle incredulity of his individuality with their surprise and amusement; for, with his mouth hanging stupidly open, he fixed his features in so vacant an absence of all expression, that he less resembled himself than some daubed wooden block in a barber's shop window.

The Doctor, perceiving the metamorphosis, smiled

in silent observance. But the friseur, who at first had smirkingly felt flattered at seeing his operations thus curiously remarked, became utterly discountenanced by so incomprehensible a change, and so unremitting a stare; and hardly knew what he was about. The more, however, he pomatumed and powdered, and twisted the Doctor's curls, the more palpable were the signs that Mr. Garrick manifested of

"Wonder with a foolish face of praise;"

till, little by little, a species of consternation began to mingle with the embarrassment of the hair-manufacturer. Mr. Garrick then, suddenly starting up, gawkily perked his altered physiognomy, with the look of a gaping idiot, full in the man's face.

Scared and confounded, the perruquier now turned away his eyes, and hastily rolled up two curls, with all the speed in his power, to make his retreat. But before he was suffered to escape, Mr. Garrick, lifting his own miserable scratch from his head, and perching it high up in the air upon his finger and thumb, dolorously, in a whining voice, squeaked out, "Pray now, Sir, do you think, Sir, you could touch me up this here old bob a little bit, Sir?

The man now, with open eyes, and a broad grin, scampered pell-mell out of the room; hardly able to shut the door, ere an uncontrollable horse-laugh proclaimed his relieved perception of Mr. Garrick's mystification.

Mr. Garrick then, looking smilingly around him at the group, which, enlarged by his first favourite young Charles, most smilingly met his arch glances, sportively said, " And so, Doctor, you, with your tag rag and bobtail there—"

Here he pointed to some loaded shelves of shabby unbound old books and pamphlets, which he started up to recognise, in suddenly assuming the air of a smart, conceited, underling auctioneer; and rapping with his cane upon all that were most worn and defaced, he sputtered out: " A penny a piece! a penny a-piece! a-going! a-going! a-going! a penny a-piece! each worth a pound!—not to say a hundred! a rare bargain, gemmen and ladies! a rare bargain! down with your copper!"

Then, quietly re-seating himself, " And so, Doctor," he continued, "you, and tag-rag and bobtail, there, shut yourself up in this snug little book-stall, with all your blithe elves around you, to rest your understanding?"

Outcries now of "Oh fie!" "Oh abominable!" "Rest his understanding? how shocking!" were echoed in his ears with mock indignancy from the mock-offended set, accompanied by hearty laughter from the Doctor.

Up rose Mr. Garrick, with a look of pretended perturbation, incoherently exclaiming, "You mistake—you quite misconceive—you do, indeed! pray be persuaded of it!—I only meant—I merely intended—be sure of that!—be very sure of that!—I only purposed; that is, I designed—I give you my word—'pon honour, I do!—I give you my word of that!—I only had in view—in short, and to cut the matter short, I only aimed at paying you—pray now take me right!—at paying you the very finest compliment in nature!"

"Bravo, bravo! Mr. Bayes!" cried the Doctor, clapping his hands: "nothing can be clearer!—"

Mr. Garrick had lent the Doctor several books of reference; and he now inquired the titles and number of what were at present in his possession.

"I have ten volumes," answered the Doctor, "of Memoirs of the French Academy."

"And what others?"

"I don't know—do you, Fanny?"—turning to his librarian.

"What! I suppose, then," said Mr. Garrick, with an ironical cast of the eye, "you don't choose to know that point yourself?—Eh?—O, very well, Sir, very well!" rising, and scraping round the room with sundry grotesque bows, obsequiously low and formal; "quite well, Sir! Pray make free with me! Pray keep them, if you choose it! Pray stand upon no ceremony with me, Sir!"

Dr. Burney then hunted for the list; and when he had found it, and they had looked it over, and talked it over, Mr. Garrick exclaimed, "But when, Doctor, when shall we have out the History of Histories? Do let me know in time, that I may prepare to blow the trumpet of fame."

He then put his cane to his mouth, and, in the voice of a raree showman, squalled out, shrilly and loudly: "This is your only true History, gemmen! Please to buy! please to buy! come and buy! 'Gad, Sir, I'll blow it in the ear of every scurvy pretender to rivalship. So, buy! gemmen, buy! The only true History! No counterfeit, but all alive!"

Dr. Burney invited him to the parlour, to breakfast; but he said he was engaged at home, to Messrs. Twiss and Boswell; whom immediately, most gaily and ludicrously, he took off to the life.

Elated by the mirth with which he enlivened his audience, he now could not refrain from imitating, in the same manner, even Dr. Johnson: but not maliciously, though very laughably. He sincerely honoured, nay, loved Dr. Johnson; but Dr. Johnson, he said, had peculiarities of such unequalled eccentricity, that even to his most attached, nay, to his most reverential admirers, they were irresistibly provoking to mimicry.

Mr. Garrick, therefore, after this apology, casting off his little, mean, snivelling Abel Drugger appearance, began displaying, and, by some inconceivable arrangement of his habiliments, most astonishingly enlarging his person, so as to make it seem many inches above its native size; not only in breadth, but, strange yet true to tell, in height, whilst exhibiting sundry extraordinary and uncouth attitudes and gestures.

Pompously, then, assuming an authoritative port and demeanour, and giving a thundering stamp with his foot on some mark on the carpet that struck his eye—not with passion or displeasure, but merely as if from absence and singularity; he took off the voice, sonorous, impressive, and oratorical, of Dr. Johnson, in a short dialogue with himself that had passed the preceding week.

" David!—will you lend me your Petrarca?"

" Y-e-s, Sir!—"

" David! you sigh?"

" Sir—you shall have it, certainly."

" Accordingly," Mr. Garrick continued, " the book—stupendously bound—I sent to him that very evening. But—scarcely had he taken the noble quarto in his hands, when—as Boswell tells me, he poured forth a Greek ejaculation, and a couplet or two from Horace; and then, in one of those fits of enthusiasm which always seem to require that he should spread his arms aloft in the air, his haste was so great to debarrass them for that purpose, that he suddenly pounces my poor Petrarca over his head upon the floor! Russia leather, gold border, and all! And then, standing for several minutes erect, lost in abstraction, he forgot, probably, that he had ever seen it; and left my poor dislocated Beauty to the mercy of the housemaid's morning mop!"

Phill, the favourite little spaniel, was no more; but a young greyhound successor followed Mr. Garrick about the study, incessantly courting his notice, and licking his hands. " Ah, poor Phill!" cried he, looking at the greyhound contemptuously, "*You* will never take his place, Slabber-chops! though you try for it hard and soft. Soft enough, poor whelp! like all your race; tenderness without ideas."

After he had said adieu, and left the room, he hastily came back, whimsically laughing, and said, "Here's one of your maids down stairs that I love prodigiously to speak to, because she is so cross! She was washing, and rubbing and scrubbing, and whitening and brightening your steps this morning, and would hardly let me pass. Egad, Sir, she did not know the great Roscius! But I frightened her a little, just now: 'Child,' says I, 'you don't guess whom you have the happiness to see! Do you know I am one of the first geniuses of the age? You would faint away upon the spot if you could only imagine who I am!'"

* * * * *

Another time, an appointment having been arranged by Dr. Burney for presenting his friend Mr. Twining to Mr. Garrick, the two former, in happy conferenee, were enjoying the society of each other, while awaiting the promised junction with Mr. Garrick, when a violent rapping at the street door, which prepared them for his welcome arrival, was followed by a demand, through the footman, whether the Doctor could receive Sir Jeremy Hillsborough; a baronet who was as peculiarly distasteful to both the gentlemen, as Mr. Garrick was the reverse.

"For heaven's sake, no!" cried Mr. Twining; and the Doctor echoing "No! No! No!" was with eagerness sending off a hasty excuse, when the footman whispered, "Sir, he's at my heels! he's close to the door! he would not stop!" And, strenuously flinging open the library door himself in a slouching hat, an old-fashioned blue rocolo, over a great-coat of which the collar was turned up above his ears, and a silk handkerchief, held, as if from the tooth-ache, to his mouth, the forbidden guest entered; slowly, lowly, and solemnly bowing his head as he advanced; though, quaker-like, never touching his hat, and not uttering a word.

The Doctor, whom Sir Jeremy had never before visited, and to whom he was hardly known, save by open dissimilarity upon some literary subjects; and Mr. Twining, to whom he was only less a stranger to be yet more obnoxious, from having been at variance with his family; equally concluded, from their knowledge of his irascible character, that the visit had no other view than that of demanding satisfaction for some offence supposed to have been offered to his high self-importance. And, in the awkwardness of such a surmise, they could not but feel disconcerted, nay abashed, at having proclaimed their averseness to his sight in such unqualified terms, and immediately within his hearing.

For a minute or two, with a silence like his own, they awaited an explanation of his purpose; when, after some hesitation, ostentatiously waving one hand, while the other still held his handkerchief to his mouth, the unwelcome intruder, to their utter astonishment, came forward; and composedly seated himself in an arm chair near the fire; filling it broadly, with an air of domineering authority.

The gentlemen now looked at each other, in some doubt whether their visitor had not found his way to them from the vicinity of Moorfields.*

The pause that ensued was embarrassing, and not quite free from alarm; when the intruder, after an extraordinary nod or two, of a palpably threatening nature, suddenly started up, threw off his slouched hat and old rocolo, flung his red silk handkerchief into the ashes, and displayed to view, lustrous with vivacity, the gay features, the sparkling eyes, and

---

* Where then stood the Bethlem Hospital.

laughing countenance of Garrick,—the inimitable imitator, David Garrick.

Dr. Burney, delighted at this development, clapped his hands, as if the scene had been represented at a theatre: and all his family present joined rapturously in the plaudit: while Mr. Twining, with the happy surprise of a sudden exchange from expected disgust to accorded pleasure, eagerly approached the arm-chair, for a presentation which he had longed for nearly throughout his life.

Mr. Garrick then, with many hearty reciprocations of laughter, expounded the motive to the feat which he had enacted.

He had awaked, he said, that morning, under the formidable impression of an introduction to a profound Greek scholar, that was almost awful; and that had set him to pondering upon the egregious loss of time and pleasurability that hung upon all formalities in making new acquaintances; and he then set his wits to work at devising means for skipping at once, by some sleight of hand, into abrupt cordiality. And none occurred that seemed so promising of spontaneous success, as presenting himself under the aspect of a person whom he knew to be so desperately unpleasant to the scholiast, that, at the very sound of his name, he would inwardly ejaculate,

" Take any form but that!"

Here, in a moment, Mr. Garrick was in the centre of the apartment, in the attitude of Hamlet at sight of the ghost.

This burlesque frolic over, which gave a playful vent that seemed almost necessary to the superabundant animal spirits of Mr. Garrick, who, as Dr. Johnson has said of Shakespeare, "was always struggling for an occasion to be comic," he cast away farce and mimicry; and became, for the rest of the visit, a judicious, intelligent, and well informed, though ever lively and entertaining converser and man of letters: and Mr. Twining had not been more amused by his buffoonery, than he grew charmed by his rationality.

In the course of the conversation, the intended Encyclopedia of Dr. Goldsmith being mentioned, and the Doctor's death warmly regretted, a description of the character as well as works of that charming author was brought forward; and Mr. Garrick named, what no one else in his presence could have hinted at, the poem of Retaliation.

Mr. Garrick had too much knowledge of mankind to treat with lightness so forcible an attack upon the stability of his friendships, however it might be softened off by the praise of his talents.* But he had brought it, he said, upon himself, by an unlucky lampoon, to which he had irresistibly been led by the absurd blunders, and the inconceivable inferiority between the discourse and the pen of this singular man; who, one evening at the club, had been so outrageously laughable, that Mr. Garrick had been betrayed into asserting, that no man could possibly draw the character of Oliver Goldsmith, till poor Oliver was under ground; for what any one would say after an hour's reading him, would indubitably be reversed, after an hour's chat. " And then," Mr. Garrick continued, " one risible folly bringing on another, I voted him to be dead at that time, that I might give his real character in his epitaph. And this," he added, " produced this distich."

" Attend, passer by, for here lies old Noll;
Who wrote like an angel—but talked like poor Poll!"

Goldsmith, immeasurably piqued, vowed he would retaliate; but, never ready with his tongue in public, though always ready with his pen in private, he

---

* " He cast off his friends, as a huntsman his pack,
For he knew when he would he could whistle them back."

hurried off in a pet; and, some time after, produced that best, if not only, satirical poem, that he ever wrote, " Retaliation."

This was Dr. Goldsmith's final work, and did not come out till after his death. And it was still unfinished; the last line, which was upon Sir Joshua Reynolds, being left half written;

> " By flattery unspoil'd—" *

To a very general regret, Dr. Johnson had not yet been named. Probably, he was meant to form the climax of the piece.

His character, drawn by a man of such acute discrimination, who had prospered from his friendship, yet smarted from his wit; who feared, dreaded, and envied; yet honoured, admired, and loved him; would doubtless have been sketched with as fine a pencil of splendid praise, and pointed satire, as has marked the characteristic distiches upon Mr. Burke and Mr. Garrick.

---

* This last circumstance was communicated to the Editor by Sir Joshua himself.

END OF THE FIRST VOLUME.